FRANK LLOYD WRIGHT

Recollections by Those Who Knew Him

Edited by
Edgar Tafel, F.A.I.A.

Foreword by
Tom Wolfe

DOVER PUBLICATIONS, INC.
Mineola, New York

Information provided in this text has been acquired from various sources. The letters, stories, and anecdotes included may not be factual or consistent due to the nature of personal recollection.

Bibliographical Note

This Dover edition, first published in 2001, is an unabridged republication of the work originally published by John Wiley & Sons, Inc., New York, in 1993 under the title *About Wright: An Album of Recollections by Those Who Knew Frank Lloyd Wright.*

Library of Congress Cataloging-in-Publication Data

Tafel, Edgar.
    [About Wright]
    Frank Lloyd Wright : recollections by those who knew him / [written and] edited by Edgar Tafel ; foreword by Tom Wolfe.—Dover ed.
        p. cm.
    Originally published: About Wright : an album of recollections by those who knew Frank Lloyd Wright. New York : Wiley, c1993.
    Includes index.
    ISBN 0-486-41731-X (pbk.)
    1. Wright, Frank Lloyd, 1867–1959. 2. Architects—United States—Biography. I. Title.

NA737.W7 T32 2001
720'.92—dc21
[B]
                                                                    00-052377

Manufactured in the United States of America
Dover Publications, Inc., 31 East 2nd Street, Mineola, N.Y. 11501

CONTENTS

CONTENTS

CONTENTS

PREFACE

The year of this publication, 1993, marks the 126th anniversary of the birth of Wright, and the 61st of the founding of his Taliesin Fellowship. My apprenticeship in the Fellowship lasted from 1932 to 1941. During that time I worked on all aspects of Wright's educational endeavors. That means that under his direction I farmed, worked as carpenter, plumber, electrician, plasterer, chauffeur, draftsman, spent hundreds of days at the drafting tables and eventually out in the construction field, acting as construction manager for several residences, and supervised such major works as "Fallingwater," the Johnson Wax Building, and the Johnson house.

It had been my intent to spend the rest of my life at the Taliesin complexes, as Mr. Wright had told us it could be. But in 1941 he changed his ground rules and would not allow members of the Fellowship to be prime architects for outside work while living under his roof. I left to start my own practice, which was soon halted by World War II. During the War I found employment in Chicago firms followed later by more practical field experience in construction in northern Arizona. I then went into the armed service, returning two years later from Air Photo Intelligence in India.

Settling in New York City, I again started my own practice by designing houses—which led to stores, religious buildings, factories, educational buildings, and interiors of all kinds. My office grew, as did my enthusiasm, as each project provided a particular interest and challenge of its own. My friendship with the Wrights continued.

I gave many historical but informal slide lectures about Wright and the Fellowship, and soon found wider audiences in the United States Information Agency abroad; also, at colleges and museums for the Steelcase Company, which brought me before thousands of people of all situations and interests. Audiences varied from the Ivy League schools, where professors hated Wright, to the enthusiastic and creative audiences both here and in far away places such as Istanbul, Athens, London, New Delhi, Madras and other foreign cities.

People kept asking me what it was like working for Wright, and that led me to my first book, *Apprentice to Genius*. This new album tells us about others' experiences with Wright. Yes, this volume should have started earlier for so many who knew him have passed away, and sadly, their recollections are lost.

Wright spanned much time and many stupidities. He was born in 1867 and died in 1959 living through one age into another. He witnessed the death of the "Beaux Arts," the birth of a dull "International Style" and, fortunately, missed the rebirth of classicism, known as "Post Modern," spewed out of computers.

For Wright architecture was a culture, part and parcel of life, continuously expanding and changing to meet new Democratic requirements. It was not a series of fads, it was too important for such trivialities.

With 27 years of the Fellowship at the end of his lifetime, with approximately 450 architectural apprentices, it is often asked, why isn't Wright's work more broadly accepted? There are many reasons— despite Wright's best efforts, his maverick approach, he did not attract the sons and daughters of affluence and influential families who set the styles and make decisions about what gets built and where.

Now, at last, more often, the pendulum swings in Wright's direction, and he is admired and revered today as he never was before. His works are treasured, and the public is avid for more and more details about his life and work—especially from the dwindling group of those who knew him.

ACKNOWLEDGMENTS

I want to offer my deepest appeciation to my many friends and others who contributed wholeheartedly to the assembly of this book. Also, I want to thank them for their willingness to share their experiences. It became apparent to me after my previous book, *Apprentice to Genius (Years with Frank Lloyd Wright)*, 1979, that many who knew Mr. Wright from different situations and times, had individual remembrances that would make a different kind of assemblage, and also this would offer an opportunity for me to expand upon some of my own experiences.

Again, my thanks, also to the Graham Foundation, that had confidence in this project, Professor Masami Tanigawa, and Jean Libman Block, who gave of her exceptional abilities, Iovanna Wright, who gave both her remembrances and permission to use her folks' letters. And special thanks to Tom Wolfe, friend and client, the only contributor who never met Wright, for his exciting introduction.

To the contributors, one and all, and helpmates galore, who contributed endless efforts. At John Wiley, thanks to Linda Bathgate, Diana Cisek, and Russell Till for their enthusiasm and professional skills, and especially to Everett Smethurst, our guiding light.

FOREWORD

In September of 1932 a young New York architecture student named Edgar Tafel applied to become an apprentice in Frank Lloyd Wright's brand-new Taliesin Fellowship out in the Wisconsin cow belt and asked Wright to "wire collect." Wright not only took him at his word and wired collect (the telegram is reproduced on page 5) but also said he was accepted "if you pay all you can now." With that Tafel got his first glimmer of the great man's way of life. Wright was chronically broke, looked upon money as an earthbound aggravation, couldn't be bothered with trying to accumulate it—he spent everything he made for designing the Imperial Hotel in Tokyo on Oriental art objects before he reached the boat to sail home—and assumed that earthlings interested in his celestial work would be willing to part with their own money on the spot, too. Today many thousands are interested in Wright's work and his singular life, and all are in debt to Edgar Tafel for settling up C.O.D. with Western Union and the celestial one so promptly sixty-one years ago, especially we who are about to enjoy the pages that follow.

Tafel spent nine years with Wright and supervised the construction of three of his most famous buildings, Fallingwater, Wingspread, and the Johnson Wax headquarters in Racine, Wisconsin, before heading off on his own distinguished career. But Tafel's talents went beyond architecture. He had the powers of a Boswell, at least where Wright was concerned. No one ever understood him better as an architect or as a man or was ever better at bringing him alive on the printed page. Tafel's *Apprentice to Genius (Years with Frank Lloyd Wright)*, published in 1979, is by far the best book on Wright ever written. In it, as in no other, we learn Wright's approach to architecture from the inside out exactly the way he taught it to his young apprentices in the trough of the Great Depression, i.e., with a verve, a showmanship, and a supreme confidence that belied the evidence of their own eyes—which was that here was a white-haired man in his late sixties who was poor as a church mouse and whose career was an absolute wreck.

Now, in this book, Tafel convenes a rollicking wake of all sorts of mortals who knew Wright personally over the course of his nine decades: apprentices, clients, contractors (grossly underpaid), employees (sometimes paid), suppliers (not paid at all), architects (notably Philip Johnson), his third wife Olgivanna, their daughter Iovanna, his sons David and Lloyd, his granddaughter the actress Anne Baxter, plus Arthur Miller, Marilyn Monroe, Robert Moses, and other famous people whose lives crossed Wright's. Tafel chased them all over the world to coax out the memoirs, tape-recorded conversations, and letters we are about to read, so that we get their recollections of Frank Lloyd Wright in their own words, and he has unearthed a gorgeous selection of letters from Wright himself. It makes for a full album and a merry hum.

We see the reigning actor of his day, Laurence Olivier, get up from his table at the Colony Restaurant in New York and go over to Wright's to pay him homage. It couldn't have happened the other way around. With his capes and kingly bearing and mile-high starched collars, Wright existed on a plane more Olympian than any other celebrity's. We see Arthur Miller and Marilyn Monroe drive Wright out to Connecticut to see the farmhouse they have just bought as a retreat from the world of gossip and publicity. Wright walks in, looks at the weary structure and the Simple Simon layout of the place and says, "Ah, yes . . . the old house . . ." America's most glamorous couple shrinks to two inches tall. We see Senator William Benton of Connecticut reach across Wright to try to kiss the hand of Wright's wife Olgivanna. Wright whacks him on the hand with his cane. Benton, a mere United States Senator in the presence of Frank Lloyd Wright, apologizes for his impertinence.

These are scenes from Wright's last years, when his reputation was grand and secure. More revealing is the testimony of the then-young people who knew him in the 1930s at his lowest point. In 1909, when he was forty-two years old, Wright left his wife and ran off with a client's and became the villain of a notorious scandal. After its brilliant start, his career now went into a grim slide that lasted almost thirty years. He became such a pariah, he moved from his house and studio in Oak Park, Illinois, near Chicago, out to Iowa County, Wisconsin, where he built a new house, Taliesin. He needed money from his mother to do it. In 1914 the scandal turned from notorious to lurid when a servant at Taliesin slaughtered the mistress, her two children, and four other people with a hatchet and burned the house to the ground. Wright rebuilt it, but in 1925 another fire, this one accidental, destroyed it again. On top of that came the Depression, and Wright's practice collapsed to dead zero. In desperation he started the Taliesin Fellowship and lived off his apprentices' tuition and manual labor. They planted, cultivated, and harvested the food, cooked it, served it, cleaned up after it, worked as farm hands, gardeners, carpenters, plasterers, electricians, plumbers, masons, cabinetmakers, chauffeurs, florists, and entertainers. (And, as we will see in these pages, most of them loved the experience.)

Wright didn't have two cents to rub together, but his daughter Iovanna recalls feeling like a princess who "lived in a kingdom" called Taliesin. He wasn't about to let her go off to school with ordinary boys and girls for an ordinary education, and until the age of ten she knew neither the alphabet nor simple arithmetic. "When I got out in the world and observed how others lived," writes Iovanna, "I couldn't understand it—something was wrong. I could not understand the way they lived, how they could live in their environment." Eventually she made it to New York City, where Wright sent her to study the harp under the great Marcel Grandgeny.

Wright was passionate about music and it is thanks to Vivaldi and Bach that we find in this book the key to his unquenchable confidence. At Taliesin in Wisconsin and later at Taliesin West in Arizona, Wright decreed musicales every Sunday evening. One evening an apprentice from China, Yen Liang, performed a selection of violin sonatas by Vivaldi with Edgar Tafel accompanying him on the piano. Wright, who was not familiar with Vivaldi, was fascinated, and wanted to know when he lived. Yen Liang told him he was born in 1660. "So," said Wright, "Bach did have someone before him to base his work on." Bach had been born a generation later, in 1685. What a relief! One less competitor! Sublime though he was, Bach had climbed up on the shoulders of giants, whereas he, Wright, had created an entire universe of architectural forms with a big bang, out of nothing. On another Sunday evening, just before Iovanna was to perform on the harp, Wright went to the piano, struck "a series of heroic chords" (in the words of apprentice Carter Manny), and said, "If I had followed music and not architecture, I could have surpassed Beethoven." Naturally. Creators of universes are, if one need edit, gods.

Wright's belief in the celestial importance of his work tended to mesmerize everyone he came in contact with, even those who didn't share the faith. The sheer *hubris* was exhilarating. He made going along with him seem like a ride with Destiny, and many went along against their own pecuniary judgment. One of the most charming memoirs in this book is by Marshall Erdman, who was a young contractor in 1948 when Wright talked him into taking on the construction of a building for the First Unitarian Church of Madison, Wisconsin. The budget was only $75,000. Erdman not only lost money on the job, but then, intimidated by Wright and Destiny, went out and borrowed more so that the church could be completed. Wright kept promising him he would make him a star. For the next five years Erdman stared down the gullet of bankruptcy, but Wright was true to his word. First Unitarian had a roof line like a ship's prow, soaring panels of glass, and an array of twelve-foot wooden oars, as they were called. It was a radical design requiring radical methods of construction. Within those five years, while Erdman wrestled with his creditors, it became one of the most famous church buildings in America, and Erdman's reputation was, indeed, made.

Wright now regarded him as part of the family. In 1954, when Erdman was trying to launch a line of prefabricated houses, Wright designed one for him gratis—to the consternation of Jim Price, president of the country's largest prefabricator, National Homes, who had offered Wright $100,000 to do just that and had been turned down.

That year, 1954, Wright was eighty-seven, a legendary figure with more commissions pouring in than he could handle. The three buildings Edgar Tafel had worked on, Fallingwater, Wingspread, and the Johnson Wax headquarters, had been the beginning of an astonishing comeback. Wright was sixty-eight when he designed Fallingwater for the father of one of his apprentices, Edgar Kaufmann. Over the next twenty-four years, until his death in 1959 at the age of ninety-two, he saw 180 buildings he designed go up, the last being the Guggenheim Museum in New York, completed not long after he died.

His claim to be Destiny's architect was now generally acknowledged. No one has ever made the point more graphically, however, than George Nelson does here in *About Wright*. Nelson, who would later achieve renown as a designer, was assigned by *Architectural Forum* in 1937 to put together a special issue on Wright.

The Johnson Wax building was underway at the time, and one day Nelson was sitting in the big living room at Taliesin when he heard Wright get into a row with some Johnson Wax representatives in a room nearby. Apparently the construction was going over budget. By and by Wright emerged and complained to Nelson that the clients had lost sight of the purpose of their own building, "which was that this was a memorial to Grandpa, the founder of this great industrial enterprise." They were approaching it with the bean-counting mentality of people putting up a speculative office building. "One of these days they're going to be sorry," he said, "because when you go up to the building you're going to see lines of buses that have just disgorged tourists from all over the country." Nelson went back to Racine to see the building in the early 1960s, a few years after Wright's death, "and what do you think I saw? A long line of tourist buses. He was absolutely right about the whole thing."

If asked to name the greatest of American architects, the architectural fraternity tends to name two: Thomas Jefferson and Frank Lloyd Wright. But here we come upon a curious anomaly. As Philip Johnson points out in his conversation with Edgar Tafel, Wright's influence on American architecture today, scarcely one generation after his death, is practically non-existent. In the universities, architecture students are not even introduced to Wright's "organic" principles, as he called them, except as a piece of history. The prodigious post-World War II commercial building boom that created the look of modern America did not draw from Wright's Johnson Wax building but from the "glass boxes" of Corbusier, Gropius, and Mies van der Rohe, the European stars of the Bauhaus or International style. This was galling to Wright even at the height of his fame; all the more so, since the Europeans had drawn heavily upon his own early work when it was published in Germany in a lavish folio edition in 1910. Maria Stone, a writer married to Wright's friend the architect Edward Durrell Stone, tells of having lunch with Wright out under a tree one hot day at Taliesin. Flies were everywhere. Wright picked up a fly swatter . . . *Fwap* . . . "That's Gropius!" *Fwap* . . . "That's Corbusier!" . . . Mies he spared, because he liked him personally and Mies sometimes gave him credit.

How did it come to pass that Wright, so revered within the American architectural profession itself, was so largely eclipsed by the Europeans? Philip Johnson, who as a young man was the Europeans' herald in America, playing Apollinaire to their Braque and Picasso, offers some down-to-earth explanations hereinafter, and others, down-to-earth or otherwise, appear in a book called *From Bauhaus to Our House*. Yet one more suggests itself. In 1970, the centenary of Dickens' death, British writers were polled and asked to name the greatest British writer of all time. There were co-winners: Shakespeare and Dickens. It is the case of Dickens that resembles Wright's. By that time, 1970, there was not a single British writer attempting to do what Dickens had done, which was to write long, dramatic, emotionally charged novels full of rich, highly realistic slices of contemporary life. Indeed, the entire trend was in another direction, toward anorexic stories told with the prestigious juicelessness known as minimalism. (Nor has anything changed in the twenty-three years since.) The truth, at bottom, may be that both talents, Dickens' and Wright's, were too utterly idiosyncratic, too hopelessly *sui generis*, to serve as shoulders for anyone else to stand on.

It fell to the apprentices' lot, and theirs alone, to bring Wright's organic architecture into the future. Apprentices such as John Howe and Peter Berendtson designed countless residences that can be immediately identified as Wrightian, and Alden Dow, an heir to the Dow Chemical fortune, built wrighteous churches and an extraordinary house for himself beside a pond in Midland, Michigan, that, if anything, outwrights Wright. Others, Tafel among them, used certain of the maestro's principles, particularly in the choice of materials and decoration, but developed their own styles.

No matter what their approach, all the apprentices realized their years at Taliesin had to do with something more than architecture. Taliesin was what would later be known as a commune. (Gropius' Bauhaus had been one, too.) Taliesin was Frank Lloyd Wright's big family and, to borrow Iovanna Wright's word, his kingdom. Ego strains between the more ambitious apprentices and Daddy Frank (a name they used, *sotto voce*, when the rebel hormones flowed) were always at play beneath the surface. Apprentice Robert Bishop's letters to his financee give a lovely picture of the doubts the boys were prone to. "Lovely" is the word, for there seems not to have been a single apprentice, even among those who walked out, who did not look back upon his years with Wright with affection. Daddy Frank was not hipped on control. Mainly, it seems, he wanted to have some energetic help and a receptive audience along for his romp with Destiny.

His widow Olgivanna kept the Taliesins alive as a school, studio, and commune for twenty-six years after his death. She was every bit as strong-willed, every bit as regal within the kingdom, as her husband had been, and every bit as difficult, as Tafel's own exchanges with her in these later years show. In fact the Taliesins without the maestro could never be much more than an afterglow. Yet it was not until Mrs. Wright's death in March of 1985—and no apprentice could ever bring himself to call her anything but Mrs. Wright—that the apprentices felt the great adventure was finally over, no matter how far they might have wandered in the meantime. Mrs. Wright's funeral at Taliesin West became a coda, and they assembled from all over the world. Tafel, who had departed the commune forty-four years before, described the funeral to an apprentice who couldn't make it, Byron Mosher, in a letter: "On the plane ride out I thought of the many days at Taliesin . . . and about a visit a few years ago, after a bout of Mrs. Wright's fury. She kissed me goodbye and said, 'Edgar, remember, I am the only mother you have.' That reminded me of how many times she or Mr. Wright would say at a Sunday evening, 'Edgar, play Bach's Jesu, Joy of Man's Desiring.' She will never ask again."

He tried to describe to Mosher what he felt on his drive back from Taliesin to the airport in Phoenix, but he couldn't find the words for it. "Maybe I felt it was what purgatory could be, or that the past was done."

TOM WOLFE

BIOGRAPHICAL OVERVIEW

1867   Born June 8 in Richland Center, Wisconsin to Anna Lloyd Jones and William C. Wright. First child of his father's second marriage.

1869–1878   Traveled with his family to Iowa, Rhode Island, and Massachusetts, where in each state his father held pastorate positions.

1878–1885   Returned to Wisconsin, where his father became secretary of Wisconsin Conference of Unitarians and Independent Societies.

1885   Quit Madison High School to take a drafting job with architect Alan D. Conover.

1885–1886   Attended University of Wisconsin.

1887   Moved to Chicago and took a job with architect Joseph Lyman Silsbee. Published first sketch in *Inland Architect*.

1888   Joined Adler and Sullivan as a draftsman.

1889   Designed and built his own home in Oak Park, Illinois; married Catherine Tobin.

1889–1893   Continued to work for Adler and Sullivan and began freelancing his own designs.

1893   Fired from Adler and Sullivan for freelancing; opened his own practice in the Schiller Building in Chicago.

1893–1901   Produced at least seventy designs, of which forty-nine were built, significant among which was the Winslow House (1894). During this time he also wrote many speeches and articles.

1901   Was subject of a feature article in *Architectural Review;* first prairie house appeared.

1902–1908   Developed and refined the prairie style; began to use materials native to the area. Significant works included Heurtley

House, Willits House, Dana House, Cheney House, Glasner House, Robie House, and Coonley House; nonresidential buildings included Hillside Home School (1901), Larkin Administration Building (1904), and Unity Temple in Oak Park (1905–1906)

1909 Left family and practice and went to Berlin to write and produce a portfolio of his works to date. He was joined there by Mamah Borthwick Cheney, his paramour and wife of a former client.

1910 Returned to Oak Park.

1911 Mrs. Cheney divorced and on Christmas Day, Wright invited her to live with him at Taliesin, which he had built for them.

1912–1914 Lived with Mamah Borthwick, during which time he produced only six buildings, notable among which were "Northome" (Little House) (1913) and Midway Gardens (1914).

1913 Visited Japan with Mamah Borthwick; obtained approval for preliminary plans of Imperial Hotel.

1914 August 14. Taliesin was set afire by a crazed employee and seven people, including Mamah Borthwick and her two children, were killed.

1914–1915 Taliesin II was completed; met Maud Miriam Noel and moved her into Taliesin with his mother.

1916–1922 With Miriam Noel, lived intermittently in Japan to work on the Imperial Hotel. He also executed several domestic designs during the period, notably "Hollyhock House" (Los Angeles, 1917).

1922 Formally divorced from Catherine in November

1923 Wright's mother, Anna, died in February; he married Miriam Noel in November.

1924 April. Miriam left him and Louis Sullivan died. Went to California, where he designed several concrete block houses. Returned to Chicago in November and met Olga (Olgivanna) Milanoff.

1925 Started practice in Chicago January 1; began living with Olgivanna in February; April fire at Taliesin II caused Wright to sell his Oak Park home to pay for repairs; Miriam began legal action against him in November; Iovanna was born to him and Olgivanna in December.

1926 Continuing legal actions by Miriam against both Wright and Olgivanna forced both into hiding; Olgivanna's former husband pursued both of them for custody of Svetlana (his and Olgivanna's child); Wright and Olgivanna were accused of violating the Mann Act; Bank of Wisconsin foreclosed on Taliesin; Wright and Olgivanna were arrested in Minnesota in October; they leave for California in November.

1927 Miriam pursued Wright and Olgivanna to California in January and attempted to have Wright arrested for abandonment; third fire at Taliesin in February caused loss of significant pieces of oriental artwork and other damage; part of Wright's Japanese art collection was auctioned in March to pay debts; Minnesota dropped Mann Act charges in March; Bank of Wisconsin sold livestock at Taliesin in April and moved to take possession of the house; Wright and Olgivanna returned to Madison in May; Miriam granted Wright a divorce in August; Wright worked to regain Taliesin with support from friends.

1928 Married Olgivanna on August 25 in La Jolla, California.

1929 After being a design consultant for the Biltmore Hotel in Phoenix, Arizona, Wright obtained a commission to design the San-Marcos-in-the-Desert Project. "Ocatillo" was constructed as a camp for Wright and his draftsmen, and construction plans for the desert hotel were made there. Plans for Saint Mark's in the Bowery apartment complex were completed. Both projects were halted after the stock market crash.

1930–1932 Few commissions were completed; Wright lectured and published frequently: Princeton Lectures (1930), Chicago Art Institute (1930), New School talks (1931), *The Disappearing City* (1932), *An Autobiography* (1932).

1932 Taliesin Fellowship opened in October with thirty apprentices.

1932–1934 Taliesin Fellowship became established and building of the Fellowship complex continued.

1935 Broadacre City was completed in March.

1936–1937 Reputation of the Taliesin Fellowship grew as the Fellowship produced Wright designs for "Fallingwater" (1936), Johnson

Wax Building (1936), Hanna House (1936), Jacobs House (first Usonian house) (1937), "Wingspread" (1937), among others.

1938–1941 Wright's practice picked up. Taliesin West was built in 1938 and Florida Southern College was begun. Many other significant buildings were designed during this period: Sturges House (1939), "Suntop Homes" (1939), Community Church (Kansas City) (1940), Lewis House (1940), Pew House (1940), Affleck House (1941).

1940–1941 Museum of Modern Art retrospective exhibit was held and Wright received several awards and honors during the exhibit period.

1942–1945 Wright endorsed conscientious objector status for some apprentices at Taliesin. Federal Judge Patrick Stone called for FBI investigation of possible obstruction of the war effort. During World War II no commissions were completed and Wright had a sparse life style.

1945 First Guggenheim Museum plans were completed.

1946–1959 The most productive period of Wright's life. The GI Bill brings many apprentices to Taliesin. During this period he received 270 house commissions and designed more buildings than ever before. He received citations or honorary degrees from at least eighteen societies or schools. Several major retrospective exhibitions were held. Thirty percent of his public buildings were completed between 1952 and 1959. He designed furniture, rugs, and wallpapers between 1955 and 1957. Significant buildings during the period included the Johnson Wax Research Tower (1946), Unitarian Meeting House (1947), V. C. Morris Gift Shop (1948), Price Tower (1952), Beth Shalom Synagogue (1954), Annunciation Greek Orthodox Church (Wauwatosa) (1956), Marin County Civic Center (1957), Wyoming Valley Grammar School (1957), and Grady Gammage Memorial Auditorium (Tempe, Arizona, 1959).

1959 April 9, Wright died, aged almost ninety-two, in Arizona. He was interred at family graveyard near Taliesin, in Wisconsin, on April 12.

Letters from
Frank Lloyd Wright

I received fifty-eight letters from Wright during my apprenticeship and after. I wrote him one hundred eighty-six letters. Most of mine concerned the projects I was supervising. In addition, I wrote hundreds of letters to contractors and subcontractors regarding matters of construction.

My first letter to Wright, not shown here, was a request for a brochure of his school. With the brochure came several weeks of turmoil for me: asking advice here and there about Wright, registering at the university should Wright not accept me, preparing and then not preparing to go to Wisconsin as my decision changed. Wright sent me a collect telegram of acceptance, which eased my mind. I have no record of responding to him that I was coming, or when, but the welcome at Taliesin was cordial.

In June of 1932, I had completed my first year in architecture and was living in New York. I had just read the Wright auto-biography and had become a fan. I looked up everything I could about him (of which there wasn't much on the East Coast). That summer I went to Rutgers University for added credits, and discovered that Wright was starting a fellowship. I wrote for a catalog, which I received later in the summer, during which time I was a counselor at a camp. The brochure was stunningly beautiful—printed dark brown on sepia paper. It spelled out the philosophy of the fellowship and by the time I returned to the city I was completely sold on the idea of studying with Wright.

My parents, of wide liberal background, who had had me attend progressive schools, took my thoughts in stride and indicated that I could do whatever I wanted; they would continue to furnish me with the $450 tuition fee they were paying, plus an allowance. The tuition, including room and board, was stated in the brochure as $675.00 per year. So, I wrote Wright the following letter. It appears that two days later, I received a return (collect) telegram.

Sept 20, 1932
175 W. 76 St
New York City

My dear Mr. Wright —

Enclosed is my application to the Fellowship. Unfortunately, I have been unable to raise more than about $450. for the year's tuition. I could have the $135 for the first payment, and break up the balance... After reading the bulletin of the Fellowship I felt my schooling in New York University quite lacking in the fundamentals of architecture, but could not see any way of being at the Fellowship under my present circumstances. Mr. Percival Goodman, an architect here, advised me to make every possible effort to be in the fellowship. If I could be there, I would do any work asked of me to make up the difference in tuition. I could leave New York immediately and do general work on or in the buildings before the term begins.

If any such arrangement could be made I would greatly appreciate it. In any case, wire collect to my above address.

In reference to any particular art expression, I have delt mostly with the crafts. Last year I worked in the productions of the Marionette Theatre at the New School for Social Research, and later assisted in making stage sets for a large adult camp. Outside of my work at N.Y. University I manage to find time to continue with the piano—keep a few Bach preludes and fugues moving—and do other work at home, such as build furniture, fix lights, dab in paint and do some amateur photography. In short, I have more or less circumscribed about architecture, but have never been able to "live" it. My childhood on a farm in Jersey left an impression I would like to get back to.

I wish you could wire me soon. Thanking you for the effort

on your part, I remain,
Yours Sincerely
Edgar Allen Tafel

EDGAR A. TAFEL
175 WEST 76 St
NEW YORK CITY

1201 S

CLASS OF SERVICE

This is a full-rate Telegram or Cablegram unless its deferred character is indicated by a suitable sign above or preceding the address.

WESTERN UNION

NEWCOMB CARLTON, PRESIDENT   J. C. WILLEVER, FIRST VICE-PRESIDENT

SIGNS

| DL = Day Letter |
| NM = Night Message |
| NL = Night Letter |
| LCO = Deferred Cable |
| NLT = Cable Night Letter |
| WLT = Week-End Letter |

The filing time as shown in the date line on full-rate telegrams and day letters, and the time of receipt at destination as shown on all messages, is STANDARD TIME.

Received at 2120 Broadway, New York   SEP 22 PM 3 25

NAW134 32 DL COLLECT=SPRINGGREEN WIS 22 202P

EDGAR A TASEL= /.08-5

175 WEST 76 ST=

MINUTES IN TRANSIT	
FULL-RATE	DAY LETTER

BELIEVE WE CAN MANAGE A FELLOWSHIP FOR YOU IF YOU PAY ALL
YOU CAN NOW STOP YOU MAY COME NOW INTO TEMPORARY QUARTERS
IF YOU LIKE MY RESPECTS TO PERCIVAL GOODMAN=
FRANK LLOYD WRIGHT..

After nine months, and through a grueling Wisconsin winter, I went home for a visit, partially for a change in scene, but also to see that my tuition would be paid. Wright wrote to me during my absence and from the tone of his letter it was clear that he had a warm feeling for me, as I had done as much as I could for him and the Fellowship. It was a great feeling to have a letter from FLLW.

Mr. Edgar Tafel,
525 Seventh Avenue
New York City

Dear Edgar: I am sorry you are not enjoying your holiday- but I hope your "hand" will help stave off money troubles. There has been quite an exodus here during the oppressive hot weather, Goodall, Montgomery, yourself, Bernoudy and Howe.
The rest of us are carrying on and getting something done. Most of your "Fellows" are heroes. We are planning a descent on the Fair (Progress) all together- with a red flag! Hope you'll be back for the event. I think my friend Johnne Breake at the Congress Hotel will stake us to a supper, a night, a breakfast and a dinner (for 40us) then home. We have cars enough to carry us in and probably out. All we need is gas. We can probably "drain" that from something somewhere.
My best to your people.

Sincerely,

F. L. L. W.

Taliesin, Spring Green, Wis.
June 19th. 1933.

After being at the Fellowship in Taliesin for another six months, I returned to New York for the Christmas holidays. I had been given a chore—to look up a piano Wright wanted to purchase. Since I was the pianist at Taliesin, and since I would be in New York, the center of musical instruments, I was given that assignment. At a later time, when he was in New York, he went to Fisher and had a carload of musical instruments sent to Taliesin C.O.D. The freight stood at the station for about 5 weeks because Wright couldn't muster the required monies.

EDGAR TAFEL:31 W 47 ST:NEW YORK CITY

Dear Edgar:

Thanks for the attention to detail. I do
not believe, however, the double B is what
we want for the solo instrument at the Playhouse. It is the same size as the one we
have now in the L.R. at Taliesin.

Let us stick to it until we locate a concert
grand Beckstein or Steinway or Mason Hamlin.

There is a full size concert grand in a private residence that a Mr. Paul knows about —
that we might get. He said it had been used
scarcely at all and price $1000.00. Why not
look it up through him —

    Chas.W.Paul:61 W.51st. Street:N.Y.C.

Sincerely,
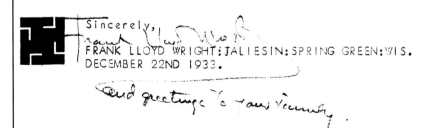
FRANK LLOYD WRIGHT:TALIESIN:SPRING GREEN:WIS.
DECEMBER 22ND 1933.

And greetings to your family.

It is the end of April 1935. Bob Mosher and I have been in charge of the exhibition of Wright's Broadacre City at Radio City. In this letter, Wright states, "The $200.00 was 'creative' at that end . . ." This remark was prompted by my success in obtaining a delinquent tuition payment from an apprentice's father. Wright had earlier asked me to do what I could to get payment.

I was instructed to promote the program in Washington, which seemed impossible. Then the telegram indicates that Kaufmann, who had financed the exhibit, wasn't ready to have it come to Pittsburgh. It went there later. Mosher and I drove the truck with the model aboard, from New York City, back to Wisconsin.

■ EDGAR A. TAFEL:31 WEST 47TH STREET:NEW YORK

■Dear Edgar - I've been rushing about since I returned, lecturing, etc - and neglected your letter. The $200.00 was "creative" at that end and immediately went to work at this end.

It is alright to go to Washington or do anything either of you can do to promote our mutual stake in the Taliesin Fellowship. Use your own judgement in such matters when you can not get a response from me. This Washington matter looks a bit undignified again. A side-show in a vestibule, made and sponsored by ourselves only. Can't we go into the Corcoran Art Gallery or some place to which we might look for, at least, an invitation and some credit? I am getting restive concerning the show. We need you boys and we need the truck. The dump truck we have acquired is going all the time on road and dam-work. Can't we pull out there shortly after the 1st without raising animosity too high?

What importance do you attach to this desire to give me an official job? I am not inclined to take it too seriously. Were there something tangible in prospect I might come down to Washington.

Have yet had no word from Tom Maloney.

Tell Bob I appreciated his letter and saw his forebears at Cranbrook. A pleasant overflow occasion. Mr. Booth, the founder, was quite flabbergasted - had never seen the like

---

at Cranbrook and began talking about building a
big hall. Another job for Saarinen, who was very
nice. The Pavilion had 460 chairs for 650 people
and several hundred had to be turned away unable
to get into the place.

        I appreciate your folk's kindness to
Bob, of which he speaks in his letter.

        Spring is here and beautiful as ever.
We need you both at home. We are again caught
short-handed and late with our work. This year
we won't have such a big garden so we can easily
take care of it.

        My best to you both, relatives and
collaterals also.

                        Frank Lloyd Wright
TALIESIN:SPRING GREEN:WISCONSIN:APRIL 28th, 193

THE COMPANY WILL APPRECIATE SUGGESTIONS FROM ITS PATRONS CONCERNING ITS SERVICE

1201-S

CLASS OF SERVICE

This is a full-rate
Telegram or Cable-
gram unless its de-
ferred character is in-
dicated by a suitable
sign above or preced-
ing the address.

WESTERN UNION (22)

R. B. WHITE
PRESIDENT

NEWCOMB CARLTON
CHAIRMAN OF THE BOARD

J. C. WILLEVER
FIRST VICE-PRESIDENT

SIGNS

DL = Day Letter
NM = Night Message
NL = Night Letter
LC = Deferred Cable
NLT = Cable Night Letter
Ship Radiogram

The filing time as shown in the date line on full-rate telegrams and day letters, and the time of receipt at destination as shown on all messages, is STANDARD TIME.

Received at 54 West 45th St., New York, N. Y.

1935 MAY 27 AM 11 36

NU79 11 XC=SPRINGGREEN WIS 27 1005A

EDGAR TAFEL=

    31 WEST 47 ST=

IF STILL LACKING MONEY FOR VOYAGE WIRE WILL ARRANGE KAUFMAN

HERE=

    F LL W.

MINUTES IN TRANSIT

FULL-RATE | DAY LETTER

ONLY WESTERN UNION
can carry your answer back by
TELEGRAPH. . *Quickly, accurately*

MESSENGERS ARE AVAILABLE FOR THE DELIVERY OF NOTES AND PACKAGES

Some two and a half years later, I had been working on Fallingwater, and in mid-August my mother had come to visit me—both at Taliesin, and on the Johnson Wax project that was under construction. My father wrote Wright wanting to hear first-hand how his son was doing. The reply speaks for itself. I like the last sentence best.

GOWNS Inc.

31 WEST 47th STREET
NEW YORK

MEdallion 3-1929

August 24, 19⁥7

Dear Mr Wright,

Since Mrs Tafels' return from Taliesen we have heard of nothing but the works and wisdom of Frank Loyd Wright and of the genuine hospitality and consideration of Mrs Wright, espeqially when Mrs Tafel had her accident. She is practically recovered now and is creating a more beautiful collection than ever, inspired, I'm sure, by the atmosphere of "Taliesen". I envy Mrs Tafel not only for her visit with you, but also the privilege of having seen the Johnson building in the making.

I believe you can appreciate the sentiment of a father who as a layman, appreciative of the afts but not a creator, lives in the hope that his son will be a creator. As parents, we have tried to do everything for our children and in compensation for the years that Edgar has been away from us, we hope that he will be,at least, a good architect. We hold high hopes for him especially because of his five year association with you.

Would it be asking too much of you to express your opinion of Edgar? We have faith in Edgar because we love him, but you alone know his capabilities. It is because of our great respect for your opinion that we ask you this.

Mrs Tafel joins me in sending kindest regards to Mrs Wright and yourself.

Sincerely,

Samuel Tafel

My dear Father Tafel: Your letter like many others has waited for an answer.

I am happy to say that Edgar has been giving a good account of himself these past two years. Up to that time he did'nt seem very serious and I did'nt count on him very much.

I have always liked Edgar. I thought he grew up in New York in the cash and carry system and had probably been infected, like the others- although I did take him on for far less than the others when he came.

But somehow Edgar seems to have escaped-his fate- and he is now one of the "trustees" at Taliesen. He is getting valuable experience and though he has paid very much less for his training on the whole than many alongside him I have felt that so long as I was a good investment for him he would be a good one for me.

In my opinion, however, he is far from having arrived at the point where he has ceased to profit by being at Taliesen hard at work.

In this process of becoming an architect he has not drawn on his blood parents very heavily and has acquired another kind of parent. A kind of spiritual fatherhood seldom rewarded in our "system" - that "system" in which you and Mother Tafel have to earn a living and to which you refer to with dislike.

I hate to see Edgar going back into that system and hope Taliesen with the help of those sons I have shared myself and my home with these past four or five years will grow up here into a different kind of effort and life.

I can't go on forever breaking in colts to pull the plough or pull chestnuts out of the fire for the system or just for themselves or for "parents". I expect to see the talk of social justice I've heard from you and Mother Tafel (and Edgar too) take effect in the future of Taliesen. But just how this is to be I don't yet know in detail. I am waiting my chance though - I think I hear Mother Tafel say - "yes - a fat chance!"

But just the same I have seen a far less "chance" grow up into a pretty fine thing while I have lived - if I kept on working.

If Edgar is as good as I think he is, he is now a son of Taliesen with affection for his New York parents but no obligation to them. And except as they find it a pleasure to be a help to him I see no reason for their being so after this year ends.

But after all Edgar is a man himself now and what he does with himself will have to go with me.

Sincerely,

WLW/37   .

By April 1941, I was married and living at Taliesin with my wife. I was supervising two Wright houses. The next two letters indicate some of the problems—money, the heating (which wasn't working well on one of the houses), and remarks about the foliage being missing. In the second paragraph he tells me to leave the house alone and then asks where the junipers are?

The second letter indicates Nesbitt sent money, and Wright passed along a total of $100 for expenses at Taliesin, which I and another apprentice were managing at the time.

MR.EDGAR A. TAFEL:TALIESIN:SPRING GREEN:WISCONSIN

Dear Edgar: Expect some money from Nesbitt with the next few days and
will send some to put where the shoe pinches worst.

By "letting the house alone" I meant to do not more than essential - like the
heating,because I am contemplating something radical where the house is concerned.

Wish I could borrow money too -- I suppose owing it overtime is much the same
thing?

I didn't mean to even insinuate that any work you do in the right spirit
(even if a mistake) is ever wasted. So cheer up, son, and carry on the happy
days.

I could see no junipers in the photographs where they were so sadly needed.
Did they perhaps blow out or something?

We'll be seeing you all soon, now -
Affectionately,

Frank Lloyd Wright
Taliesin West
April 7th, 1941

TALIESIN WEST PHOENIX ARIZONA

Dear Edgar: Here is $50.00 to apply where the shoe pinches most, gas, etc, I suppose or whatever.

I am sending Frances $50.00 for household. Will pay up the bills there soon as I can. We must leave here fairly cleaned up and its a problem. Have spent so much on building this year – nearly nine thousand dollars. Not much, but ye Gods!

Wes leaves here next Monday to get his affairs in order – pigs, cattle, etc.

The electric connection can wait now until we get there and Peterson can wait for Wes.

What about Ed? Who is doing the milking? Carey should help milk I should think. We need a good farmer at the Midway – and more cows. Taliesin expects every man to do his best where needed most. I think I am entitled to a fortnightly report of the why and how of what you are doing.

Best

Frank Lloyd Wright
April 10th, 1941

In the fall of 1941, my wife and I left Taliesin for war work in Chicago. We sent the Wrights a Christmas present. My wife's name was Jean, but Wright always called her "Sally," because his secretary was named Gene Masselink and the Wrights thought there would be confusion. Wright asks that I help him with some situation with his client, which indicated to me that he wasn't so furious at my leaving after all.

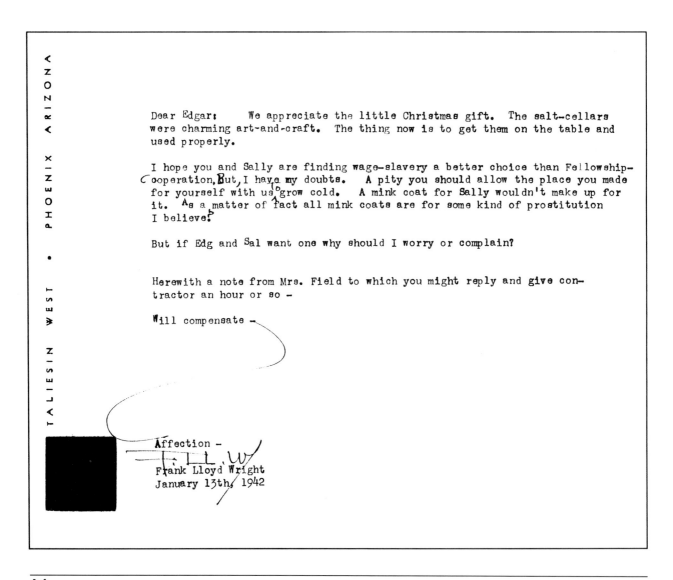

Dear Edgar: We appreciate the little Christmas gift. The salt-cellars were charming art-and-craft. The thing now is to get them on the table and used properly.

I hope you and Sally are finding wage-slavery a better choice than Fellowship-Cooperation. But, I have my doubts.   A pity you should allow the place you made for yourself with us grow cold. A mink coat for Sally wouldn't make up for it. As a matter of fact all mink coats are for some kind of prostitution I believe.

But if Edg and Sal want one why should I worry or complain?

Herewith a note from Mrs. Field to which you might reply and give contractor an hour or so —

Will compensate —

Affection —
Frank Lloyd Wright
January 13th, 1942

*By June 1942, we were living in Flagstaff, Arizona, where I was
involved with construction related to the war. Wright's letter is in
response to a birthday telegram sent to him.*

Dear Edgar: Thanks for the birthday-gram. I meant to answer your very good

letter long ago.

Your Appleman finally wrote but we are working out a new policy — not ready to

receive short-time apprentices yet. I am writing directly to him. First

we want a strong central group (say nine or eleven) intrenched here in these

hills, interests centered here. Then we will take an inflow and outgo of short

time apprentices, longest stay — four years.

Meantime we intend to take it easy "for the duration" (the British taught us to

say it that way).   There are now only about nineteen of us and likely to be five

less in a few months, because conscientious objectors go to war when in a pinch, etc.

I hope you and "your gal Sal" are happy because that is all that matters in any

show down — but I hope really happy deep inside with a sense of satisfaction in

doing well what you want most to do — square with the inner man, so to speak.

Conscious of high-minded devotion to a cause worth while.

We'll be seeing you now and then, I hope —

Faithfully,

Frank Lloyd Wright

TALIESIN: SPRING GREEN: WISCONSIN   June 12th, 1942

LETTERS FROM FRANK LLOYD WRIGHT

By November 1942 it had occurred to me that I should have a letter of recommendation from Wright for future use and needs. His letter is in common with others he wrote for other apprentices—he was not accustomed to helping us through letters of recommendation, which I fully understood. The length of time one spent with Wright bore no relationship to the content of the letter of recommendation. Those who were with him for only a short time got letters that were almost the same as those he wrote for apprentices like me, who were with him for many years. But my request gave him an excuse to write the accompanying letter, which tells of his inner thoughts at the time, both personal and political.

TALIESIN • SPRING GREEN WISCONSIN

Dear Edgar: Somehow I regard the advent of another Tafel in the world as of inferior consequence compared to a Tafel able to carry on a work in the world with loyalty based upon right-minded ideas - instead of selfishness. And violence. I can understand why you should be pleased however -- as you would be at getting some thing to build, for yourself.

It is probably ungracious and maybe a little ungrateful to say that there are too many babies-already and too many parents who are "let us then be up and doing" for us. And too many architects wanting to build something for themselves with no greater capacity to see anything as greater than themselves.

From my standpoint of course that is where you choose to be and I can only wish you (as I wish the others in your same case) a pleasant time at it -- knowing it is not of much consequence anyway.

And I have met the housing Crat as he exists. He is drinking of the vanity of office -- blessed with a little brief authority. What the Crat is is best seen in what he does -- a thorough inferiority. But it is good enough for him because he is inferior.

I will be glad to write a recommendation for you, however, to becom one of them if you choose. I guess you can't feed yourself and Sal now not to speak of a baby unless you do get your feet into a public trough somewhere, somehow.

It was nice of you to take an interest in the camp. We will send Hans there presently.

Page 2

And nice to send us a letter even though you were prompted to do it because you wanted something from us. I don't know if anything more than a recommendation for a job and the gal Sal ever got to you in your ten years at Taliesin. Only Time will tell -- and Time is not telling yet? Meantime it looks as though you and all the others must go to fight to preserve the capitalist system and as as actual fascism (whatever the name it is given by Roosevelt) a conscript. I understand all restrictions -- wives, babies, defense work or no defense work are all off.

So I expect to eventually hear from you all in the armed forces before another year is out and the "freedom to produce" is either stalemate or briefly triumphant. Meantime I hope you make the most of the pennys-worth of freedom still left to you -- on the tires that you now own.

The money matter won't save you nor save anyone else, much longer. The more permanent the position now the worse, really, for the future.

Why don't you and Sal go to Russia and enlist to fight the Germans on the only front that seems to matter?

Affection
Frank Lloyd Wright
November 30th, 1942

TALIESIN · SPRING GREEN WISCONSIN

TO WHOM IT MAY CONCERN:

This is to certify that Edgar Tafel has been a member of the Taliesin Fellowship, working for me for about ten years. He is capable and intelligent. I recommend his services to anyone interested in building good buildings.

Frank Lloyd Wright, Architect

Taliesin

Spring Green

Wisconsin

November 30th, 1942

This letter was sent to me in the Army, when I was stationed in Calcutta. I had written Wright in behalf of former apprentice Yen Liang, who was living "over the hump" in Kunming, working for the U.S. Army in design/construction. Yen wanted to come back to the United States with his wife. In a handwritten postscript, Wright remembers "Sally."

By December the war was over and I had been discharged from the Army. I found that my marriage had failed while I was away.

Dear Edgar: Your letter shows you are still awake.   You can grow.

I suppose we are Yen's best bet for getting over to this country. I am willing, but I don't deceive myself thinking his devotion to me is the motif for coming. So all will be well.   Some of you fellows have waked me up concerning my place in your horoscopes.

Affection –

Frank Lloyd Wright
Taliesin West
Scottsdale
Arizona

April 4th, 1945

Whereas "Sally" ever? We don't see her this summer at the "West" Hee

*In 1946 I returned to New York. During this time I was in-
volved with many thoughts and possible projects. I had already
completed one residence and was starting on more. Edgar
Kaufmann Jr. and I had thought up a concept of publishing
a photo album of all of Mr. Wright's completed works. I had
arranged some of the financing for the project and I presented
my idea to Wright.*

*I had visited Taliesin by then and I was pleased with Mr.
Wright's reference to me as "little Tafel Boy."*

Edgar Allen Tafel
60 West 68th Street
New York City 23

Dear Edgar: Go ahead with your project when you
are ready. We will cooperate.

It was nice to see that little Tafel Boy back
here where his home was for so many years.

Affection,
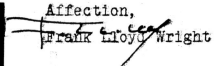
Frank Lloyd Wright   August 3rd, 1946

The Usonian Homes project was starting. I was asked to be on the list of approved architects. But summing up its construction theory, I feared I would have no control of my own design. The idea was that the group would have a committee to review designs and approve or disapprove of them. The approved design would then go to Mr. Wright for his comment.

I wrote him that I didn't take issue with his being the design head, but that I didn't like having to submit my designs to the college of cardinals. I didn't mind going to the pope himself. Usonia went ahead without my participation.

Edgar A. Tafel
47 West 12th Street
New York 11

Dear Edgar: Glad to see you anytime, but
concerning the Co-op project -- no worry.

If they like the idea I submitted we will work
it out. If not, it is all right with me. We will
work it out elsewhere,

Plenty of opportunities waiting as <u>you</u> ought
to know -

Frank Lloyd Wright   June 27th, 1947

Joseph Salerno was a New York-based "Chicago" architect who had written a fine piece on Mr. Wright's work that I sent Wright.

"To Lucille!" refers to my second wife. We had visited the Wrights at Taliesin, and he never forgot a beautiful lady.

Our correspondence dwindled from then on, I was always welcome to visit, and I saw him from time to time at the Plaza Hotel in New York.

Edgar A. Tafel
228 West 11th Street
New York 14
N. Y.

Dear Edgar: Thanks for the
bouquet. Salerno's piece is
near right -

To Lucille. .

Affection,
Frank Lloyd Wright
January 27th, 1948

Relatives

Frank Lloyd Wright was born on June 8, 1867. He was the first of three children born during his father William's second marriage. William Wright's first wife, Pamela, died in 1864, leaving the widower with three children. In 1866 William married Anna Lloyd Jones, who was to become Frank's mother.

Thus, Frank Lloyd Wright had three older half-siblings, Charles, George, and Elizabeth, and two younger sisters, Jane and Margaret Ellen (Maginel).

Frank Lloyd Wright was married three times. His first marriage, to Catherine Tobin, which ended in divorce, produced six children—four sons, Frank Lloyd, Jr. (Lloyd), John, David, and Robert Llewellyn (Llewellyn), and two daughters, Catherine and Frances. His second marriage, to Maud Miriam Noel, which also ended in divorce, was childless. His third marriage, to Olgivanna Milanov, produced a daughter, Iovanna. Olgivanna also had a daughter, Svetlana, from a previous marriage to a Russian architect.

This section contains reminiscences by two of Wright's children—David and Iovanna. A nephew, Franklin Porter, and a cousin by marriage, Robert Moses, also offer their recollections.

DAVID WRIGHT

David Wright, who was born in 1895, is the third son from Wright's first marriage. He became a businessman and now lives in Phoenix in a house designed by his father. David's older brothers, Lloyd and John, became architects, and his younger brother, Llewellyn, was an attorney who lived in Washington, also in a house designed by his father.

MY FATHER

I always like to think of my father in humorous situations. There were very few serious situations. He only disciplined me once—he spanked me, and not very hard. Here's an old story. Dad and I were driving down to Camelback one day and he turned to me and said, "David, is there any truth to the saying that if you take a drink before you're 45 you're a fool, and if you don't take a drink after 45 you're a greater fool?"

*   *   *

One time shortly before he died he came to my house and knocked on the door. It was early evening and we had just finished eating supper. He said, "Let's go down to the Biltmore and have dinner." He added, "I'm sick and tired of everything at Taliesin, with Olgivanna trying to work up some of this stuff. I want to get away from there." I said we had just finished eating dinner but that I would go and eat with him at the Biltmore. He was fed up with Olgivanna and a joker from the newspaper doing weekly columns with her—social notes about the famous people who came to visit the Fellowship. So we went to the Biltmore and had dinner. When we had finished the maitre d' came around, and I asked for the check. "Oh we never give Mr. Wright a bill." I said I was taking my father to dinner and that I wanted the bill. And they gave me the bill. That was shortly before his death.

*   *   *

Early pictures of David Wright's house in Phoenix, Arizona

In 1923 I was with him in Chicago at the Congress Hotel when he got the telegram from Tokyo about the earthquake. I was with Dad in his room there, and Sullivan was there too, I believe. Dad lived at the hotel at the time. That's when he had offices in the Pullman Building on Michigan Avenue. That was a tough time for him, but then I don't think he ever had an easy time. He made his own problems. He was responsible for the furor and the hardships and the controversies, as well as the misrepresentations by the media. It all helped to make him famous. He didn't mind that.

* * *

When they brought Mies van der Rohe over to become professor at the Armour Institute, he got quite a go-around and the architects of Chicago got together to honor him. Dad and the family and I were there. Everyone was lauding how they brought Mies van der Rohe over and so on. Finally after all the kudos—none of the speakers had even alluded to the fact that he had been influenced by Frank Lloyd Wright—and telling about what they had done and how great Mies van der Rohe was, they asked Dad to present him. So Dad walked up the aisle, got up on the platform, turned to the audience, and said, "I give you Mies van der Rohe," turned around and walked off the stage.

JOHN LLOYD WRIGHT

While he worked for his father on the Imperial Hotel in Tokyo (1920), Frank Lloyd Wright's son, John, an architect, was instructed by his father to complete a set of six drawings (two are shown here), present them to the client, Viscount Inouye, and collect the fee for his father. John did as he was asked, kept his unpaid back pay, and sent the balance to his father, who was then in the United States. On receipt of the balance Frank Lloyd Wright sent son John a cable-wireless, firing him. In John's book, My Father Who Is on Earth *this anecdote is told in a chapter entitled "He Fired Me."*

John Wright went on to conduct a successful practice in Indiana, and later in Southern California, and remained close to his father.

Plans herewith were given to me by a Japanese historian, who claims there is no record of a Viscount Inouye, and the house was never built.

The first floor plan shows no principal stair to the second floor, but the second floor plan shows an impossible stair location to the first floor. John must have produced the plans hurriedly.

JOHN LLOYD WRIGHT

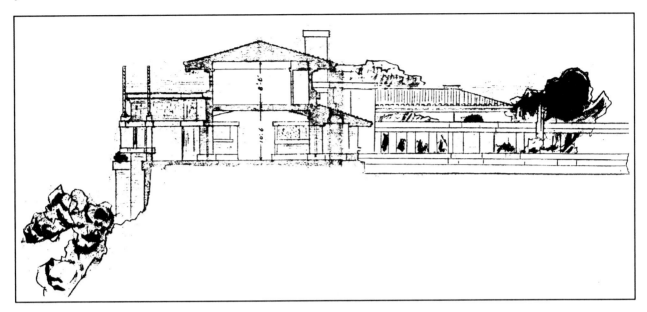

Residence for Viscount Inouye in Tokyo. It was never built.

IOVANNA WRIGHT

Iovanna is the child of Wright's marriage to Olgivanna, his third wife. Born in 1925, she grew up in the environs of the Fellowship and was educated in schools in the Spring Green and Scottsdale areas. Our friendship stems from when I taught her piano; she later studied the harp as well. She has always been an independent person, and followed a life of music and writing; she now abides in California.

REMEMBRANCES

When the Taliesin Fellowship began, I was seven years old. I couldn't read or write, and had no knowledge of numbers. Daddy was dead set against academic education because of his university experience in Madison—remember, he left in his junior year to go to Chicago. When I was nine years old, the principal of the grade school in Spring Green, on finding out my age, put me in the fourth grade—but I didn't know the alphabet. One of the apprentices, Chandler Montgomery, tried to teach me arithmetic by holding up cards with pigs drawn on them. I didn't like it. Then he had a great big drafting-room-size paper with marshmallows drawn on it, and you were supposed to use a watercolor brush to make them blue or pink—Renoir or Gauguin would have loved it.

I felt my childhood was completely different from other children's. When I was about eight years old, Mr. Gurdjieff* came to Taliesin and said to my mother something to the effect of "Your daughter must go to school . . . she needs the association of other children . . . you absolutely must send her to school." So mother worked on Daddy, and that's how I finally was sent—or perhaps today I wouldn't know how to read and write.

*Georgi Gurdjieff was philosopher-founder of a movement based on enlightenment through meditation. Gurdjieff established his Institute for the Development of Man at Fontainebleau, France, where Olgivanna lived and taught.

Frank Lloyd Wright and Iovanna (pronounced EE-ovahna) when she was about nine years old.

Eventually, I went to school in Spring Green and in Arizona—on and off, back and forth, half a year in each place. My arithmetic fell out the door en route. I was a boarder at the school in Arizona for a while, then I went back to being driven in. The apprentices took turns driving me. One of my drivers was Aaron Green—I was thirteen at the time. Blaine Drake also used to drive me—he was the worst driver and once I fell out the door. He didn't help me back in—an awful man. I never graduated from high school, leaving near the end of my junior year. So I don't have a high-school diploma.

Daddy treated me as a princess. In the chapter of the *Autobiography* entitled "The Merry Wives of Taliesin," where he speaks of some of the women who were there—such as Mrs. Moser and one of the Japanese ladies—he says that what Taliesin needs is a little princess. I felt that I lived in a kingdom. I remember

Aaron Green once saying "I remember a wonderful king." He was speaking about my father.

When I was very young Daddy kept a hairbrush for those times when I was mischievous. I remember this hairbrush: it was a light ivory color, round, with a handle, and amber trimming. Daddy would pull up my skirt, pull down my pants, and spank me with the back of the hairbrush. I would put out a great yelling, but the spanking never really hurt.

When I was about twenty—mother told me this years later—Daddy had my room wired, with my room hooked up to an alarm clock in his room. This was so that if I came home at two or three o'clock in the morning, I would step on the wire coming up the stone staircase. The alarm would go off in his room, he would wake up, open the Dutch doors into mother's room, storm in, and say "OLGIVANNA, *your* daughter came in at two o'clock this morning—do something about it," and he would go back to his room. *She* had to do something about it. He never said a bad word to me about it, he never bawled me out. He would only say "Dearie, did you have a nice time last night?"

But sometimes he did have a temper with me. You see, there's something in the Lloyd-Jones blood that isn't good. They all had very strong tempers. Once he and I had a fight in the living room—mother and Aunt Maginel were there—and he slapped me and said "There is no more filial piety," and he walked out of the room. I understood what he did because I knew I had done wrong.

I took it as natural that I should be living in this special environment. When I got out in the world and observed how others lived, I couldn't understand the way they lived and how they could live in their environment.

I might have had a poor academic education, but I had a great education in music. My parents told me early—when I was about ten—that I must master at least one musical instrument, and that I may have a choice. Mother tried me out on the cello. Sam Sciacchitano—a professional cellist who was spending the summer at Taliesin—became my teacher. My parents bought me a baby cello, and I cried and cried when I played it, until the tears fell down onto the cello. Poor Sam sat there not knowing what to do, and poor mother was terribly upset. I also tried the piano and the recorder. I couldn't stand the recorder, so my parents said that I must choose—or else. I chose the harp. I started with an Irish harp,

IOVANNA WRIGHT

Iovanna and her father, mid-1930s.

Iovanna and Frank Lloyd Wright.

which I didn't like, and worked my way up until finally I obtained a concert grand. The harp has fifty-two strings, which all have to be tuned every fifteen or twenty minutes. It was a hard instrument. I studied with Margaret Cooper in Madison, and got a good foundation, and then she suggested to my parents that I go to the master harpist Marcel Grandgeny in New York, and that's how I hapto to get to New York.

I have never gotten over the unity I felt with Svetlana, my mother's daughter by a previous marriage. When I was three, Svetlana was eleven. Mother kept photographs—so precious to me—of Svetlana and me out playing in the snow together. Maybe those were the real days for me. Svetlana always addressed my father as "Daddy Frank." She was a big help in my life: she had wonderful advice to give, and had wisdom far beyond her years. It was never as though she were my half-sister. She was my full sister, and father loved her every bit as much as he loved me. She was my only sister—as nobody else ever was. She had no reason ever to think of her blood father, because mother had done a lot of travel-

Living room at Taliesin West, with Iovanna's harp.

ing with Svetlana when she was very, very young, in the years prior to coming to New York.

Mother and father were, as one would say, wildly and passionately in love with each other. The only problem was my father's extreme jealousy of my mother. He was violently jealous. If a man kissed my mother's hand he couldn't stand it. He would bawl her out for a long time afterward, even when she had absolutely nothing to do with it. Here's one case I clearly remember: the apprentices took weekly turns working with me in the stable. Once, a man named Jim helped mother onto her horse after he had saddled it. My father, coming down the court, saw this. And just afterward my father fired this man, and the man had to leave early that afternoon. That was bad. Another incident occurred in New York, at the Plaza Hotel. My mother and father were leaving and Senator William Benton leaned over my father to kiss my mother's hand. My father, on observing the senator's reach, struck Senator Benton's arm with his cane. Senator Benton apologized at the door.

When I started dating, I could talk only to mother about it, never to father. Father was against my dating altogether. That wasn't right either. He just wanted me to be a princess forever. When I was seventeen he called me into the living room once and said "Cheeky"—his pet name—"I don't want you to get married until you are forty years old." I was amazed at what he said, because a couple of my friends had already gotten married. I was only seventeen, and at that time in your life forty seems terribly far away—you might die before you get there!

My first trip to Europe was when I was twelve. My father had been invited by the Royal Institute of British Architects to accept the Sir George Watson chair. So my parents took me along, and we went on the *Queen Mary*. We went to England, then to France, and then to Yugoslavia, which is where Mother was from. In Yugoslavia, we met my Uncle Vlado, rented a limousine, and drove around the countryside. We went to Dubrovnik and Sarajevo and Zagreb. That was my first long trip away from home. I loved it—I began to see the world!

I left Taliesin in 1943 for New York. I continued with the harp and I began formally studying dance in New York with Elizabeth Delza. I also studied composition and harmony. We went to New York in the winter of 1948–49, and Mr. Gurdjieff was staying at the Wellington Hotel. We stayed at the Plaza, of course. We used to go to dinners at the Wellington, and after my parents left I stayed on in New York with Mr. Gurdjieff. He completed his stay with the New York group that was then established, then Mr. Gurdjieff and I went to Paris together on the *Queen Mary*. This was three years after my first divorce. Mr. Gurdjieff had a large apartment in Paris; he had given up Fontainebleau some years before. Mother had been at Fontainebleau for about six years, I think from 1918 to the end of 1923. When I returned from Paris and Mr. Gurdjieff, I went back to Taliesin. Then I started a group in philosophy in Chicago—that would have been 1950 or 1951. I commuted between Taliesin (Wisconsin, of course) and Chicago, and would stay at a hotel in Chicago. As an adult, I was always very proud to be referred to as Frank Lloyd Wright's daughter. If you have a famous man for a father and people like your father, then people like you; but if

IOVANNA WRIGHT

people don't like your father, then they don't like you, automatically, no matter who you are.

I was with father when he passed away. I was there for three days and nights in the hospital in Phoenix, with Uncle Vlado and Gene (Masselink). How can I ever forget those moments? I do not think of my father's death constantly—I couldn't live that way, no one could. But it does come back every once in a while.

Some time before the recent removal of my father's remains from Wisconsin to Arizona, I had discussed this matter with my mother. We were sitting together in the cove in the house in the desert, and she was saying how awful she thought it was to have this coffin underground, with the worms chewing through it. It's much more beautiful—much more airy, free, and sunny—in the desert, and the desert seemed far more appropriate. The graveyard had begun to be such a doleful, sorrowful place to visit. Moving the body was the very best thing to do. I was surprised at the idiotic, perfectly nasty reactions on the part of the Tobins (father's children by his first wife, Catherine Tobin). I really was. That was bad. They started the controversy, they stirred it all up—Llewellyn, David, and the others. Very, very bad. They had no right to cross my mother's wishes. Besides, really, if you stop to feel about it, remains are remains, they're simply symbolic. They're nothing else.

FRANKLIN PORTER

*Franklin Porter is the son of Frank Lloyd Wright's sister, Jane,
and her husband, Andrew. He was brought up in both Wisconsin and Oak Park, and graduated from Swarthmore College.
He went on into businesses of various kinds, and now lives in
Richardson, Texas.*

WHAT IT'S LIKE TO LIVE IN
A FRANK LLOYD WRIGHT HOUSE

"D'ya know sompin'?" asked one of my ten-year-old companions,
addressing two other members of The Club as we were working to
assemble our crystal wireless sets, "Frankie lives in a crazy house—
the kitchen's upstairs!"

That was the first time I had given any thought to what it was
like to live in a Frank Lloyd Wright house. Though I did love it, my
twelve-year-old playmates never let me forget that it was the crazi-
est arrangement they had ever heard of. I didn't like them to tell
anyone else about this oddity, as I always felt embarrassed about it.
There was, however, a compensating factor. Under the large down-
stairs living room and bedrooms, there was a most magnificent
crawl space housing a network of pipes and brackets. In this space
was a dolly upon which we could roll from one end to the other;
and when one of the other Club members brought his greasy con-
veyance over from his father's garage, we staged noisy, dusty, exciting races. We spent many rainy afternoons racing around this
marvelous arena, emerging sweaty and dirty for a treat of lemonade
and cookies in the upstairs sunporch off the kitchen.

Another secluded area under the house on a platform above
a storage room was filled with trunks, suitcases, and travel chests.
It was surrounded by a balcony from which you could peer down
at the space. By climbing on boxes we could grab the floor of
the platform and then the railings of the balcony and swing into the
wonderfully private reserve. Here, among trunks and suitcases, The

Japanese postcard, Heurtley House, Oak Park, Illinois.

Club was allowed to establish its Laboratory, consisting mainly of a Gilbert Chemical set. Our favorite experiments were mixing things that would either explode or smell like rotten eggs. If the noise was not too loud, nor the stench too extreme, we were left alone in our Club's exclusive domain, snugly isolated from the beauty and comfort of the living space for which the house is known to admirers of its architect.

As I grew up, I came to love the house in a way more in harmony with the intentions of my uncle. But I have always loved best the Wright house in which I was born, Tan-y-Deri (Welsh for "Under the Oaks.") Built on a hill in southern Wisconsin, the house looks across a park-like valley to another hill, upon which, as though a part of it, is my uncle's house. Tan-y-Deri affords a better

Heurtley House, Oak Park, Illinois

view of Taliesin than Taliesin itself, though the house has never been honored by inclusion in a collection of Frank Lloyd Wright's work, nor noted by any critic. Tan-y-Deri in its simplicity, in the sense of space you get as you walk into the living room from the entry and look out over the porch to the hills beyond, in the wide, protecting eaves, in the sturdy, massive limestone chimney offers suggestions of Wright's masterful touch.

After my mother's death, I sold Tan-y-Deri to my uncle. As we reached our final agreement, I became tearful at the prospect of parting with it. Uncle Frank understood, and with a tenderness that admirers of him know little of, said, "Franklin, you can come back here any time for the rest of your life and treat it as your own." After Wright's death, Olgivanna faithfully made good his word, and made it possible since his death for me to spend a few cherished days every summer in the house of my birth.

ROBERT MOSES

Robert Moses and Frank Lloyd Wright were brought together by a distant connection between Moses' Wisconsin-born wife's family and Wright's and the two families' common Welsh ancestry. Formally, they were second cousins by marriage.

Moses's accomplishments were in the field of public works and the attendant politics from the shores of Long Island to the northern New York State frontier. Between these two geographical extremes he transformed the faces of the city and state with state parks; city playgrounds; miles of parkways, bridges, and tunnels; low- and middle-income housing; thousands of beaches; golf courses; tennis courts; and conservation areas.

I don't know which of the two affectionate sparring partners labeled Wright the skylark and Moses the mole—but Moses did see to it that Wright's single New York monument was accomplished. The following Moses talk was given at the Guggenheim Museum dedication in New York City after Wright passed away.

I gave Moses a copy of Tafel's first book on Wright—included here is the letter of gratitude from Moses. His arithmetic with respect to both his and cousin Frank's genius is, however, faulty. Genius is an unquantifiable absolute, which each possessed beyond measure.

—ARNOLD VOLLMER

ROBERT MOSES AND COUSIN FRANK

Aside from a roundabout family relationship to Frank Lloyd Wright, and a long-standing friendship with Harry Guggenheim, I can claim credit here only for successful efforts to keep cousin Frank close to, if not quite within, the law. I have other disqualifications as a roughneck in matters artistic and as an ex-officio trustee with janitorial privileges at the Metropolitan Museum of Art.

Fortified by a devoted wife, cousin Frank believed with all his Celtic fervor that genius rises above codes, and his battle with the city department of buildings is famous wherever inspiration clashes

ROBERT MOSES
ONE GRACIE TERRACE
NEW YORK, N. Y. 10028

June 6, 1979

Mr. Arnold H. Vollmer
211 E. 70th St. - Apt. 25H
New York, New York 10021

Dear Arnold:

I read the FWLW book last night when we were back at our digs and found it loyal, appealing, and a bit too worshipful for me. The pictures of Frank are excellent but too posed. This book raises the same old questions which have always puzzled and plagued Frank's friends - how much is genuine architectural genius and how much fakery? I say 25-75%. Them's high marks in the arithmetic. I wouldn't want to defend such arithmetic in the court of last resort, wherever that may be. I certainly would not hope to get anything like these marks if applied to me in the form of how much accomplishment and how much pure cussedness.

Love to your bride from both of us.

Best,

P.S. - I rate Shakespeare as a dramatist - 80 percent genius and 20 percent fakery.

with bureaucracy. The commissioner of buildings has to live by the book, and Commissioner Gillroy tossed the book at cousin Frank. I was always doubtful whether Commissioner Gillroy's successor would come through at last with a certificate of occupancy.

Editor's note: *When the building department continued delays in giving approval for construction of the Guggenheim Museum, Moses called the department commissioner saying "I will have a building permit on my desk at 8 A.M. tomorrow or there will be a new building commissioner." The approval was received on time.*

We need not debate how much of cousin Frank was genius and how much was, let us say, showmanship. Genius even in small proportions is very rare indeed, and we should always greet it with cheer.

Cousin Frank always reminded me of his distinguished uncle, Dr. Jenkins Lloyd Jones of Chicago, who went on the famous Ford World War I peace ship. I met uncle Jenk at the pier when the ship returned and asked him what he had accomplished. Uncle Jenk stroked his white whiskers reflectively and replied, "We made a deep impression in the neutral countries."

And that, my friends, is just what his nephew did all of his life. He may not have conquered all his enemies, but he surely made deep inroads in the neutral countries.

With all his pretended extravagant contempt for New York, cousin Frank was convinced in his heart that the big city could not survive without at least one major building designed by him, and we are now conferring the ultimate honors on the maestro in absentia.

It is very sad that cousin Frank was not destined to see this museum finished. Other great men have glimpsed the promised land from a distance. We miss him, and yet he is here. After almost 92 years, his body wore out, but his mind, Dei Gratia, was undiminished to the end, and his youthful crusading spirit will surely live, for no man of talent was ever less awed by his enemies or more certain of artistic resurrection.

As to the contents of this museum, I readily subscribe to the fifth freedom—that is, the exploitation of art, which I cannot understand. And I shall fight to the death for the right of the avant garde to exhibit organic architecture, abstract painting, stabiles, mobiles, and symbolism, which just can't mean what I think it means. There are to be sure also comparatively recent works of great beauty and some of coming young artists, which I fondly think I understand.

As to Solomon R. Guggenheim and his family, who have given this museum to the public, we salute them as model citizens, proud of their city, bold and progressive in their outlook, and generous in their countless benefactions. If I cannot honestly say I comprehend all that goes on here, I can admire hospitality to new ideas, for it is only the open mind which insures progress.

Friends

Of the thousands of people who would never forget him, two are recorded here. People who met him or were brought into his presence fell into two classes—those who were impressed and liked him and his style and those that hated him from the start—there seemed no in-betweens.

PHILIP JOHNSON

Philip Johnson graduated from Eastern schools before entering Harvard during the Gropius period. He started the New York City Museum of Modern Art with Henry-Russell Hitchcock, and after the war he kept a position there as head of the Museum's architecture department. At this time he began his architectural practice, which continued—with various partners. His works are well known: museums, schools, residences, etc.

PHILIP JOHNSON ON FRANK LLOYD WRIGHT, AN INTERVIEW

E.T.: What do you think architecture would have been today if there had been no Frank Lloyd Wright?

P.J.: I think what would have happened is the German invasion would have been even more overwhelming on the one hand, and the Beaux Arts revival would be still stronger. That's all. He is the type of genius that comes only once every three or four hundred years. To ask what architecture would be like without Wright is like asking what Bernini would have been like if Michelangelo hadn't existed. You see it's a question you can't possibly answer. Frank Lloyd Wright is in every one of our mentalities, but you notice that the influence of the actual forms and shapes is minimal. That's the curious thing, you see. The International Style was eminently copyable, adaptable, and quite broad. Richard Meier's work, for example, is quite a broad interpretation that's still successful. Another interpretation is that of Norman Foster. His goes on in various ways directly, but where is the direct line to Wright? I mean both the direction of Meier and the direction of Norman Foster are quite original in their own rights although the ancestry is perfectly clear. And in my case it's clear for many reasons, but not from Mr. Wright, and yet there isn't a day that doesn't go by without my thinking of Mr. Wright; there isn't a day that I don't feel—when I have a pencil in my hand anyhow—that the man isn't looking over my shoulder. It's funny. I've never thought of that before.

E.T.: You could remember, I'm sure the first moment you met him—you met him probably in 1929, 1930. . . .

P.J.: '32, '31, . . . when Russell and I drove up to Taliesin East.

E.T.: That's before your show at the Museum of Modern Art?

P.J.: Yes, before the show—so it was 1930. We drove up to Taliesin, Wisconsin, Russell and I; we visited him and he was very cordial. He didn't have a telephone, of course. He was very, very poor. And I remember the room I stayed in was propped up by a 2″ × 4″ because he couldn't afford to strengthen the beams. Of course later Wes Peters took care of that with steel without telling Mr. Wright.

E.T.: Didn't we always?

P.J.: Didn't you always? [*Laughter*] You had to go back and build 'em for him eh? Well that's what I loved about him—he had the right attitude.

E.T.: Where were you exactly when you heard that he died? Do you remember?

P.J.: What year was that?

E.T.: '59. I heard it on the radio.

P.J.: No, I don't remember. I'd lost track of him by then. '59—that was after the Seagram Building. Oh yes, I did meet with him, of course, because I remember his remark about the Seagram Building. I visited him at his suite at the Plaza.

E.T.: What was his remark about the Seagram Building?

P.J.: Whiskey building on a pink tray. He had wonderful expressions.

E.T.: So you probably last saw him at the Plaza?

P.J.: Probably at the Plaza. He called me one day without announcing who he was; the voice sounded familiar. He said, "Who's this, do you think?" And I said, "If I didn't know better, I'd say it was Frank Lloyd Wright." It was. He never called anybody, you know.

E.T.: What did he want? He always wanted something.

P.J.: He wanted me to have dinner with him.

E.T.: Oh that's nice.

P.J.: Wasn't it. We had a stroll. I brought Phyllis Lambert along; I thought it was good for her education. Most charming man in the world. And then once I had supper with Frank and Moses, Robert Moses.

E.T.: Did he tell you what he thought of your work?

P.J.: Oh lord no. He had more sense than to do that. He was a tactful man. Oh yes, he visited the house. All those stories are all published.

E.T.: Of course it's been documented in those letters about his not being happy about being included in the International Style show at MOMA in 1932.

P.J.: Oh yeah, vicious about it. He had every right to be. But I notice he did one, I mean that house in the show and "Fallingwater" demonstrate that he absorbed anything that there was for him to learn.

E.T.: That's where we would disagree.

P.J.: All right. I think he did much better, but he certainly knew what it was all about.

E.T.: Well what do you think his reaction would be if he were alive today and saw his work included in an exhibition of postmodernists?

P.J.: Oh is it really?

E.T.: No I said *if*.

P.J.: He'd be mad. I wouldn't blame him one little bit. He was way above all that, but he was desperate in those days. It's hard to believe that in 1930 the atmosphere was so different from what it is now.

E.T.: Did he talk about the evils of the city to you?

P.J.: No, we didn't discuss much. Well he was very proud of Broadacre City. At that time he was beginning to think of the Mile High idea and that has the opposite connotations of his country stuff. He was able to switch around to suit his mood.

E.T.: To what extent and in what ways do you feel that Mr. Wright's personality and lifestyle helped to shape today's image of the architect as a cultural celebrity?

P.J.: Well in so much as he was the main figure probably in that famous novel, *The Fountainhead*, by Ayn Rand, he changed it a great deal. I never knew if it was a novel or Frank Lloyd Wright himself. Of course he changed the whole architectural world including Mies van der Rohe and all of them. He was very influential on everybody in the Dutch and German-speaking world. He certainly changed the image of the architect for our time.

E.T.: When Henry-Russell first suggested to you that Mr. Wright be included in the International Style exhibit, you replied, "Isn't he dead?" Is that true?

P.J.: No, of course not. What is true was that I did refer to him in public as the greatest architect of the nineteenth century. That was a quote, but I certainly never said he was dead. We all knew he was still alive.

E.T.: Do you think young architects ought to be exposed to Wright more than they are?

P.J.: I wish they could be—I've often been thinking of that—and that's what I meant when I said earlier that we lose track of him and yet we have him with us always. It just seems impossible. Think of the disquisitions there are on Mies that everybody professes now to dislike, but every magazine now has long articles on the exegesis of an unknown discovery of a little sketch by Mies. Where are the similar scholarly articles on Wright? There are lots of publicity books, appreciation books, but there's very little scholarly criticism.

E.T.: And the critics run down the sale of anything of his, don't they?—They say, for example, "Why should someone spend $80,000 for a chair?"

P.J.: Oh all that. That just shows the public knows better than the critics. Critics are difficult people to deal with, as they exist today.

E.T.: They have to turn out this garbage every week, every month, don't they?

P.J.: A friend of mine says a critic is no good unless he pans something he hasn't read. They all want to be read. Then they get mail in and then they follow the mail.

E.T.: Then they go to a better magazine?

P.J.: But there isn't enough on the greatest architect of our time. Maybe do you suppose, Edgar, that is true because his work was so personal it is almost impossible to take off from it? I mean you could handle, let's say, the Nebraska State Capitol, you could handle Goodhue, you could handle Richardson—obviously many, many people did. Richardson was not only a great architect, but he was the most influential. He was very influential on the look of a city. You can't miss a building built in 1890 in any city in the United States—Richardson, Richardson, Richardson. And four years after Mr. Wright's death, you couldn't say Wright, Wright, Wright. Maybe in some Indiana towns. I remember we used to drive through the countryside and have a competition. . . .

E.T.: And in the residential field? . . .

P.J.: Only in the residential field. And that stopped. Because then he changed. The best residences—the ones I like best—are the California ones. Maybe that's because I've seen them last, I don't know. But, you see, he changed himself, and yet nobody really took off from the block houses—unbuildable in the first place. But that wasn't the reason; the reason I can't figure out. I mean why didn't Schindler and Neutra take off more from Wright? When they were alive I didn't ask them. There we had a manmade, godmade tradition right at hand.

E.T.: Also Antonin Raymond.

P.J.: Yes, and Raymond. He took Corbusier all right, and yet he was a Wrightian; god, we all know that. But is it harder maybe? You know best.

E.T.: One of the most difficult things for most ex-apprentices, excluding myself, is that when they sit down to draw, they wonder, "What would Mr. Wright think of what I'm about to do?"

P.J.: That's what the Miesian apprentices do too. It's very natural.

E.T.: I like to bury myself in the problem and the client.

P.J.: Of course. Just let Mr. Wright be a present seed. It's the only way.

E.T.: Otherwise you die very young.

P.J.: That's the danger of apprenticeship, but the advantages are greater than the disadvantages. You learn more surely from there than anywhere else in the educational centers.

E.T.: Wright gave you as much responsibility as you wanted to take, and you don't get that in the educational system.

P.J.: No, I'd abolish the whole educational system. But I'm not very popular so I don't say that out loud. You only go to school if you have a guru like Wright or like Mies whom you want to study closer, but school in itself doesn't teach you anything.

E.T.: The schools are all trying to copy each other, aren't they?

P.J.: Oh yes, they are all just taking in each others' wash and they're sinecures for people that don't get enough to build, and they become professors.

E.T.: Did you know Mrs. Wright at all?

P.J.: Well, sure, I saw her every time I saw him—no, I didn't, because she didn't come here. And I saw her after his death.

E.T.: What do you think this great romance about Wright is—the books keep coming out; people are anxious to know. . . . They want a hero, do you think?

P.J.: They want a hero the way they wanted that hero in *The Fountainhead*. Someone who's pure and undefiled, against the grain, the romantic hero who really conquered all—and Wright did.

E.T.: Why don't we have any heroes?

P.J.: Heroes have all gone—I put that in my recent speech for the AIA in Orlando. There was a great period from Wright down through Mies and Corbu. Then there were some interesting architects of our time, but no heroes at all, and really no form givers. There's no one person living about whom you can say, "Well, you may not like it, but look at his forms. There's something there." I think we're objective enough to do that, and I don't think either of us knows anybody. What happened to the source, I don't know. I guess you wait a few hundred years until the constellations are right. I don't think you can give a sociological or economic or a Marxist interpretation of this fact that geniuses just happen. Absolutely amazing. Maybe he wouldn't have happened just the way he did without Sullivan or Richardson, but I don't know. It would have been different.

E.T.: I wonder if Wright had been thirty-five years later what would have happened.

P.J.: Well, I love that kind of speculation, but it doesn't lead very far because it happened the way it did, and the influence was the other way around. The tributes of Berlage and Mies in 1910 to 1914 were extraordinary. I mean, the American out from the colonies would be the leading architect in the world? That was hard for them to take, but the good ones did.

Wright also changed my life. I was at the Museum of Modern Art and I was building my house, and he said to me, "Philip, you've got to choose, do you want to be a critic, or are you going to be a practicing architect. You can't do both. And of course it was so obvious, but the fact is that he was the only one that said it. Imagine his knowing me well enough, and being confident enough in his own judgment, that he would say that. Most people would just think, "Well, I'll butter this guy up because I might get a show," or something. We gave him a show every other day, if you remember. But he was that strong.

E.T.: Can you just elaborate a little bit on how you think of his work each day?

P.J.: As I work, I'm afraid I say the same thing everybody says, "How would he have approached this problem? What are his solutions to this particular type of problem?" Yesterday I was working on a building about the size of the Larkin Building and, of course, it came to mind, among other things; lots of things flit through your mind, but they can't flit through your mind without Mr. Wright. At last, after many years, I have a house to do, and you can't think of a house without thinking of Mr. Wright.

E.T.: We haven't touched on Taliesin West.

P.J.: Yes, sad story. Well, the famous anecdote—I'm afraid this is much published—when I visited him there once—in the forties or fifties—he was sitting at the end of his room, which he considered his throne, and he said, "Come sit here, Philip.

After all, the prince visits the king." Isn't that marvelous—complimenting me and taking his place carefully in the throne. And I just thought that was delicious. Of course his conversation was peppered with epigrams, one just wishes one could recall.

E.T.: I only called him Frank once.

P.J.: Did you?

E.T.: But this was as follows: he came over to the drafting board and naturally we stood up in deference to the boss, etc., and he looked at something. He didn't like what I had been doing, and he changed it and he said, "And Mr. Tafel, now you see how it is to be done." And I said, "Yes, Frank."

P.J.: You didn't.

E.T.: He called me Mr. Tafel only that once.

P.J.: He deserved that one.

E.T.: He loved a joke so long as it wasn't on him.

P.J.: Yeah that's right.

E.T.: I think he felt when he came east that he was coming into enemy territory.

P.J.: I think so. But that's why I think he called me that night. I think he wanted company—like anybody living in a hotel in a strange town. He didn't like me particularly, but I stirred him up, anyhow. So he just called.

E.T.: And you were the enemy camp?

P.J.: Well I think he always thought so, no matter how many shows I gave him at MOMA—"Fallingwater" or anything like that.

E.T.: After the war you gave a big Mies show and I went there with him. Oh, he got furious. You had blown up a sketch to the size of that wall.

P.J.: Mies did that.

E.T.: Oh, Mies did that?

P.J.: Yes, he did all the installation. Wright thought that was awful, huh?

E.T.: Oh, to take a little doodle and make it into that.

P.J.: It's alright. The dislike was mutual. I remember I was visiting Mies in Chicago and I went up to see Taliesin, came back and said, "I want to see you, Mies, I just got back from Taliesin. I'll tell you all about it." He said, "Oh I'm busy tonight." Mies was never busy—all of a sudden, he became very frosty.

E.T.: But he was the only one of the bunch that Wright would have any truck with.

P.J.: And Wright was the only one of his generation that Mies would talk about. He wrote that nice article about Wright.

E.T.: It might have been also that Wright had turned down Le Corbusier and Gropius and he was tired of that same thing. He changed all the time.

P.J.: Oh sure. Wright was a very protean type. I mean he was in the middle of writing me these awful letters and we'd get together and joke, like the time we met Robert Moses together. Wright was a very genial, loving man—very forgiving. I mean I wouldn't have forgiven that little snot Philip Johnson. Why would he? Because I was always, as you know, indiscreet and yappy. He was a very great man.

E.T.: You spent time with him and Robert Moses?

P.J.: Oh just a lunch we had. Nothing happened. I naturally wanted some fireworks or something.

E.T.: They got along though, it seems?

P.J.: Yes, in a friendly, distant way. Moses was an extremely bright man.

E.T.: I have a wonderful piece, an Op Ed piece, that Moses did at the dedication of the Guggenheim in which Moses calls him "Cousin Frank." They were second cousins by marriage.

P.J.: Yes, I remember. Well, your tape has run out.

MARIA STONE

Maria Durell Stone, a writer, spent all of her adult life immersed in art and architecture. It was early during her marriage to internationally famous architect Edward Durell Stone that she met Frank Lloyd Wright.

After Stone's death in 1978, Maria continued writing on many subjects for different publications. She has written two novels, one of which has an architectural setting.

It was the spring of 1954 when I first met Frank Lloyd Wright, a season that is symbolic to the creative person, a time for planning, growing, for visions of things to come. This was an auspicious time to be at Taliesin.

I was very young, working on my first job on a new magazine. This was only my third assignment—I was to report on a day in the life of Frank Lloyd Wright. Because of my youth and inexperience, I was somewhat intimidated at meeting this important and controversial figure who was finally receiving a flood of long overdue recognition.

When I reached Spring Green, Wisconsin, I found out quickly that any apprehension was unnecessary. I had no need to worry about what questions to ask, or what architectural ground to cover, because the moment I stepped on Taliesin soil I saw that the answers were written on the building that hugged that gently rolling hillside. In the quietude of this setting, Frank Lloyd Wright welcomed me warmly, putting me at ease. His charisma was overwhelming. He was energetic and spirited. I was immediately drawn to him and knew that I was in the presence of a remarkable man. "You look like one of the ancient queens of Egypt," he said, appraising me. "Hatshepsut, or Nefertiti." I hadn't any idea what either queen had looked like, but by his tone I knew I had been complimented. "And eyes," he said, "I read eyes. Yours tell me you're an honest woman."

If I had never received another compliment in my life this would have made up for it. My purpose was to spend one day, during which I hoped to be his shadow. Four days later I was still listening, following, mesmerized with this man I had known only through books and articles. Most of the books and articles were written by his peers, who often used the printed word to attack his individuality.

From this encounter numerous truths have stayed with me and stimulated my thinking over the years. Wright's message that an "individual must be true to himself" has served me well. I learned that architecture, to be sincere, must have "organic character" and must be conceived according to nature. He taught me that "architecture is the highest cultural expression of man."

A few hours after I arrived at Taliesin we dined with others outside under a large tree. Flies, for some reason, were prolific on this warm spring day. Wright remedied this annoyance by having a fly swatter next to his chair. As a fly landed, he would pick up the swatter and take precise aim. "That's Gropius," he jovially exclaimed, and then he would take aim again at another unsuspecting fly. "And that's Corbusier," he would add, until dead flies littered the table and he had struck down the so-called hierarchy of modern architecture. If only it had been as easy to rid the landscape of some structural abominations, too.

I had not met Gropius (I was to interview him later in Japan), or Le Corbusier, or Mies van der Rohe at this time, but they were architects I heard much about during my visit. Wright explained to me about "that foreign flavor" that was "strangling the flow of expression" in the design schools and in the buildings being constructed around America. That "International Style dogma," as he called it, was being forced on us.

Later, after this informative luncheon, we walked through the fields. Wright, his cape trailing dramatically behind him, pointed out the miracles of nature, letting no bird, tree, or small animal escape his vision. He explained that a day, to be productive, must be a combination of different elements. For example, a short nap was a must. It divided one day into two and helped to refuel the creative spirit.

Subsequently, I saw how this diversity worked, and how skillfully he utilized his hours. Time was spent at the drafting board, then a walk with nature, an hour at the piano. Perhaps there would be tea and a talk with his young students, followed by work on the books he was writing, or visits from admirers who made Taliesin their pilgrimage. The well of creativity was never allowed to run dry.

Change, realization of dreams, purpose, nonconformity, fellowship, and, as Thoreau said, listening for the sound of "a different drummer," were some of the things I came away with from that journey to Wisconsin. Heady stuff for a girl just out of school.

Wright talked about his favorite writers, Blake, Thoreau, Whitman, and Tennyson, to name a few. Emerson's line, "what a man does, that he has," was tacked on the drafting room wall.

One of the improprieties that bothered me at the time was the way in which the architectural profession treated Wright. How often I read about the *"enfant terrible."* It took time—in fact several years—before I, in my innocence, realized that this animosity was prompted by his peers' own inadequacies. It seemed impossible that men of cultural attainment could be weighted down with the base instinct of jealousy. Wright spoke about this, and later I was to read his comment on it in his book, *A Testament.*

"No jealousy is comparable to professional jealousy," he wrote, "so this trait was to be expected by the new architecture to say nothing of the new architect."

Our paths were to cross often in Wisconsin, Arizona, San Francisco, and New York. I married Edward Durell Stone, who was one of Wright's greatest admirers, and they were close friends. Edward, though usually gregarious, chose to listen when Wright spoke, not only out of deference, but because he appreciated the wisdom of this brilliant man. Wright admired Edward's work and often complimented him on his accomplishments. He especially applauded Edward's departure from the International Style.

Edward and Wright shared many friends. One friend, Dorothy Liebes, the talented and well-known weaver, had worked on projects with both of them. One evening in San Francisco, Dorothy gave an elegant black-tie party. I hesitated going to Dorothy's soiree because I was expecting a child, due any day. I felt uncomfortable and my ungainly appearance in maternity clothes did not enhance my feeling or soothe my vanity. But Edward insisted. As we arrived, Edward was suddenly surrounded by old friends he hadn't seen since Harvard days. In the confusion and crush of people I moved to one side. I spotted Wright on a nearby sofa, also a prisoner of admirers. He was flamboyantly dressed in a white suit with a brocaded vest. He beckoned to me, ignoring those who stood at attention. "Come, my dear," he said, as if sensing my discomfort, "I'm

William Wesley Peters, Maria Durell Stone, Frank Lloyd Wright, and Edward Durell Stone. [Photo credit: Charles Rossi.]

not allergic to beauty." He rose and came toward me, kissing my outstretched hand. "Is it my good fortune to have you alone?" he asked with a glint in his eye. It was obvious he was trying to help ease my distress. "The most radiant face is the face of an expectant mother. Do you realize you are the most beautiful woman in this room? And the youngest," he said with a chuckle.

That feeling of ungainliness evaporated. His graciousness and sensitivity got me through that long, tiresome evening. A few years after this event, we took our son, Benjamin Hicks, to Arizona so that Wright could see the child.

Wright was enchanted by Hicks, who was a bright, spirited boy with handsome black eyes. Wright immediately expounded on the importance of being Italian, though Hicks was a mixture of Scotch and English as well. Hicks, who was still interested in Ba-

bar and Winnie the Pooh, listened intelligently as Wright talked at length about the land of romantic art and threw in facts about Vivaldi, Palestrina, Giotto, and Leonardo da Vinci. Wright, impressed with Hicks as a youthful listener, declared he would like to be the boy's godfather. We all readily agreed, forgetting that Wright, now in his eighties, and Hicks, just past three, might never have the opportunity to cultivate a mature relationship.

Later, at a simple luncheon in Hicks' honor, we ate baked beans with brown bread. Wright looked at what was being served and said, "In architecture you never know if you'll be eating caviar or beans. One is only a few steps ahead of the bill collector." Apparently it was a lean time for the Taliesin group, but other than the simple fare, austerity seemed remote, judging by the richness of their life style.

As coffee was being served, Hicks chose to play with the sugar cubes in a bowl on the table. Wright took the boy on his knee and patiently though energetically showed him how to build a tower. His elegant commentary was illustrated with a platform of cubes, with subsequent cubes laid north and south, and, on top of these, cubes laid east and west until the structure grew tall and miraculously stayed that way—a simple monolith, or, as someone remarked, "the Mile High tower." I regretted that we didn't have a camera at that precise moment. I'm sure Hicks—a Harvard graduate and an architect—would relish such a photograph if it did exist.

Visits to New York were something Wright, though he protested otherwise, truly enjoyed. He was recognized everywhere, even by New York cab drivers, who had seen him on television. He enjoyed good restaurants, and the Colony, no longer in existence, was one of his favorites. On several occasions we dined there with him. Though the place was always filled with celebrities, all eyes focused on Wright when he was led to his table. Even the maitre d' bowed with more than the usual obsequiousness. On one particular night, Laurence Olivier was seated nearby. Olivier came over to shake Wright's hand. The two worlds of theater and architecture met. It was rewarding to see the silent gratification that appeared in Wright's eyes.

Walking down Park Avenue with him was one continuous lecture on the way modern architecture was "on the skids." I consider myself truly fortunate to have tagged along with Edward and Wright on their excursions around New York. No eager student at Yale or Harvard learned more in a semester than I did on a ten-block walk down this thoroughfare. Wright labeled the tall build-ings going up as "boxation architecture," or as "anachronistic bosh." To him they were "boxes next to boxes," "glassified landscape," "style for style's sake by the glass-box boys."

Resplendently erect, his silvery mane blowing in the breeze, his walking stick used like a preceptorial pointer, Wright would elo-quently denounce it all. At times people would gather, attracted by his stateliness. An audience only heightened his declarations. "Human cages," "social strangulation," "atrophy of man's spiritual capacity" were terms he threw out to all of us. My favorite of all his statements was that Park Avenue was a "crevice in a glacier." He called the speculators who built the buildings "the money-changers in the temple." In front of Lever House, he called its architects, Skidmore, Owings and Merrill, "Skiddings, Own-more and Sterile." He found the work of this large office particularly offensive, and he called the architects the "hucksters of internationalism."

Observing the skyline, he grew pensive, and, turning to Edward, said seriously, "Ed, we can do away with all this." He took in the whole skyline with his cane. "Four of my mile-high sky-scrapers lined up the length of Manhattan would do the job. The rest could be left to pasture." Edward loved the statement and quoted it often.

One evening Wright came to visit us in our east sixties town-house in New York. An admirer approached him just as he rang the bell.

"Is Edward Stone a pupil of yours?" the fan asked.

"No," Wright replied. "Not a pupil, but a pal." When Wright entered the house and strolled through our gallery floor, which was where we displayed a great many works of art, he became quite thoughtful as he studied the different pieces. Using his cane again as a pointer, he went about making quick and witty judgments about each one.

"Lessons in finger painting," he remarked about a huge abstrac-tion by a well-known American painter. Observing the work of an Italian artist, he confided, "This fellow should have looked to his heritage instead of over his shoulder." "Substitute for talent," he labeled a tortured bronze. Had we not been good friends we might have been hurt by his sharp appraisal of our so-called treasures. But his remarks had a mixture of truth and candor, and who could take exception to that?

His comments continued until he walked into an 1875 panelled room and the warmth of the wood and its history seemed to satisfy his romantic side. The focal point in this room was a rare twelfth-century Japanese screen from a temple in Nikko. Edward had given this to me as a birthday present. It was something we both treasure; a mixture of ink, color, brocade, and silver leaf. Wright studied it for some time. His fondness for Japanese art was well known, and he had once shown us several prints he had collected when he was designing the Imperial Hotel. At one time he owned a vast collection, but many were burned in the tragic fires at Taliesin, and others were sold when money was badly needed. He nodded his head as he continued to stare at the oriental figures that graced the screen. "The twin ideas of mercy and salvation," he said. "In Sanskrit it is the Lotus of Truth." He continued to talk about the importance of the screen, pointing out things we had not seen or known. He ended the enlightening monologue with "Now this I would like to own."

Edward looked at me in desperation. I could read his mind. He was always very generous, and I could see he wanted me to give the screen to Wright. I was torn between the love I had for this beautiful antiquity and the desire to present it to this remarkable man. Somehow, though it was difficult to refrain, I didn't offer the screen. It was my birthday present and I was young and sentimental. I lived to regret my reluctance. Frank Lloyd Wright died a year later, and I always felt that this unusual screen might have given him a year of joy.

I have many memories of Frank Lloyd Wright, several drawings scribbled on restuarant napkins, and a letter he wrote to me after publication of the article written about my first visit. Through the years he always found reason to compliment me. When Edward designated the United States Embassy in New Delhi, it was Wright who named it the "Taj Maria." To this day the Indians still call it that. What greater accolade could he have bestowed on me? How often in history is a beautiful building in an exotic land dedicated to someone?

Frank Lloyd Wright was the American dream come to fruition. He contributed to humanity far more than he received. It might be another hundred years before someone of his stature comes this way again. His last words to Edward were, "Love your work, love your wife, tell the truth—that's all there is to life."

Clients

Wright's clients ranged from those who could afford a few thousand dollars to those who wanted mansions, museums, hotels, colleges, banks, and schools. What deeply hurt him was that his home state of Wisconsin never employed him, his adopted state of Arizona gave him but one opportunity—a performing arts building (when he was near his death) and the federal government gave him no embassies, nor anything of importance. When a State Department official was asked why so, he answered that "Wright hadn't sent in a resumé."

INTRODUCTION

To Frank Lloyd Wright, architecture with a capital "A" was a way of life. It was not the building design alone; it was not an expression of copied lines from past experiences, learned in school from old books. Architecture as practiced in his youth was learned by studying in an approved school on the East coast, followed by a requisite trip to Europe, where students absorbed the old traditional forms for future use at home.

Wright felt the Midwest was fertile ground for something appropriate to the American way of life, divorced from the European past. And the people he found in this part of America, and elsewhere, in the course of his life—people who were clients and gave him the opportunity to build his vision apart from the traditions of Europe—held a particular place in his work.

Wright's friendships and involvement with clients were as varied and specific as the buildings he designed. The grammar of a house was the same throughout, as was his rapport with its owners. He kept his buildings and people as separate as the ideas he had for each structure.

The feeling clients had for him was equally unique. Most of the time Wright was in direct contact with the couples he built for, but for one reason or another, and only occasionally, apprentices presented drawings and supervised. William Wesley Peters was the general contractor for two Wright homes, and I did a stint as supervisor for a house in Amherst, Massachusetts. From our recollections of those times, it was clear that clients who'd met Wright personally were completely bowled over by him. As one woman in Indianapolis for whom Wright built a home said, "he was the architect in our life, and this house kept his spirit alive." For those people we apprentices worked for, it was as if we were extensions of Wright, and they treated us with great respect.

Whenever any of us came back from a trip where we'd visited Wright houses, we would tell him about them. He'd always be very interested, asking about the condition of the place, about the owners, the landscaping. Then he related to us the circumstances around the clients and his relationships to them, and too, the problems of the building process itself.

In the 1930s another apprentice and I drove all around Chicago trying to look at "his" houses, getting into as many as possible. We told Mr. Wright about it when we got back to Taliesin, and gave him regards from the Sherman Booths. (He'd built them a house in 1915.) "How were they?," he asked. "And the house?" He told us they'd cut down the size of the original house as he made it in plans. We relayed that Mr. Booth was sorry now that he hadn't gone ahead with the original larger house.

Once, on a trip to Arizona with Wright, we stopped to see houses along the way. Near Tulsa, Mr. Wright phoned his cousins the Richard Lloyd Joneses (their house was built in 1929) and got us invited not only to visit but to camp overnight in the place. Jones was a cousin, and a local newspaper owner. He and the architect exchanged old family stories. From there we went on to Witchita, Kansas, where Wright arranged a visit to the house he'd done for Henry J. Allen. Mr. Allen was quite cordial; they exchanged remembrances of things that had happened while the building was going on.

Perhaps one of the strongest friendships between client and architect was the one between Herbert Johnson and Wright. They met at a time when Mr. Johnson had recently been divorced and was deeply involved with building his administration building (1937–1938, Johnson Wax Building). Later, when Mr. Johnson remarried, he asked Wright to design a house for his new family—there would be a master wing, for the couple and his daughter, a service wing for the three boys. Mr. Johnson not only made a program, but drew up a diagram of a center core, with the four wings emanating. Mr. Wright took this theme and called the house "Wingspread."

Mr. and Mrs. Francis W. Little, for whom Wright designed two homes in his lifetime, were also clients of stature in his view. The relationship between the Littles and the architect changed as both aged. In 1902 when a young Mr. Wright designed their first home in Peoria he referred to them as Mr. and Mrs. Little, as he would continue to right through the period of a long letter in 1912 explaining to them his personal trials, and referring to the bad press about his recent "affair." Wright hoped they would not think badly of him. Years later, the architect called them by their first names.

The Littles were active members of the Chicago Art Institute and were great music lovers, so, in the grand scheme for the second home, Northome House, Wright designed a large recital room. As correspondence of the period shows, the client–architect relationship was not easy. A letter from the client dated 6 February 1912 reports: "I would prefer to have you rather than anyone design our house. . . . but you have made a very strong but unsuccessful effort to persuade us to like and accept something we don't like and don't want." The restored "music room" from this house is at the Metropolitan Museum; the long wall of windows may seem an obvious Wright idea. But the architect originally wanted to use much colored leaded glass, and the client argued that this would cut out the light and interfere with the lake view at the foot of their hill. After many arguments, Mr. Wright settled for clear glass windows decorated around the edges with geometric design of colored glass pieces held by lead mullions.

Another client friendship that lasted many years was with Ben and Ann Rehbuhn of Great Neck, New York. Ben was a free-thinking publisher and mail-order businessman, selling body building and health books. The story goes that he had once studied with Frank Harris in Paris; he had a fine library that was called pornographic at the time. He published books on sex and health, like a *Girl's Guide to Sex*. They were elementary school texts really. He was a strong advocate of freedom of the press.

Mr. Rehbuhn read an article in a 1937 issue of *Coronet* magazine about the architect written by Meyer Levin. He and his wife wrote Mr. Wright, and said they would be deeply honored to have him design a house for them. He designed the house. I worked on the preliminaries and came to New York on vacation. It was my job to present the drawings to them, and it was the first time I was entrusted with such an event!

We made the working drawings, and Wright selected a builder who had worked on another Wright house. There were problems, but not many. The house was designed with an existing tree coming up through the dining area. There were skylights above, and floor heating below. No one told the roots not to send up sap all year long, and when the leaves began to grow in winter, they died and so did the tree.

Some of the furniture was Wright designed and other pieces were chosen by Ann Rehbuhn who was a dress designer. Though the house wasn't experimental really, Mr. Wright was especially fond of it and its owners. He liked them and often visited when in New York, enjoying the fact that one of his designs had reached the "enemy camp" (his term for the eastern seaboard).

About the same time as the Great Neck house, Mr. Wright designed a home for his old friend, the newspaperman Lloyd Lewis. He'd known Lewis since the 1920s but this old friendship didn't prevent the client from insisting on several changes that he thought would make the house better. One particular contention involved a balcony parapet. Lewis felt it was so high that when seated in the living room he could see the river flowing below. I was asked by Lewis to ask Mr. Wright if he would lower the balcony. Mr. Wright promptly said, "no." They argued about this balcony back and forth. One day Lewis became insistent and said, "Goddamn it, Frank, I have to live in the house. I want the parapet lowered." Mr. Wright turned to me and said, "Edgar, he's a client, let's give him what he wants." We lowered the rail.

Sometimes there were unbuilt commissions. In the 1950s Arthur Miller and his then wife, Marilyn Monroe invited Wright to Connecticut to look at land they'd bought for a house. As the playwright recalls, "It was Marilyn's idea to bring Wright up, and one day the three of us drove up. Wright went to sleep in the back seat. I got a speeding ticket for doing 48 in a 45 mph zone. It was a gray afternoon by the time we got up there. We had smoked salmon and a few cold things. Wright warned me against pepper but I had a little anyway. He and I walked up to the high ground where there was an old orchard above a pasture, which faces north but has an endless view over the hills. He took one look and then peed and said, 'Good spot,' and we walked down."

That afternoon, a car driven by several apprentices was following the entourage. Marshall Erdman recalls Miller and Monroe driving the architect up in their Rolls Royce. When it was over, Wright got back in their rented car, and Erdman asked him, "How did you like Marilyn Monroe." And Wright said, "she carries herself well."

Drawings of a house arrived. Watercolor sketches, Miller recalls. "They were simply impossible." The architect had designed a circular living room with ovoid stone columns covering a sixty-foot diameter. A native stone swimming pool jutted out over the grade which would have meant twelve-foot or more retaining walls. "The place was very formal with very little sleeping room." Wright had envisioned an entertainment house, something fit for a corporation not two people in the country. "He simply had it all wrong," Miller adds.

Then there were those clients who hadn't met Wright. They sent letters, photos of their sites, and programs, and he went ahead and "drew-up" the plans. Something was lacking in these relationships. The architect was designing for an imaginary client; the owner was fearful of the "genius" conception; and, always, there were problems of running over budget. One eastern client in this category told me we were a "bunch of wild Indians out there" (meaning at Taliesin), and another in northern Wisconsin feared that any communication with Mr. Wright would lead to trouble. But the true believers—those who made the trip to Taliesin, saw the Fellowship in action, got to know those of us who worked on the buildings—had special excitements, experiences, and results that they lived with and cherished for the rest of their lives.

*   *   *

Following is a story related to me by Eugene Masselink, Mr. Wright's secretary. I call it "The Lutherans are Coming."

A building committee from a Lutheran church came to see Wright; they discussed a program and went away, being told to come back in two weeks. When the two weeks were about up, Gene suggested to Wright they call off the visit to see the plans— they hadn't been started—at the last minute. Mr. Wright had the plans for an abandoned job, a small shopping center, brought out of the vault, and he changed the titles on the areas: the bank became the sanctuary, the supermarket became the Fellowship hall, the stores were entitled classrooms, and on and on. The Lutheran title was inscribed just as the Lutherans arrived, and Mr. Wright showed them the drawings, with accustomed gusto and aplomb. After he finished his talk, the pastor said: "Let us pray," and went on, as heads were lowered: "Lord, we thank thee for leading us to a great architect, who has designed in your honor, a great edifice we will use and enjoy. Amen." Heads were raised; the clients departed; end of story? The building never got built.

THE LITTLES' HOUSE

In 1902, when Mr. Wright was 35 years old, Francis W. Little engaged him to design a house and stable in Peoria, Illinois. Not long after, D. D. Martin, of Buffalo, New York, visited the house, when considering Wright to be his architect—and the Martin visit eventuated in Wright's design of the Larkin Building and five residences in that area.

Little later helped finance the drawings and production of the German publication of *Ausgeführte Bauten*, and undoubtedly Mr. Little knew the circumstances of Wright's trip to Europe, accompanied by his former client, Martha ("Mamah") Borthwick Cheney.

It was Mr. Wright's custom to tell stories about his clients, their occupations and lives in general, while in the drafting room, and/or going through photo and drawing files—but never a word was said about the Littles. But the Martins were always and often the subject of stories.

In 1911 the Littles moved to Minneapolis and again engaged Wright to design a house out of the city on a lake—a country/weekend structure. Apparently they were awaiting Wright's return from Germany to begin drawings.

Wright had left his wife and children and had gone to Europe with his former client's wife Mamah Borthwick Chaney, and apparently Wright was deeply concerned that the ongoing unfavorable press regarding his personal life would hamper his design of the Little country house. The following letter to the Littles indicates Wright's appeal. At this time Wright was 45 years old.

The house was completed in 1914. After the Littles passed away, it was inherited by their daughter and her husband, who lived in it until 1971.

TALIESIN
Spring Green
WISCONSIN Jan 3d 1912.

600·610·ORCHESTRA·HALL·CHICAGO
TELEPHONE·HARRISON·457

Dear Mr and Mrs Little —

I assume that the nature of my situation here was pretty well known to you — I could not very well have informed you more in detail as things stood — but want you to know I am not insensible to much that you have done. however it may seem. The long expected news paper out break has come — and the situation no doubt has reached you — in bad line and false colors — the usual caricature of any thing touching sex or family. made for the man in the street and aimed at his moral predjudices for respectability. —

I dont care to whittle away at them and sandpaper them to my ideas in the idiotic fashion of "good" fatherhood — but I love them. I love my work — my mother and sisters, my aunts here and the few friends I possess. I had very few — fewer than most men. I have not been a very good friend — and I love this woman who has cast in her lot with me here not wisely but too well. She too has her remunerative work — as I have. She is quite able to supply her own needs — and we work together — But above all them all I believe I love the Truth in my own soul — that which is the God in me and commands me — and so — no christian. for I have not lost my soul in order to find it except to the vision in my soul and now I am the slave of Truth only. I want to die no less devoted than now and would you wish me to "wake up" as you call it? Believe me sincerely grateful and happy in the thought that you cared enough to help me if you could —

As always your friend
Frank Lloyd Wright.

N.B. —
The phaeton awaits mothers advent — this is her home as well as mine and she is expected soon. F.LW.

TALIESIN
Spring Green
Wisconsin Jan. 3, 1912

Dear Mr. & Mrs. Little—

I assume that the nature of my situation here was pretty well known to you—I could not very well have informed you more in detail as things stood—but want you to know I am not insensible to much that you have done—however it may seem. The long expected newspaper outbreak has come—and the situation no doubt has reached you—in bad line and false colors—the usual caricature of anything touching sex or family—made for the man in the street and aimed at his moral prejudice for respectability—and his salacious weakness for profit. All was invented absolutely except a statement of the facts I saw fit to make because I didn't want anyone to employ me in ignorance of the facts or to neglect to do so either for that matter. But it was perverted in many sentences and belied my sentiments in important particulars. Small matter. It will soon be forgotten.

I am only sorry that when they were through I had seemed to apologise and complain whereas I did neither.

Never have I reflected upon Mrs. Wright in any way or upon her attitude in this at any time—nor ever will. I took the privilege of acting according to my sense of right no matter what it cost her. She is entitled to the same privilege even though it pains me. It is beyond question now that I could never live in the married state as it now exists. My marriage was no worse perhaps better than the average in some respects but I was constrained in it to feelings I ought to feel and did not—shamed by subscriptions to principles I knew in my heart to be only predjudices—the whole atmosphere in which I lived an established property in human souls—wherein one *must* give without the impulse, *be* without *choice,* irrevocably bound to a condition I had learned to hate with my whole strength.

My children as are other children were infected by the idea that father and mother existed solely for them—the slavist sentimentality of a perverted Christianity; victims of the delusion that marriage confers rights which only sympathy can claim. In short it was death to any freedom loving spirit—were there no other woman and no other children on earth.

Mrs. Wright and I only angered and stultified one another. The children were demoralized by that depressing consciousness in the atmosphere. Of course all I have and may earn is theirs still and will continue to be and there is no real happiness for me unless I can help them. It might have worked out differently for me in a fairer way to all if I were a different sort—I would do it now however as it has been done were I confronted by the same situations—no one can judge those situations but myself—So you see I am as Mr. Little said, "a hopelessly selfish piece."

The now high sentimentality that puddles the foundations of property into place nauseates me. The animosity of current morality hisses like a snake in my ears, The "Jones conscience" of which I once stood in awe manifests itself chiefly as *fear,* the *dread* of wills sick with ambition; dread to be accounted less than their pretensions would leave them, Respectability is thin—but no less desirable on that account I believe. Our skins are thin but serve to contain the blood that circulates within them—the blood that is life. But this Christian "respectability" of the world is a sallow skin stretched over human bones—no blood beneath it. "The Corpse in the Cargo."

But this is no tirade. I am the fool now—but honest—at least: A barnyard fowl I never was! For twenty two years I tried its in common and in competition with fowls good for nothing else! I may be no more than a peacock destined to feathers and a struts but—*as one is:* to be the best one sees: in that is manliness & heaven enough for me—and may God be merciful to me for what lies I told and lived to get there and credit given for those I would not tell. In marriage there is no *giving* there is no *choice*—for all *belongs* any way. There is *no being* except as one may happen to live wholly, when all other questions die in that fact and few find it. So the institution is like a relentless clamp from without and which with property turning the screw soon binds manhood and womanhood and childhood in perpetual slavery or—the sort of disgusting thing one hears and sees revealed as its price wherever men congregate and talk of themselves. I hope the women are more discreet. But if this sounds like the cry of a wounded egoist, pessimism of the day—it is not so. There is no complete home happiness for me or mine now—There is love in my heart still for life at its height and a desire to serve—I really live only when I can feel my life in keeping with me, as I am: Once I wrote a poem—many years ago—a cry of the ego rampant—I called it "As I Am" and like a fife and drum corps coming down the street it was too much for almost anybody—but I have it—and value it yet. I love my children with an agonizing love and the desire to be something that will count with them—something helpful in their lives is stronger than ever. I must be something that they will have in their veins with pride and conscious of its strength.

I don't care to whittle away at them and sandpaper them to *my* ideas in the idiotic fashion of "good" fatherhood—but I love them all—I love my work—my mother and sisters, my aunts here and the few friends I possess—I had few—fewer than most men.

I have not been a very good friend—and I love the woman who has cast in her lot with me here not wisely but too well. She too has her remunerative work—as I have. She is quite able to supply her own needs—and we work together—But above them all I believe I love the truth in my own soul—that which is the God in me and commands me—and so—no Christian for I have not lost my soul in order to find it except to the vision in my soul and now I am the slave of Truth only. I want to die no less devoted than now and would you wish me to "wake up" as you call it?

Believe me sincerely grateful and happy in the thought that you cared enough to help me if you could—

As always your friend

Frank Lloyd Wright

N.B.
The phaeton awaits mothers advent
—this is her home as well as mine and she is expected soon.
F.L.W.

During the preparation of material for the 1938 Architectural Forum, Wright made a trip to Minneapolis to direct the photography, taking along then apprentice John Lautner, who remembers that the Littles were not there. He and Mr. Wright moved the furniture about for the photographer. We know that almost all of the furniture in the house was brought from Peoria.

In the early 1970s I wrote a review of a new Wright book for the *A.I.A. Journal*, but before sending it in, I realized it would be best to have a former apprentice review it. I sent it to John Howe; we had shared many years together, much of it in the drafting room. John was then practicing in Minneapolis, and when writing back his approval, mentioned the Little House in part of his letter, reproduced on the facing page.

The Howe information generated a series of phone calls on my part. I called John for details. I called the Lovnesses, Wright clients in Minneapolis (who were friends of the daughter of the original owners). I asked Don Lovness to investigate the possibility of the house going to the museum; he called back within an hour and said he had a verbal "hold" on the house for that purpose. With the thought that the Little House would be a wonderful exhibit for the Metropolitan Museum of Art in New York, I called its architect, Arthur Rosenblatt. Arthur and I met that same day and reviewed photos of the house. The next morning Arthur presented the idea to Thomas Hoving, the director, who thought it would fit for the museum. In fact, he had spent the last summer on the lake bordering the Little House and had already admired it.

Soon I ventured to Minneapolis with two curators, and they, too, loved the house. I stayed on with the Lovnesses to do some planning, and returned to New York happy to have been a principal in saving at least parts of a Wright house from extinction. Some months passed, and many of us who were concerned traveled to the Little House to bid it farewell. We did this with mixed feelings, for while we did preserve some of the house, it would never again be part of the environment in which Wright had created it. And, I knew that Olgivanna would vehemently disapprove scattering the parts.

On returning, I called Arthur Rosenblatt and suggested that Director Hoving would be the best person to break the news to Mrs. Wright. (I had told Wes Peters about the Metropolitan's plans already, but he exclaimed he would not be the bearer of ill tidings, for she would be angry at him. He also stated it was not one of Mr.

7601 WAYZATA BLVD. • MINNEAPOLIS, MINN. 55426 • PHONE 544-7022

A R C H I T E C T

October 13, 1971

Dear Edgar,

I was delighted to get the preliminary draft of your review
of "Genius and the Mobocracy". I think what you have written
about Mr. Wright is very good, and gives some badly needed
insights into what he was really like, and what those times
were like.

The big F. W. Little house "Northome" on Lake Minnetonka is
about to be torn down. Mrs. Stevenson, the daughter, inherited
the house many years ago, feels it is only a burden, and is
building her French provincial dream house in the side yard.
The price tag on the big house is too high for anyone to consider
buying it, taxes are exorbitant, and the community (Deephaven, a
part of the suburb of Minnetonka) couldn't care less. There
was an article about it in the Minneapolis paper and I have
heard that some members of the AIA were trying to organize a
protest group, but I have not been contacted and I do not think
anything has come of it.

Saving important buildings has become a case of "crying wolf"!:
There is an outcry for preservation every time an ugly old
Victorian house or warehouse is threatened with destruction,
so few really care when a real masterpiece vanishes.

As ever,

Jack

Wright's best works, though I disagreed.) I concocted a letter for Hoving to send to Mrs. Wright in which I said that I considered her husband the greatest architect of all time. I wrote, "It has been brought to our attention that the house was to be demolished and could not remain intact. After checking all other possibilities, we decided it had to be saved and done immediately." I added that I hoped she would understand. Hoving sent Mrs. Wright my concocted letter, and soon thereafter I received a letter from her—soft at first, for my wife had recently passed away, and then the essence of it:

OLGIVANNA LLOYD WRIGHT
March 23, 1972

Dear Edgar,

    Of course you added one more disappointment to the already hard life that has struck Taliesin of late. It seems to me that on ethical, even spiritual, basis you would have contacted me about any building that Mr. Wright had built, the fate of which had to be decided one way or another. I believed that love and respect of me and my judgement would have prompted you to do so. Interior values are not always measured by prestige nor are they measured in terms of dollars and cents. I know that you were prompted by good intentions, but sometimes when man omits a higher duty, even material benefits suffer from it.

    Personal contact from time to time -- of which there is so little left on this earth for everyone -- is essential as your meeting the payment of your next bills. I cannot believe that you have not learned that from your terrible experiences you went through of late.

    I hope to see you soon at Taliesin.

With love
Olgivanna Lloyd Wright

Wes must have told her everything, for upon receipt of her letter, and feeling betrayed, I called Rosenblatt to ask whether Hoving had ever sent "our" letter. He said not only did it go, but Mrs. Wright wrote a thank you letter, posted the same day as the letter to me:

OLGIVANNA LLOYD WRIGHT

March 23, 1972

Dear Mr. Hoving,

Thank you for your letter informing me that your museum is going to preserve the "fragment" of the Francis Little house designed by my husband. However, that in itself is violating his principle of organic architecture. It is too bad that Minneapolis was not up to preserving this great building on the site and in, the environment for which it was designed.

I wish you as much success as can be expected under such circumstances. I hope that you are able to re-erect the Great Living Room in such a way as to preserve its original quality of lines and space.

Sincerely,

The living room is now in the American Wing of the Metropolitan Museum of Art in New York and the library is in the Allentown Art Museum, which I designed. Parts of the furnishings and stained glass windows are in many museums around the country.

I often think back historically: If there had been no Great Depression, Wright would not have started his Fellowship. That Fellowship was directly and indirectly responsible for the reemergence of his practice; and we who were there, working the fields, pushing pencils around the drawing boards, being part of an organic architecture—would not have been around to help save, directly or indirectly, some of Wright's works for generations to come.

LEE ACKERMAN

Lee Ackerman, a real estate developer who resides in Phoenix, was graduated from Harvard with a degree in engineering. He was a newspaper writer on several newspapers including the New York Times *and the* Boston Globe. *Later he went into banking and then the advertising business, before moving to Arizona, where he conducted land development programs. It was during some real estate development activities that he employed Mr. Wright.*

In early 1954, as a fledgling real estate developer, I received an opportunity to purchase 160 acres of land, the site of an old airport in Paradise Valley, Arizona. I believe the purchase price was $125 per acre with approximately $500 down and the balance to be paid over a lengthy period with interest rates at 5% or 6% per annum. (Today, this site is filled with shopping centers and subdivision homes, and I would estimate the value to be about $8 a square foot, or over $30,000 per acre.)

Sometime during the early part of the year, I was in a discussion with some people concerning the fact that trailer house living had been a second- and third-class mode since the outset of the use of mobile homes during World War II. Further discussion led to the fact that it was a shame that something better could not be afforded for people who live in these homes, since the mobile homes themselves were starting to be tremendously upgraded. It occurred to me at the time that perhaps a mobile home park might be an ideal use for my desert acreage.

I considered all the possibilities and decided that the best way to approach changing trailer-house living would be to get a top-flight, nationally known architect. Since I was aware of Frank Lloyd Wright's internationally acclaimed reputation, and because I was aware of his presence in Scottsdale at Taliesin West, I decided to contact Mr. Wright as my first choice.

I telephoned Taliesin West and found that Mr. Wright was in residence in Spring Green. I telephoned him to see if he would be interested in the project. As I best recall the conversation, I said, "Mr. Wright, I don't know that you are the best architect in the entire world," and he replied "We think we are." I said, "But I do know that if you would tackle this problem of changing trailer living from second class to first class, a great deal of attention could be focused on the project, and I might be able to get it off the ground."

He invited me to come visit in Spring Green and I readily accepted. I had no money, but I borrowed $250 from a friend to make the trip. I was met at the airport in a nearby town by Wesley Peters, who was then a young assistant to Mr. Wright and who later headed the Wright foundation. If my recollection serves me right, Mr. Peters drove a Rolls Royce. At any rate, it was a great deal more of an automobile than I had been used to riding in.

When I arrived at Taliesin, I was impressed both by the serene beauty of the setting and the contrasting bustle of scurrying young architects. I was introduced to Mrs. Wright first, who took me into a small dining room where she and I and Mr. Wright had lunch. During the course of the meal, a pay telephone on the wall rang about four times. The first call was from the University of Mexico asking if Mr. Wright would address a seminar in Mexico City. The phone was answered by one of the young apprentices, and Mr. Wright, I believe, acquiesced in that engagement.

The next call was from the American Institute of Architects of New York City, asking Mr. Wright to speak at a forthcoming convention of architects. As I recall, Mr. Wright rejected that meeting because of a conflict in his schedule. The third call was from Florence, Italy, asking if it were possible to have Mr. Wright's traveling exhibit available to them after it left Rome. I do not remember the answer to that question, but I do remember being more than slightly overwhelmed at this point, although my hosts had me at ease as far as personal conversation was concerned.

I did manage to ask him why he had the pay telephone on the wall, and he explained that, with so many students from all over the world, more than occasionally they had gotten homesick and run up very costly long distance bills, which they were unable to pay and he not willing to pay, so he had decided to put in the pay telephone as a defensive measure. As we were finishing lunch, one of the young students came in and advised Mr. Wright that he had a business meeting with a gentleman from Bartlesville, Oklahoma.

Mr. Wright asked me to come along with him and sit a few minutes outside his office while he took care of his business. The partitions in his office were thin, and I could hear everything being said. The gentleman from Bartlesville said, "Mr. Wright, I would like you to design a home for me in Paradise Valley, Arizona, and an office building in Bartlesville. I intend to spend about $2 million for my home and about $20 million for my office building." Mr. Wright responded, "If we decide to take on the project, you realize that our fee is 10%?" The gentleman said, "Would you like me to write out a check to you for that amount?'

At that point, sitting in the hall, no money to my name and there on borrowed funds, I had a deep, sinking feeling in the pit of my stomach. Shortly after, Mr. Wright concluded his meeting and I was ushered in to sit down with him. I believe I said, "Mr. Wright, I have to explain to you that I do not have any money to do this project. My hope was that you would do such an outstanding job that I would be able to finance the project from people's desire to be associated with your new concept." Mr. Wright said, "Lee, don't you have any money at all?" I replied that I did not. He asked me if I could dig up any money, and when I asked how much, he said $250. With my promise of $250 he agreed to do the job and said that he would not wait for the money to begin working. He said that he was particularly interested because it was challenging and different, and because he had never done anything other than Taliesin in Arizona and wanted to do more.

I flew back to Phoenix, got together the $250 and sent it off to Mr. Wright with an agreement that we would pay a substantial fee if and when the project came to fruition. He apparently had not waited for the money, because within a week I got my first sketch of the project. Unfortunately, in his desire to create something beautiful, Mr. Wright had also made the mobile home sites over an acre each, and it would not have been feasible to develp the project accordingly. I got on the phone to Mr. Wright and explained the problem, again with some trepidation as I had heard that he was very difficult to work with.

He said, "Lee, we can do anything to make this feasible," and within two weeks I had another set of sketches cutting the size of the lot to a quarter of an acre, which although still four or five times the size of a normal mobile home lot, did at least make the project appear feasible. There were, I believe, a total of four or five differ-ent drawings, with each one on lovely parchment containing a one-line missive saying "Is this okay, Lee?" or "Call me when you have a chance to review this information."

I went around with the drawings to the local building authorities and tried to get the property zoned. Given the design, they were inclined to go with me, but asked for figures on the cost of bringing in water, sewers, and other utilities. Although all of these items are on the site today, at that time they were neither nearby nor were the utility companies willing to bring their lines anywhere vaguely close for me to develop the property on an economically sound basis. I spent about a year trying to solve those problems, and finally abandoned the project. All during the course of this time and in several visits to Taliesin West for dinner with the Wrights, Mr. Wright could not have been more kind and more solicitous, and all the stories that I had heard about his cantankerous manner and temper were, at least in my experience, not true. When he died in 1959 I felt that, although I had not had much contact with him in recent years, I had lost a wonderful friend, and that the world had lost an outstanding architect and one of the most outstanding personalities of his time.

Some time later Mrs. Wright asked to have the drawings returned and I agreed to her request. However, I did not give up my one-line letters from Mr. Wright, which are in my safety deposit box and which I intend to bequeath to my children and grandchildren as a legacy of a wonderful experience in my life.

ARTHUR MILLER

Arthur Miller is the well-known author of many successful dramas. He met Wright on the one occasion described here in order to have Wright design a house for himself and his wife at the time, Marilyn Monroe. Here is the self-typed response to my request of his recall.

ARTHUR MILLER

3/7/86

Dear Edgar;

We had bought an old, rundown farm. The old house was naturally near the road and, besides, needed a great deal of work. It was Marilyn's idea to bring Wright up and one day the three of us drove up. Wright went to sleep in the back. I got a speeding ticket for doing 48 in a 45 mph zone, an inauspicious sign.

It was a gray afternoon by the time we got up here. We had brought smoked salmon and a few cold things. Wright warned me against pepper but I had a little anyway. He and I walked up to the high ground where there was an old orchard above a pasture which faces north but has an endless view over the hills. He took one look and then peed and said, "Good spot," and we walked down the hill back to the house. His vitality was amazing, never drew a deep breath going up.

Some time passed, how long I can't recall, probably a couple of months not more, and the drawings arrived. He had never solicited our ideas or even our needs, and what discussion of this kind there had been I initiated, emphasizing that we wished to live simply, would not be having big parties, etc.. (I had been vaguely put on notice when, on his entering the farmhouse he looked about and with what I thought was a certain amusement if not contempt had said, "Ah yes, the old house.") But of course it could have had no interest for him as an object; on the other hand, we we were looking for a place to live, first and foremost.

2

ARTHUR MILLER

The drawings, actually water color sketches, were simply impossible. A circular living room with ovoid stone columns covering a sixty-foot diameter, if I recall, was more of a conference room. And, indeed, there _was_ a conference room, too, with long table and a dozen chairs, just like in the movies. Plus a native stone swimming pool jutting out over the grade which would have meant retaining walls twelve or more feet hight at one end and would have cost a mint all by itself. The place was very formal but with very little sleeping room, rather an entertainment house fit, I thought, for a corporation and not two people in the country. He simply had us all wrong.

Finally, I did not think he had much interest in what the thing was to cost, and furthermore had no actual idea. He said something about $250,000, which was absurd even in the mid-Fifties for that kind of construction.

So it was allowed to simply lapse, and gradually we got to like the old house more and more, and did some basic restoration to make it liveable as a weekend place. I returned the sketches to Mrs. Wright soon after he died. We only saw him the one time.*

He was, I thought, a great romantic, a man of ▬▬▬ style, a theatrical type of the old school who Orson Welles would love to have played.

*On second thought, I recall ahe other meeting at the Office in...was it the Plaza Hotel? Where he showed us a vast drawing of a new city he had drawn up for some Middle Eastern king, a vision of minarets and towers connected by airborne highways and monorails, It was quite wonderful although even then one had to wonder whether it would ever materialize. I suppose he never lost his childhood imagination, did he, or the strength to insist on his own vision, a blessed quality but hard to live with, I should think.

I never got the chance to sit down with him about his drawings, having gotten the sense that it was a take-it-or-leave-it proposal. But since it so lacked the slightest relation to what we would have wanted I never thought there was any point in contacting him about the house again.

Best,

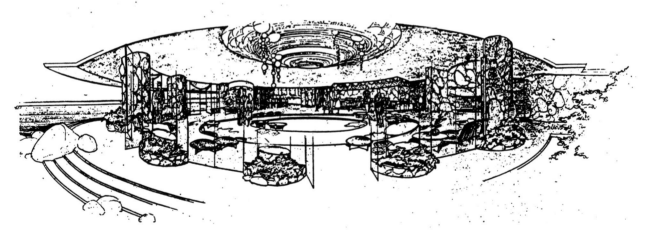

Drawings for the Arthur Miller House, Roxbury, Connecticut, that was never built.

THE WILLITSES

Mr. Wright always enjoyed relating stories about former clients, and relating the people to their buildings. He also had a captive audience that consisted of a core group of apprentices who always wanted to hear stories about Mr. Wright's adventures. The following story stands out as a story that Mr. Wright did **not** tell. In this case, Llewellyn, Mr. Wright's son, told me the first part and Wes Peters told me the second part. I believe these stories have never been told.

Mr. Wright had built a house for Mr. and Mrs. Ward Willits of Highland Park, Illinois, in 1901. The Willitses and Wrights were connected socially and were friendly. By 1905 Wright and "Mamah" Borthwick Cheney were seeing much of each other. The Willitses knew about this situation, and in an attempt to bring Wright's wife, Catherine, and Frank together, they helped finance a trip for themselves and Frank and Catherine Wright to Japan. This was the Wrights' first trip there, and they travelled with the Willitses. Together, the two couples went to San Francisco by train, sailed from there to Yokohama, and finally took a train to Tokyo.

Soon after their arrival, the story goes, Mrs. Willits spent an afternoon looking for her husband Ward. After quizzing the hotel concierge, Mrs. Willits found out that perhaps, if she were lucky, she would find Mr. Willits and Mr. Wright at a certain bath house, bathing. Mrs. Willits took the nearest rickshaw to the bathhouse and grabbed Ward out of the waters. They went back to the hotel and took the next train to Yokohama, and retraced their steps back to the United States. Frank Lloyd Wright did not see the Willitses again until about thirty-eight years later.

Wes Peters recounts: during World War II, Wes was driving Mr. Wright to Chicago, and their tour took them through Highland Park, along Sheridan Road. Suddenly, Wright says, "There's the Willits house. Let's drive in and say hello." They drove up, Mr. Wright pressed the door bell and the door soon opened. An elderly lady appeared in a house dress, apron, and curlers. She took one look at Wright, turned and shouted, "Ward, Ward, Frank's here."

House of Ward Willits, Highland Park, Illinois.

With that, she ushered them into the living room, where they had some coffee and chatted. Soon Mr. Wright said, "Wes, we have to be getting along." They bid adieu and left. According to Wes, Mr. Wright said nothing about his relationship with the Willitses, except that Mrs. Willits had been an attractive woman. Wes had never heard Llewellyn's story.

THE BRIDGE

In the late 1940s Robert Chuckrow, then a young builder, worked for Wright building houses in the "Usonia Homes" project some 30 miles from New York City. It occurred to me that, based on his experience there, he could easily bid and then build some of my work, and it proved so. He was low bidder on four houses I was doing in the area, and we became friends. I also designed a house for him and his family. Later, I designed stores for his firm, as he went on to a dazzling career of large projects.

One day Chuckrow related this experience: Wright was to design a house at Usonia. Chuckrow was directed to pick him up at the Plaza Hotel and to drive him up the scenic Saw Mill River Parkway to see the proposed site. Near the end of the journey, they crossed a bridge made of tensile steel, the supports and swoop of

Photo of the bridge.

At the site. Second from left: Robert Chuckrow; Frank Lloyd Wright; man pointing, Henken, instigator of Usonia.

the rods covered with brick and stone. Seeing this, Wright stated it was a very worthy and interesting bridge, made of natural materials. Furthermore, he went on, if he had not been an architect, he would have wanted to have been a bridge engineer. Bridges, he stated, took man over water and valleys; he spoke eloquently about the mobility of man's trespassing over rivers and gorges.

When he arrived at the foot of a hill, which was the proposed site, Wright emerged briskly from the car and led us up the steep hillside—the client, the Usonian development member, an ex-apprentice, and myself following. Wright pronounced the site fine for the house. He then proceeded some 50 feet farther, relieved his bladder, and came back to the group. There was a silence, nobody knowing just what to say. Then Wright pointed his cane at the spot where he had been and said, "Something meaningful will grow there."

We all descended. Wright and I took to the car and drove back along the same route. When he again saw the bridge that had been the object of his favorable comments, he declared: "Look at that terrible, inorganically designed bridge. Imagine placing masonry on tensile steel. It's insane and an outrage. The design engineer should be put in an asylum, or jail, for making such a foolish structural error."

Not another word was spoken all the way back to the Plaza.

Draftsmen

Before the Fellowship, Wright's work was produced by employed draftsmen, from 1893, when he began his practice, to 1932. In this section, three of his draftsmen from this period recall their experiences.

KAMECKI TSUCHIURA, DRAFTSMAN FROM JAPAN

Kamecki is a Japanese architect who worked for Wright on the Imperial Hotel during its construction in Tokyo. He came to the U.S. afterward to work for Wright at Taliesin, and later returned to Japan to continue his work.

FRANK LLOYD WRIGHT FROM 1921 TO 1925

I first worked for Frank Lloyd Wright during August 1921, when he had his office in an annex of the old Imperial Hotel in Tokyo while he was building the new Imperial Hotel. Antonin Raymond and William Smith came from Taliesin to help him. Arata Endo and several other Japanese architects were also working there together. The perspective drawing of the new Imperial—which Mr. Wright had drawn—was displayed on a large table in Mr. Wright's office at the old Imperial.

In March of 1923 I was called by Mr. Wright and went to his temporary office in Los Angeles. He was working on the Doheny development and the Boat House at Lake Tahoe, with his son Lloyd Wright as his partner. These two projects were not actually executed; however, some concrete block houses were built in this area during the period. They are the Millard, Storer, Freeman, and Ennis houses. Only William Smith, myself, and my wife were in the office in Los Angeles to help the architect.

The earthquake hit the Tokyo/Yokohama area on September 1, 1923. We all had long days of anxiety about the Imperial Hotel until a cablegram from Baron Okura brought very good news: the hotel building was totally undamaged. It was some time later that we heard about the other buildings that Mr. Wright designed in Japan. Jiyu Gakuen, School of the Free Spirit in Tokyo, and Yamamura House Ashiya were saved, whereas Fukuhara House in Hakone was completely destroyed by the quake.

While we were in Los Angeles, the internationally famous competition for the Chicago Tribune building took place. Mr. Wright's *Lieber Meister*, Mr. Louis Sullivan—by that time retired from architectural activity—sent a letter to Mr. Wright with photographs of the winners of this competition and his comment that the second prize design by Eliel Saarinen was much better than the first by Raymond Hood. I remember this very clearly.

We went back to Taliesin in December 1923, but Lloyd Wright stayed in Los Angeles. Werner Moser of Switzerland and Richard Neutra of Germany participated with us, and A. Feller of Germany was with us for just a short period.

At Taliesin, a project of a large building in Chicago for the National Insurance Company was being planned. But this project was not executed, leaving only sketches of the plan and perspective drawings. The Nakoma Country Club—we worked on those drawings at the same time—was not executed either. We were busy, however, on the drafting boards for these projects. In those days, Mr. Wright was contributing an article every month for the *Architectural Record*; he often read them for us. Sometimes, he put colors with colored pencils on the perspective drawings we made. He did it very pleasantly; he seemed to enjoy himself in doing that. He used the waxed Japanese rice paper that he brought back from Tokyo with him. It was better than tracing paper for coloring, and he liked to use it. Drawings for the cover and the title page for his book published by Wendingen of Holland were also designed during these days. I think it was perhaps spring of 1925 when Erich Mendelsohn visited Taliesin. He was traveling in the States, and Richard Neutra—who was then at Taliesin—had been Mendelsohn's partner in designing the Berliner Tageblatt. We all gathered in Mr. Wright's living room; Mrs. Neutra played Bach with her violoncello and Mr. Mendelsohn drew various sketches of the Einstein Tower on many sheets of paper again and again, so fast.

Soon after that, Richard Neutra and Werner Moser left Taliesin, and Olgivanna came to Taliesin as Mr. Wright's new wife with her daughter Svetlana. The new life began there. William Smith, my wife, and I were still there, and one evening when we all were in the dining room that was located away from the main building, a fire broke out and destroyed a large portion of Taliesin. It was the second fire that burned Taliesin, and most of the fine arts Mr. Wright had collected during his stay in Japan were lost. But the

Kamecki Tsuchiura, Richard Neutra, Frank Lloyd Wright, 1923, at Taliesin. Photo by Werner Moser.

drafting room and the guest room were saved along with his famous collection of Japanese prints.

William Smith and I worked on the drawings for reconstruction of Taliesin; it was our last job there. My wife and I left there in November 1925, and did not see the new Taliesin.

DONALD WALKER, DRAFTSMAN FROM KENTUCKY

Donald was a professional draftsman at Taliesin in the late 1920s, when work on many projects was started but none finished, except for one house for Wright's Tulsa cousin. Donald returned to Kentucky and kept in touch with Marcus Weston of Spring Green, whose father was Wright's chief carpenter–contractor.

Never shall I forget the kindness and sympathy shown me by Frank Lloyd Wright as a cub-draftsman from 1928 to 1931. My progress through life has never been without the spirit that emancipated me from the classic architectural schooling of the time to the new school of American architecture began about a century ago.

The time is 1928, the Master is back at work after the Golden Years and the lost years and now the "comeback" at sixty three, having come through the merciless judgment from the public, now free, hoping to stay "above ground" for at least another 15 years more.

I came to work as a draftsman in October and became good friends with Cy Jannke, from Milwaukee. The first work was six perspectives of the Biltmore Hotel for Albert Chase McArthur. Our drawings made a good showing. Then we started work on the Richard Lloyd Jones house in Tulsa, Oklahoma, of which I was in charge. The house was ready for building, but Mr. Jones rejected me as site superintendent after Mr. Wright discussed the construction terms. It was a mixed blessing, as the plans were full of plain mistakes that later showed up in the house itself.

St. Marks-in-the-Bowery, New York: a projected scheme that came straight from the blue sky on Christmas Day, 1928. Mr. Wright entered the studio (I was alone) and asked me to put some paper on his board. I stood by, watching for four hours, until he put his pencil down and said, "Don, that is architecture. Make me some working drawings."

Then in the first few days of 1929 we left Taliesin, in subzero weather, for Arizona and the first camp there. Mr. Wright said later

Price Tower, Bartlesville, Oklahoma. This was originally designed for St. Marks in the Bowery, New York

that I was the hero of "Ocotilla," the desert camp. I kept busy and in May we returned to Taliesin, where there were the first five draftsmen. The first signs of the Great Depression were showing.

Many things were started again that we had left behind, including the Kahn lectures and the restoration of Hillside. The traveling exhibit was underway and I traveled with it to Princeton, New York, Chicago, and Madison. Few people saw the exhibit, and little money came from it—there was no publicity.

The Great Depression. A cold winter ahead. A carload of coke on the siding in Spring Green and I was to unload and haul it to Taliesin with no help from the boys. I was tired of the seven day week, not enough to eat, and cold weather—the end was near for me. Mr. Wright had been to Chicago trying to get work when he came into the studio, after dark, on December 7. I had just unloaded the coke and let him know it was in the bins. I told him I had decided to leave. He was completely let down, but the reasons I had for leaving were understood by him.

The final talk lasted some time, then he mentioned money. I had always seemed to have a little bit to tide me over until he could pay up. He asked me if he had ever paid me, and I said no. He went into the house and came back with eighty dollars, forty of which he gave to me. Also, he figured how much he owed me and gave me an I.O.U. for one thousand dollars (which I returned to him on his next birthday). He gave me his book, and, with a handshake, I walked out into the dark, cold night on my way to other adventures.

I always wondered why he did things useful for young men and concluded he did it for America. In the following years, in many places, there was always a warm greeting from him. After he passed away I used to visit the Westons in Spring Green and one night, after a long talk, Will Weston said "Don, you loved the old man, didn't you?"

HENRY KLUMB

When the Fellowship started, Henry Klumb had been the senior draftsman for five years. During this period, he took exhibits for Frank Lloyd Wright's works to Europe, worked on the sketch of the ill-fated San Marcos Hotel in Arizona, and was generally in charge of activities of the first year of the Fellowship. He stayed at Taliesin until September 1933—when leaving, he said he had had enough of the "kindergarten" and wanted a life of his own.

After Taliesin, he worked with the Museum of Modern Art in New York City on exhibitions, was with the Los Angeles Planning Commission, and went to Puerto Rico in 1944 as chief architect for Public Works, later having his own practice there. In the 1950s he employed Robert Mosher for a spell, and conducted a fine practice until his demise.

In 1980, Donald Hoffmann, then architecture critic of the Kansas City Star, having written much on architecture, wrote Klumb for an explanation of the kinds of drawings illustrating Wright's "Princeton Lectures." The following is most of Henry Klumb's reply (This correspondence was given to me by Klumb's son Richard):

Now the history of the abstract rendering of the Robie House (and others).

Returning from the desert camp near Chandler, Arizona, in May 1929, after finishing the construction drawings for the resort hotel San Marcos in the Desert, we settled down at Taliesin East where architects from far away came to work for Mr. Wright—Takehiko Okami, Japan; Michael Kostanecki, Poland; Rudolph Mock, Switzerland; Valdimar Karfik, Czechoslovakia, and George Cronin of Oak Park, Chicago.

Having come from Germany, I was aware that in Europe, the younger architects, especially the critics (after the 1926 publication of Frank Lloyd Wright by H. de Fries), had a strong negative feeling about Wright's spiritual and poetic exuberance inherent in his work, considering it an expression of the superficiality of American culture. Anything that did not fit the contrived formula of intellectual rationalization was considered a crime against their rigidly adhered to formula of their two-dimensional architecture, the so-called "International Style."

Those most outspoken in their criticism lacked the capacity to understand that Wright's work was born of inner essence, ever a creative act. As the acclaimed intellectuals of the two-dimensional age, they could not comprehend, feel no stimulation, only react to optic contrasting black and white graphic architectural statements, the understood and prevailing fashion of the day. Statements were even made that Frank Lloyd Wright was an overrated American of questionable genius.

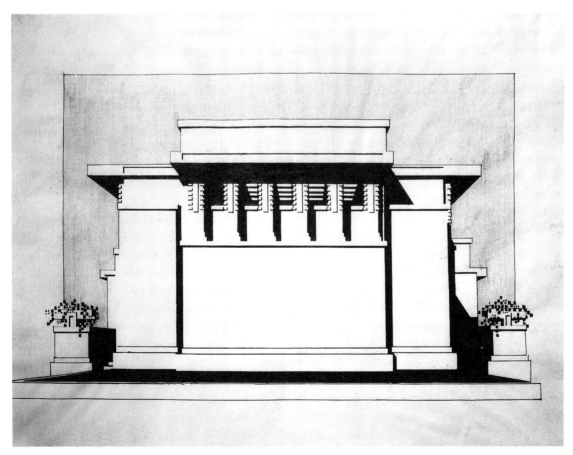

These drawings of Unity Temple, Oak Park, and Larkin Building, Buffalo, New York were made specially for Frank Lloyd Wright's Princeton lectures

Assembled and sitting with Frank Lloyd Wright around a fire
in the studio one winter day in 1929, discussing this and other
matters of "organic architecture," I suggested that we might try to
reduce his delicate renderings of his best known buildings to two-
dimensional black on white graphic presentations that modern
architects were addicted to. His answer: **"DO IT."** Okami and I
went to work and produced several, including the Robie House

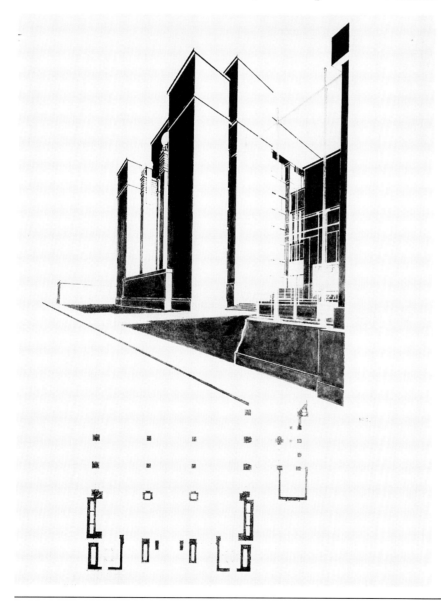

(drawn by myself), the Winslow House, Yahara Boat Club, Bock Atelier, Unity Temple, and the Larkin Building. All were drawn in ink on roll-up window shades. The result was that even the stark graphic black on white surface presentations did not produce a two-dimensional effect; rather they emphasized the depth of his poetry and the power of the third dimension. Nothing that international architecture had to show could equal it.

The drawings were not made for any specific purpose except for the reason stated. They were ultimately taken to Princeton as part of an exhibit shown during Wright's Princeton Lectures in May 1930. In October 1930 they were included in the Chicago Art Institute Exhibit where Wright gave his lectures, "To the Young Man in Architecture." Later they were used as illustrations in the publication of the Princeton Lectures.

My association with Frank Lloyd Wright extended from early January 1929 to late September 1933. In 1931 I spent 10 months in Europe arranging the first European Frank Lloyd Wright exhibit sponsored by architects H. T. Wildeveld and Erich Mendelsohn. This exhibition opened in March 1931 in Amsterdam, Holland, and went from there to Berlin, Stuttgart, Brussels, Antwerp, and Rotterdam.

Apprentices

In 1932, Wright attracted some 30 apprentices to his newly established Fellowship. The basic philosophy was "learning by doing," and the principal learning took place in the drafting room. To this day I recall all three drafting rooms, the first at Taliesin itself; then over the hill at Hillside, a half mile away, where the Fellowship moved about 1935; and then at the canvas-roofed drafting place in the desert, in Arizona, also built mostly by the apprentices themselves.

Most unforgettable was the almost daily Wright entry into the drafting room early after breakfast, and his loud "Gute Morgen!" We would rise from our drawing boards and nod. The drafting room was his main life and concern. That is where ideas would gel for him into the start of reality. We were not just drawing for the sake of drawing. The reality was getting the design of a building built.

We watched while he drew his lines with verve and excitement—erasing wherever he felt changes were necessary, talking all the while, moving from table to table, often then strolling back to his office and returning with gusto to read a letter from, or to someone—or trying out an article on us. We often could hear him on the telephone, with his deep emphatic tones or smoothing reassurances. There was never a dull moment, and when needed, we worked into the night—there was no set rule.

Here, presented alphabetically, are articles written by eleven of Wright's apprentices.

ROBERT F. BISHOP

After obtaining his BA at Swarthmore College and completing a year in an architectural office and the T-Square club in Philadelphia, Robert Bishop joined the Fellowship on a "working scholarship" in August 1932. He worked on all phases of the early remodellings at both Taliesin and Hillside and left for reasons of his own, only to be asked back to work on the "Broadacre City" model and exhibit in the Fall of 1934. During this project Bishop wrote some 44 letters to his love, Lydia. They later married and raised a family in Philadelphia, where he conducted a practice that completed some 200 projects. His widow generously gave me her typed copies of his letters for use here; the following extracts form a colorful illustration of life in the Fellowship.

EXCERPTS FROM LETTERS TO LYDIA, TALIESIN, 1934–1935

My darling,

There is alot to tell you already, though I only got here last night. I found more old friends here than I expected, and the place changed alot. It is hard to write because I am not well settled by myself, writing this in a friends room and all the trouble of finding a bed and settling down still ahead.

Mrs. Wright has been pumping me on subjects near to our problem, and I guess my mind and heart have been running ahead. I remember her last advice to me when I left here last spring was to not get married for four years. Quite different now, darling. Mrs. Wright and I agreed that marriage was advisable for anyone as soon as it could be managed. I haven't told her about you, though she obviously wants me to, but she was actually eloquent on the subject of how life begins only with marriage. I suspect she is already wondering about a Mrs. Bishop at Taliesin. I hope you are as tickled as I am that she is taking to the idea, because this might be a good place for us to start out, if the Fellowship can only get a few decent commissions. There are now two in the office and this Pittsburgh trip of Wright's is very promising. The man with the pull there has a son here, and he is sold on Wright and the boys. I never felt friendlier toward the Wrights. (Mostly, of course, because of you, sweetheart.)

*   *   *

I wish Mr. Wright had offices in the city. The country is all very beautiful, but I am very tired of the semipublic life one has to lead here. It is especially irksome in contrast to the private life I have imagined with you. When I had more friends here and no one to love away from here, it wasn't so bad. Together we put up with it.

*   *   *

Gee, I feel stupid to have come here, anyway. So many irresponsibles that I will have to finish the model [Broadacre City] myself, and I am sorry to say I think the model itself is a rather stupid idea. I have been writing as if a couple of commissions would make Taliesin a fine place to stay indefinitely, but I think now that there is something in the natures of the Wrights that makes this place impossible for mature people.

*   *   *

One day this place seems just perfect (if we could be here together). And the next, it is full of petty personalities and Mr. Wright's god complex. I last wrote you after a day when Mr. Wright had been particularly charming. But really it wouldn't do to stay here long, and it would be the worst place I can think of to start out our common life. A nice retreat for a summer later on, or even a longer stay. It is hard to tell how many of the problems here would be abolished with more income. I know it would be very different.

*   *   *

There is talk of the Fellowship moving to Arizona for part of the winter. Maybe that will be my chance to leave. Or maybe I'll go and find something there.

*   *   *

In spite of his best line about the good old soil on one's hands, the maestro is at his best in Park Avenue apartments. A recent illustration is a gorgeous new outfit from Chicago. He has been urging us all to give up these silly conventional clothes and to design and have made more sensible all-around suits, with shorter, jacket-like coats and trousers fitting tight around the ankles. And now after many of the boys have spent all their funds on such effects and made themselves, with the help of a ham dressmaker in Spring Green, more or less ridiculous, the boss comes back from his southern trip clad in the smartest suit, overcoat, shoes, and beret you ever saw. All perfectly tailored by his special Chicago tailor, and as beautiful as can be. And terrifically expensive. I couldn't dare guess high enough. He says in rationalization that he meant these "sensible" numbers for work suits, not to replace the dress-up suit. I suppose one should be very incensed over such extravagance, when the man has so many obligations. But it is impossible not to love him for it. First, because he is so darn handsome that you feel he deserves nothing less fine, and second, because he is so darn likable strutting around—like a little girl in a Shirley Temple dress—pretending not to care. Then, too, he is by far our best publicity man, and one cannot doubt that the Taliesin reputation abroad is an excellent one with Mr. Wright traveling about looking and feeling like a king.

* * *

Edgar just came to tell me Mr. W. just sent a wire telling his secretary to buy the new truck. That seems to mean we are going west. It will be fun to have a nice brand new Ford truck for just the two of us. Much better than most of the run down passenger cars here. But the wrong "two of us," dearest.

The only entertainment of note was Edgar's rendition of a Brahms Capriccio last evening. He is not a bad pianist, when in practice, especially with Brahms. He tells me that it is the last Capriccio in Opus 116, in D Major. It is awfully hard to play I guess. I love it. We have a beautiful Bechstein piano in the theatre. About as long as a Rolls Royce, it looks and sounds as patrician. You would have fun with these pianos here. Almost one in every room. Periodically the apprentices get the urge to become pianists, and all pianos storm at once with the same stupid little tune they all start out with. I have got only to scales.

* * *

I am fired with a new enthusiasm for our model since Mr. Wright got back and showed us the layout of the New York exhibition where the model will be shown. It will be part of the Annual Exhibition of Industrial Arts in Rockefeller Center, and space sells

Frank Lloyd Wright wearing a splendidly tailored suit.

for five dollars a square foot. For no particular reason Mr. Wright has given $6000 worth of space right in the center, and $1000 for building the model. It should be a fine show.

*   *   *

I am writing under difficulties, dearest, in the studio, around the corner from Mr. Wright, who is opening his mail and making wisecracks about it. He is in an excellent humor, and always charming when like that. I am interrupted every sentence to be called in to laugh at something. It would be fun to be famous. More crazy letters from cranks and institutions, addressed to Professor, Doctor, or Reverend F.L.W.

*   *   *

I have decided that Mr. Wright and I will never have any more arguments. If he is wrong, I shan't mind, because I am more sure than ever of his genius. I am relieved at this decision, and I think it is of some importance, because it makes the future happier. There is really no justifiable danger in apprenticing oneself to such a person, I feel. If one is big enough to absorb the principles, instead of just copying the forms, one's own individuality will come out regardless, and there is no point in closing one's eyes to one's practice of the principles in the petty fear that one will be bound by the particular Frank Lloyd Wright forms.

*   *   *

Gad, but Mr. Wright is a grand man when one gets him more or less alone. It makes me resent this Fellowship in a way. He takes so much time giving out sermons and identifying himself with the creative spirit of our times when he feels himself the guiding light of our colony, that it is swell to be with him when he lets down and gets human. There have been many things here, which I felt Mr. Wright was incapable of understanding—things connected with friendships between apprentices. I found that I was all wrong. He has grasped all the situations I had wondered about, and talked most generously and frankly about his attitude. We discussed at length his inability to have close friends, and he "confessed" that his worst weakness, and the most conscience-pricking, was his unconcern for others as people in their own right, to be cherished, remembered, and befriended. It was much fun to have him off his pedestal. He has an excellent "line on himself," actually. He knows his limitations, abilities, and acknowledges his good luck. But to see him as official master of these thirty apprentices you would think he was Jehovah himself. Or think that he thought he was. And so I wish he didn't have a Fellowship. If there were only a few of us here—only those truly and deeply interested in his work—he would be much more of a perpetual inspiration. Instead, he is playing schoolmaster to a bunch of immatures who are having a nice life—are scared of him, but do not really appreciate him.

I wonder about Mr. Wright and Louis Sullivan thirty years ago. It must have been a very faithful young man to work in such close harmony for seven years with someone as conceited and vain as Sullivan was. Odd too, and I can hardly understand it, for you know how dead sure of himself Mr. Wright is now. I imagine he was very naive in his twenties, that he was extraordinarily humble toward Sullivan. I know he smothered his own opinions always, and was almost literally, as he says, "a pencil in lieber meister's hand." And yet he has clearly outshone Sullivan as an architect, and developed entirely away from anything Sullivanesque. Where Sullivan was great was his ornament, of course. We have lots of examples here, as well as many drawings. Very, very beautiful, darling. But more nearly sculpture than architecture, I guess.

* * *

I had a big discussion with the maestro this evening, developing out of my criticisms of the trees on the model. They don't look like trees and I think they should. So we got off on abstraction, and what it means "to abstract" a form or quality. As always, Mr. Wright has a very ready theory: abstraction is only justified as it gives the essence of a thing more truly than a realistic copy. But that is just what he doesn't do in his own abstractions. He jumps on some momentary and quite superficial aspect and works it up into a nice pattern, which doesn't say anything about the original object. So I am trying to figure it all out for myself, just where the subject matter counts, and what, if any, value a "pure" abstraction might have.

* * *

The Broadacre City model is looking pretty good. I really don't object to it—to the architecture. I object only to Mr. Wright's claims about it. I wish he would stick to architecture instead of going off half-cocked into economics. For as a social savior he has himself all "out of drawing." But God how his imagination works with forms! And that's why I am here, after all.

* * *

You must think this is a very childish place, dearest, where grown, or practically grown, men do things like cooking. It would be, except that the cooking comes beside the regular work, and it is a necessary relief to the regular kitchen staff. It is funny to have these Sunday night dinners attended by lots of millionaires from the San Marcos hotel in Chandler, when so many of us are so poor. It makes me wonder just why Mr. Wright is so true to his architectural ideas. Many of his clients have been such insensitive dolts. I felt the same way toward the Chestnut Hill ladies who wanted the studio. An organic architecture is not for them, or shouldn't be—it is for the poor students at Yale, Penn, and Swarthmore who smell something bad in the academic training they are having handed them. It is for you, for me, for those of us who care enough for something good to want to try to make it. And then you look at who lives in these houses! But maybe it does them good. And maybe there are enough who get the idea to make up for the others. Oh well, it's fun to build them.

*　*　*

I thought all last evening when the guests were here of how I would write to you after they went home. But then I stayed in the living room as Mr. and Mrs. Wright began to talk over the guests and pick them apart, and I stayed all evening for fear of missing something. You know that Mr. Wright really does take this Fellowship *so* seriously, as if it were his family. And he talks over all strangers with us almost as freely as he would with Mrs. Wright. He has grown in human understanding in the past three years, and at times, like last evening, he comes quite close to "his boys." The tie that kept me from my letter is almost a feeling of kinship, though probably more on his part than on mine. Dearest one, I do want you to know the Wrights and be "taken in," as it were. I think we will someday work here awhile together, if only for a short time. And I see things picking up for him already. I am glad he has come through the depression so well, for now his professional foolishnesses are no longer public gossip. And I believe he will be more free to do great things in the next ten years than he has in the past twenty-five.

*　*　*

It is inspiring to have Mr. Wright on hand fifteen hours a day, and hard to keep up with him. And so good night, darling, and I hope I dream about you and not acres of trees.

*　*　*

We are all set to leave Taliesin early tomorrow morning. One good omen was a slight rise in temperature. It has been very cold the last few days, and the paper predicted colder still, but this morning it seems to have warmed up a little.

I expect to spend the day finishing the packing of the truck. My it is enormous. The model is up top, covering the whole load, with a canvas covering over all. There is a big red (Taliesin Fellowship Emblem) swastika painted on the canvas —our sign. There is an awful lot to be done of course with all the office, studio, dining room, and kitchen supplies as well as a bunch of mattresses and food and blankets.

It will probably be hard to write en route, as Mr. Wright has it all planned caravan-style and every meal will be a public picnic, and we will have to stop at tourist camps. Edgar and I will have to drive a couple hours longer a day, because the truck is new and can't go fast. Fortunately we'll have most of the food.

I will be letting you know of our progress, if only by post card. We are off! to pack. Good bye, sweetheart.

* * *

"Dining Room" at Taliesin West during the first year. Every meal was a picnic.

Dear L. darling,

I bet you are ready to kill me for not writing during the trip. But after I tell you all about it you'll know that it was pretty hard to do. It seems months ago that we left Spring Green, tho' it has been just a week, and so much happened that I won't be able to remember it all. I'll start with our arrival here and work back, or I will forget this too.

Arizona is marvellous. It is now about nine in the morning and getting hot as blazes. We are lying out in the patio of the Hacienda. I am starting an early sun-burn, with my shirt off. The Hacienda is just perfect for our purposes here. The plan of it is like this:

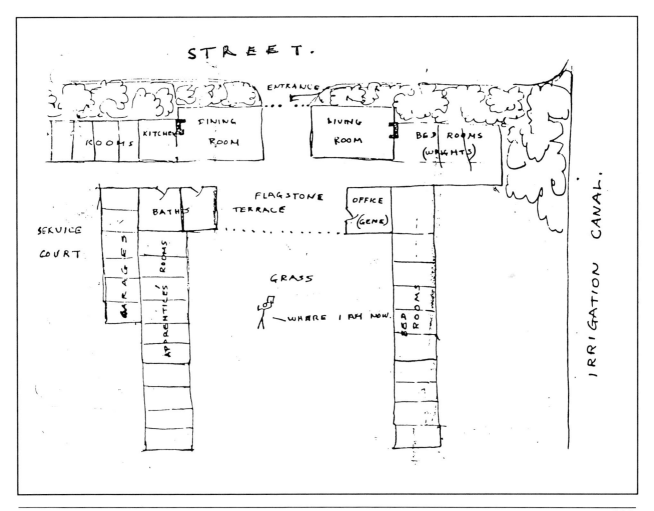

We have a new apprentice who has studied all over the world. Incidentally, he is a darn nice person. Edgar Kaufmann, one of Mr. Wright's latest god-fathers, the Pittsburgh department store owner who is helping finance the model and who is going to build a house. Young Edgar has the charm of the "born to have it" wealthy cultured Jew, but his folks have had him all over the world studying, and as a result he can't take anything from Taliesin without first finding a parallel in Renaissance art. He will probably write some very scholarly books one day, but I doubt if he will ever design a thing.

Funny, I don't know where the distinction comes in, between creativeness and logic. Mr. Wright seems so very logical, but he is of course essentially creative and the logic seems often to be the result rather than the step by step process.

*   *   *

Last night the whole gang went out. We were invited to the San Marcos Hotel to hear a piano concert. The evening was saved early by the senior Kaufmanns who invited the whole fellowship in to have highballs before the music. The hotel has no rooms that are not under individual roofs—it consists of a bunch of little cottages, —and it was in one such that the Kaufmanns stood us up to drinks. It was swell. Irish and Scotch, and so many. Mr. and Mrs. Wright were in a tough spot. They couldn't say a thing, as their flock tried to get quite cockeyed under their very noses. There were three quarts of whiskey there when we arrived and we soon ran out and Mrs. Kaufmann insisted that her husband send for more. And they had too a couple of pints of milk for the apprentices who were brought up that way. Do you remember what Irish whiskey tastes like, darling? It is almost as heavenly as your opera was, I think.

Edgar Kaufmann, r., Frank Lloyd Wright, and Edgar Tafel.

*   *   *

Sunday night (Feb. 17, 1935) was a gala one, for we entertained all our Godfathers at once. The Kaufmanns, clients and parents of one of the boys, are on from Pittsburgh at the San Marcos hotel in town here. They are delightful,—young, smart, and very attractive. He is my idea of a good capitalist. Incidentally, he owns the largest dept. store in Pittsburgh. I guess I like them most for their sympathy here, and their real sincere humility toward the "boss."

Other guests were Dr. Chandler, who is nice enough, and some prigs from the hotel, none of whom have any real sympathy for Taliesin, or the artistic. I think they liked the show,—we were all dressed up and played some Brahms and Debussy (Tafel, as usual) which sounded professional,—but I doubt if they would think much of us to see us at work, unshaven, and covered with paint.

*   *   *

When the Broadacre City exhibit was completed in Arizona, Mr. Wright selected four of us, two Edgars (Kaufmann and Tafel) and two Roberts (Bishop and Mosher) to drive the models from Arizona to Radio City Music Hall for installation. We went through dust storms, and long days of driving, in both the truck and Kaufmann Jr.'s convertible. Upon our arrival, Mr. Wright appeared, and directed us four in the installation work. Kaufmann left to join his parents' store, and directed a department of modern accessories and furniture. Bishop returned to Philadelphia to start his career. Mosher and I tended the month-long exhibit. Why was I selected? Perhaps because of my abilities, and perhaps more, because my folks had an apartment with bedrooms for two extras within walking distance of the exhibit, . . . free.

When the exhibit was over, Mosher and I drove it back to Wisconsin; later it went to Pittsburgh and Philadelphia and more. By Fall of 1935, the Fellowship went to Chandler again, during which time we produced the construction drawings for "Fallingwater" and the Hanna House. The next winter was spent in Wisconsin, for Mr. Wright was ill and couldn't travel, and the following winters the Fellowship went to Taliesin West, Scottsdale, and has wintered there ever since.

ANDREW DEVANE

Andrew Devane studied architecture in his native Ireland before coming to Taliesin in 1946. Some years later he returned to Dublin where he headed a large firm designing various projects. After his family was grown, he left Dublin in order to help the poor; he now lives in Calcutta doing charitable endeavors.

THE MATRIX

It is over forty years since I first met Frank Lloyd Wright in that splendid setting of Taliesin West and the Arizona desert. I can only repeat my words—expressed elsewhere: "Suddenly the truck was slamming diagonally toward a rhythm of white sails, raked beams and stone walls viewed through passing cacti and desert scrub. A long, low magnificent ship anchored securely in a sea of desert, stone masses and tilted white planes counterpointing the mountains, which spiked the haze behind it."

I remember, but I could never describe, the release and joy I felt as I walked through these truly wonderful buildings. Here, for me, was—and I hope still is—the purest architecture of our time that it has been my good fortune to see, and, in part, to help build. Nature, material, and space were fused and distilled, with indescribable variety and discipline, by the sure hand of a master. For once, here, for me, there was, between the ideal and the reality, no shadow, no doubt.

Under a low deck, into a beautiful luminous space built with canvas, redwood, and stone—a space that flowed into courtyard and desert and which was contained by vistas, mystery, and pools of light and shade. A scatter of artifacts, Eastern and Indian, some obviously priceless; water splashing outside and the sound of children playing. An incomparably lovely living space still, in my mind's eye; still supreme in comparison with all those places and spaces seen since. White haired, head high, small yet somehow standing tall and relaxed. Keen questing eyes, formidable, yet friendly. A gentle resonant voice, words flowing easily. An extraordinary face that I came to know so well in a short time. Gentle and reflective, humane and ruthless, sad and proud. A succession of faces, moods, characters—a tilt of the head, for all the world a conquistador or a pirate; a dreaminess of speech, then pure, withdrawn, like a contemplative close to the ultimate; a row, an argument, a brazen word, and a sidelong look, face and actions as willful and hard as a spoiled tycoon; sometimes a face shining with love, humanity, and humility when he touched truths in life and nature and released them in words or crayons.

First of all, to me he was, and ever will be, a dear and true friend, a warm-hearted, endearing, fallible, sometimes maddening human being. I owe him and all in Taliesin at that time a great deal in life and in work, and I am deeply grateful to him, particularly as I had so little to give, in ability or any other way, which was worthwhile to him in return. He certainly gave me, and others like me, a sense and an appreciation of our varying philosophies of life such as we never had before, and, in addition, he gave us a deep and personal understanding of what I believe to be the true essence and nature of architecture—an understanding that has been used well or badly by us, his apprentices and followers, according to our own lives, talents, and circumstances. Each of us lives inevitably (sometimes painfully) in his "shadow," because in art and architecture, all of us, including him, live and grow or fade and die, in a light that is god-given. I believe he understood this very well, for, notwithstanding his egotism, sometimes his superegotism, he was at the core a really humble and simple man, "sensible in the arrogance of his achievements," and truly good in heart and in spirit.

The gods alone know the heart or mind of any of us, but I always sensed, rightly I believe, that, in and through his ideals, within the bounds and shades of the reality of his own existence, there flowed that deep and mysterious amalgam of love, hope, and truth, which generated and guided what was often a wordless comprehension of the essence he sought to express (sometimes, it seemed almost desperately to express within limitations of mind, matter, and measure) in his own life and work and time. I believe this "matrix of creation" lies deep in the spirit and sense of all of us, but only a few are blessed with the gifts to reach it, channel it, and share it truly with humanity in art and in architecture as he did in will and in reality—a reality that we recognize and respond to, instinctively and deeply, in heart and will before we accept or reject it in intellect or imagination.

Frank Lloyd Wright

In Orissa, at Konarak on the shores of the Indian Ocean, stand age-old ruins of a temple of the sun. At dawn, the sun rising out of the sea strikes, hot and brazen, through the entrance gates, suffusing with fire those dark iron-hard stone buildings massed together in primitive power and progression, and lighting the carved erotica, much of it still razor-sharp, which smothers every ponderous wall and projection. It could not be a more different building—in concept, discipline, and use—from Taliesin West (although the nature and colour of the iron-fired stone is common to both). And yet it is quite clear, in the sight and the sense and the power of each, that both buildings have grown out of this same "matrix," albeit in differing civilizations and channels.

In the Nature of Materials?

Take, for example, the cathedral at Chartres and consider solely the essential nature and use of its materials. Only two main materials are used in this great structure—stone and glass. In the hands of the master builders, these materials are defined and spun out empirically, sparely, beautifully, to the very limits of their capacity and delight, in function, form, and aspiration—once again growing and flowering out of that same "matrix."

Consider likewise the gothic-like order of Frank Lloyd Wright's T-square-set square modular disciplines linked with his deep, sure sense of materials and one can speculate what would have been born if he had drawn freehand as did his master, Louis Sullivan. I asked him about this once, and he replied, with surprising simplicity and humility, that he drew "T-square and set square" because he couldn't do anything else, which was not true—but good.

Space and Form?

Again (although personally I find it difficult to appreciate Renaissance architecture generally) I never cease to marvel at those two great related Roman "spaces"—one internal, one external—considered through the eyes and hands, but not through words, of two other masters of enclosures. The first, Michelangelo's San Pietro, is internally an extraordinary spatial tour de force, the original "enormous room" with never a fault in mass-scale proportion or detail. It was fashioned a few years before he died when he was, like Bramante before him, "an old man in a hurry," but whose spirit and senses were rock-like and timeless in forging what he did not live to see. The second, and intimately related to this externally is Bernini's Piazza San Pietro, surely, in terms of space and enclosure alone, a triumph of rare sensitivity and occasion—a really splendid place. Both of these men in these works were, once again, children of that same definite yet indefinable "matrix."

As for Frank Lloyd Wright, he probably above all of our time had this deep incommunicable measure and understanding of form and enclosure, of space, which again can be tested and verified by our own eyes and senses, but never in words. An understanding that was instinctively related to his own dimensions, as the tall ones soon learned painfully in Taliesin with banged heads, with no consolation from his Olympian advice that anyone over five feet ten was "a weed," grown beyond nature's norms! Be that as it may, in all my wanderings and wonderings in and around buildings over the earth, I have never seen anyone with a greater sense of and mastery of form and space, than that which gifted Frank Lloyd Wright. It was integral and whole in him, like breathing.

I think that anyone who has sat with him and watched him draw, in those great Taliesin drafting rooms, will understand what I mean, particularly at the initial design stage: plan overscored on plan, section overlaid on section, all on beleaguered rubbed sheets of details paper, drawn ceaselessly over and over each other in layers, in what first seemed like a chaos of graphite and crayon and eraser. One watched, with growing trepidation, as to how this labyrinth was to be unraveled, unscrambled, into its separate parts and at the same time marveled at the freedom and sureness of the holistic vision of form and space locked in the maze of lines and rubbings—a vision whose origins were far beyond intellect or theory, welling up from the depths of the matrix.

As for art and architecture, even in the bedlam of confusion of today it must be evident to all who know or care, that they generally, in artist and architect, have really lost their way. No doubt it has been happening for a long time, and the reasons are many and varied, and still difficult to identify: hidden symptoms of manifest sickness, conceived deep down and long ago in intellectual, and in man-made error. Was it perhaps (still) born in Schopenhauer's nihilistic nirvana, which led ego, as surrogate lord of creation, into loveless and empty deserts, with dire consequences to art and artist not yet really understood? Or again, more pragmatically, how much actually has the positivism (and negativism) of the camera, linked with a wilderness of words, of word-made-fact, darkened and distorted our whole natural architectural vision and sense, separating us from realities of form, space, and material?

However, above all else, in our time, there is surely one main inescapable reason. It is quite clear that materialism (whether consumerist or dialectical) is the loveless swampland in which art and architecture sink lower and lower, along with almost everything else of real value in our lives, in a great mindless waste of words and images; money (or power) being the only positive self-centered, brutal objective, with the media (or propaganda) as the vacant vulgar arbiters and manipulators of our existences with almost everything that is barren, synthetic, and often thoroughly bad. We live an existence that has no place for the natural norms and laws of creation, let alone for a master builder, an existence that clogs and smothers almost any access to the truth and beauty of the matrix, which, nevertheless, still lies buried deep and sure beneath it all.

Surely it is high time that all artist and architects with integrity, consciously and courageously abandon our mushy, wordy, golden gods and gurus, and wade out of the swamplands into a clear, spare, better postmaterialist world, which is truly here now for any individual who has the faith and heart to enter it, live it, and share it in small, simple, and sane ways. How good it would be to be a true artist or architect—no longer an empty ego-deus before Moloch, but a real individual in his unique and proper place as mediator of creation for all humanity, out of the matrix—almost alone perhaps at first, but small and beautiful, in living and in service, with hope, truth, and love. All this, of course, is a total folly and fantasy to the swamis of swampland, but in truth, it is already growing and flowering now for many a one with the vision and the integrity to see and live it.

In all this—in our time—Frank Lloyd Wright and others like him are clearly and urgently relevant, not, it should be stressed, for imitation nor for innovation, but for a real and personal understanding by us of the right order and truth of their origins, their ethos, and their work. Like other good men of genius he was the child of his time, and also, in certain ways, master of the past and the future. The essence of a genius, and of all true art, is not superego or innovation (although he had plenty of both); it is that god-given, matrix-based gift and ability to see, sense, and understand more truly and clearly than others do the love, truth, and hope in the wordless immutable laws and rhythms of creation, nature, and humanity; and the gifts and the power to forge this matrix with reason, passion, and imagination into incomparable reality.

This I believe Frank Lloyd Wright did, instinctively before intellectually, with faith and with love, as no doubt did also those Orissian sun-worshippers, those medieval master builders, each one of them, in his own way and time, born out of that same unchanging infinite matrix. The principles each of them worked to were both simple and profound; and they are just as valid today as they were a thousand years ago—as they will be a thousand years and a billion words from now. The practice for each of them was of course different and difficult, as it will be for us, but the essentials were a common gift to all. They were there at the beginning of time and will be there at the end, for all those who have the love and the faith and the will to seek, within themselves, these greatest gifts, and who have the humanity and integrity to use them and share them well, as I believe Frank Lloyd Wright had—and did.

JOHN HOWE

John Henry Howe, II was one of the first apprentices and stayed at Taliesin from 1932 until after Wright died in 1959, except for a time in prison as a conscientious objector during World War II. He made many hundreds of drawings and stayed close to the drafting rooms, first at Taliesin, then at Hillside. When at the latter, he tended a flower bed outside the drafting room. He would work for an hour or so, walk out to his garden, work there for a while, and soon return to continue his drawing.

My table was near Jack's. We worked on many projects together, including the Hanna House, where he was in charge of construction documents. Every few days, the client's wife would send Jack instructions for changes she wanted. These were written on small blue sheets, and all pertained to requests for changes in bathrooms, kitchens, closets, etc. Jack stacked them neatly on his shelf adjoining a window. He said he would make the changes some time, all at once, and get it over with. The pile kept stacking higher and higher. One day Mr. Wright entered the drafting room (for him always spelled "draughting") and said, in a commanding voice, that all the windows should be opened for fresh air. Of course when we opened the windows a gust came through and blew all of Jack's blue sheets outdoors. No one moved to retrieve them, and the house was built without the client's requests.

After leaving Taliesin with his wife Lu, Jack settled finally near Minneapolis, began his own practice, and designed over 100 residences.

In high school in spring of 1932, in Evanston, Illinois, an area with many Wright buildings that Jack had seen and admired, he attended a lecture by architect Charles Morgan of Chicago. Morgan had worked for Wright and had made the exciting renderings of the National Life Insurance building (that didn't get built). The following excerpt is from a telephone talk with Jack.

E.T. How did Morgan start his lecture?

J.H. He arrived from offstage doing cartwheels to gain attention, and ended the talk later by taking cartwheels back. I was so impressed, I went backstage, introduced myself, got to know him, and was invited to his office at 333 Michigan Avenue, which he had shared with Mr. Wright. I told Morgan that I wanted to be at Taliesin. He said that Wright was starting a fellowship, that he was going up there to visit, and asked if I would like to come along. I said, "Would I ever," and soon we drove up together. We stayed overnight in the main house's loggia; Morgan slept on one side of the space, and I slept on the other. There was no other space for guests at the time. Next day, talking with Mr. Wright, I can't remember what he said the tuition was. I said I hadn't much money.

E.T. It was $675 per full year.

J.H. No wonder I didn't have it. I did have about $350 available. Mr. Wright said there wasn't any room for me at the moment; they had to make spaces available at different parts of Taliesin. And then, hearing of my lack of full tuition, he said I could stay if I kept the fireplaces and hot water boilers going. All he had for fuel was wood. As I remember, the first year, there was so little hot water that Mr. Wright was unable to have a hot bath. But, I did keep the fireplaces going, which kept me in the studio, and I was instructed to help with the cleaning. Often, when we were more apprentices, he would come into the studio (drafting room) and say: "Where is everybody?" He had forgotten that he had sent them outside to work on the dam, roads, or buildings. Back to the fireplaces, I remember he couldn't pass an unburning fireplace without wanting it burning. And I had to keep them all burning.

E.T. When I arrived, in late fall, do I remember your room being in the house, right under Mrs. Wright's room?

J.H. I was there for a time; we were moved around. At that time, some left soon after arriving, for reasons of their own. It was somewhat confusing. Recently, Wes claimed he was the first apprentice, and also did Yen.

E.T. Do you remember the first job you worked on in the studio?

J.H. I vaguely remember working on the details of the first Willey house, details being done by Henry Klumb; and I learned a lot from him. [*Editor's note: Klumb had been with Wright for some five years.*]

E.T. I've wondered how many renderings you drew when you were at Taliesin, I bet there were hundreds.

J.H. Yes, and did you see that there were hundreds I did at the recent exhibit in Scottsdale?

E.T. How did you feel when you walked among them all?

John Howe in Marin County Center, California.

J.H. Oh, some drawings, I felt, were more successful than others, but in general it gave me great pleasure to see them.

E.T. On the "Fallingwater" drawings, did you lay out the famous shot from below the falls?

J.H. No, well, you would know more about that than I, maybe I did.

E.T. I laid out the perspective from the rear, that was an impossible view, and Mr. Wright obliterated it by drawing a strong line through it. . . . but, maybe it was Bob Mosher who layed out the famous one mentioned. I do remember that after several days of Bob's working on the below-falls one, Mr. Wright came by, told him to start all over again, taking it further to the right and higher up, which he did. Jack, years later, didn't Allen Davidson do those blue renderings?

J.H. Yes, he did. His night renderings really were marvelous, Davy was very capable.

E.T. Well, I guess the important thing to remember is that you and Mr. Wright had a wonderful working relationship, and he wouldn't let you out of his drafting room sight.

J.H. Yes, that's because my table was the first table around the corner from his office, and when he wanted something done, there I was. Often, he would wake up early in the morning with an idea he had had during the night, come to the bottom of my stairs and call up to me to come down to the studio, to put the idea on paper.

E.T. What year did you leave Taliesin?

J.H. Lu and I left soon after Mr. Wright died in 1959. Just before leaving, I was one of the Taliesin Associated Architects, and my most notable achievement was the design of the Tucson Creative Dance Center. We left for San Francisco. I worked for Aaron Green and Lu did secretarial work. Some of my most beautiful drawings I made were of Aaron's designs. We were a very agreeable group in Aaron's office.

YEN LIANG

Yen came from his native China to continue architectural studies at Yale, M.I.T., and Cornell, and ended his first stay in the U.S. with his arrival at Taliesin in 1932 as the first apprentice. He returned to China, but his practice was interrupted by the Japanese invasion. He came back to the U.S. after working for the U.S. Army in Kunming, and after another stay—albeit brief—at Taliesin, he became a chief designer in the New York firm of Harrison and Abramavitz. His accomplishments include the Stamford Church, known as the "Fish," much of the United Nations, Battery Park projects, and the Albany Mall. He retired to California to make music, pottery, and the furniture he lives with.

FIRST APPRENTICE

After graduation from Tsing Hua College in Beijing, China, I decided to go to the United States and take up architecture. All I knew was that an architect designed buildings. Interviews with a few practicing Chinese architects who were graduates of the University of Pennsylvania influenced my decision to register there in the fall of 1928 for the five-year architecture course.

That school year found me studying French and calculus, doing meticulous drawings of the Roman orders and charcoal sketches of plaster casts, solving design problems by using Renaissance motifs and, of all things for a Chinese student, learning the intricacies of grinding Chinese ink sticks into ink for use in renderings. So, at the end of my first school year, feeling that I was not getting architecture, I decided to change to a better school. To pick a new school I looked at old copies of *Beaux Arts* bulletins to determine which school had won medals most frequently. Yale, M.I.T., Cornell, and Harvard were all very close. Thinking that pure engineering was perhaps the direction I should follow in order to become an architect, I registered for summer school at Cornell.

There, I soon had my fill of empirical formulas and was getting nowhere nearer to an understanding of building principles. I began to see that learning to choose the appropriate eclectic veneer—be it Roman, Gothic, or whatever—was the prevailing architectural objective in America and Europe.

After some more summer work at M.I.T., I transferred to Yale and was able to finish the five-year course in three. Then I enrolled in Harvard graduate school for advanced study, but still felt no closer to understanding architecture. Moonlighting in a Boston architect's office offered no help. I did not see how I could force Roman orders and the like on buildings—when I returned to China to practice—and still call myself an architect.

But during that year in Boston, pure luck brought me a copy of Frank Lloyd Wright's *An Autobiography*. Of course, I had heard about Mr. Wright and his work, but nothing was taught about him in the architectural schools, and there was no material on him in the schools' libraries. Looking back, I realize there was a silent boycott, a kind of taboo.

My awakening from reading *An Autobiography* was ecstatic. "This is architecture," I excitedly told myself. Therefore, with a sense of urgency (for I had already spent too much time studying the wrong things) during the middle of the spring term at Harvard, I dashed off a short note to Mr. Wright, asking to work. He answered with a similarly succinct note for me to "come along," together with the first draft of his Taliesin Fellowship application form typed by his then-secretary Karl Jensen. Thus, I became the "first to accomplish the Taliesin Fellowship" as Mr. Wright later wrote on the fly page of the first edition of his autobiography.

I was twenty-three in 1932 when I drove up to Taliesin in a two-seater gray and black Stutz with a rumble seat. I approached Taliesin the wrong way, up a steep back road and stopped behind Mr. Wright's Cord convertible. I was struck by the beauty of the place every which way I turned. Mr. Wright was away in Chicago, and Karl Jensen directed me to take my things to a basement guest room below Mr. Wright's quarters. As I moved my luggage to the basement, I passed a woman who was washing some laundry by the fountain outside the kitchen. It never occurred to me to speak to her. I found out later that it was Mrs. Wright, and she was very angry at me for not greeting my hostess, deeming me arrogant and ill-mannered. She never let me forget that incident.

The following day I was summoned to the studio by Mr. Wright. He shook my hand and I immediately knew that he was a man different from any other I had ever met. He moved gracefully. He dressed very elegantly. He was concerned about my having spent money on such a fancy car, funds I could have spent at the Fellowship. I didn't know, and never did know, how he had found out about my purchase, but I told him that I needed a car to come to Wisconsin, so a Chinese classmate who had spent four years in Chicago and knew the ropes had taken me to a second-hand car dealer; I emphasized that it was really only a used car. At any rate, that car became a great favorite at Taliesin, carting groceries and other supplies. And because of its strong pipe bumpers, it served as tow car and tractor when emergencies came up. [See Wes Peters's recollections of Yen Liang and the Stutz, page 160.]

Taliesin was designed by Mr. Wright to hug the hills with the hilltop exposed, affording the stroller a panoramic view of the valley over the low sandstone parapets. And through the seasons of the year, Taliesin wore the mantles of the changes well. The snow of winters piled on the serene Buddha, adding to his passive countenance on top of the grand stairway at the entrance. The sight of a pine branch through the clerestory window, with a couple of birds chirping away on it, was subject enough to inspire a painter in the spring. When I plowed (trying hard to get a straight row) in the corn field in the spring, I often got distracted by looking up at Taliesin to admire its loveliness from down below.

Fall came with a blaze of colors. Husking corn was better than a party! When I was told about the legendary rite of a kiss from the girls when you husk a red ear of corn, I worked like a demon to reap the corn. It was the introduction to living so closely to the earth that gave me an understanding of the cycle of living as nothing else did. A stable, a pig sty, a garage, and a woodshed—all usually ugly places in the average establishment—were, at Taliesin, beautiful because of their design. From the driveway, one structure looked like a clean, nice building where people could live without shame—but it was the stable. It spanned the back drive and had tall two-by-fours with muslin between. The floor of the stable had a hole where the droppings and straw could be swept down a chute below. The pig-sty, a semicircular structure, at the end of the apple orchard, housed the pigs. It was, to me, the most elegant living quarters a pig could ever have. Sandstone walls and pipe structure with mesh overhead formed the sty. No pigs in the whole world had it that good!

Aside from the revelations, which opened new vistas on architecture for me from close contact with the fertile mind of Mr. Wright, from living at Taliesin—rich in architectural ideas and heartbreakingly beautiful—from working in the drafting room, and from actual hands-on constructions in masonry, carpentry, plumbing, furniture building, and even lumber milling, I learned, without realizing it at the time, a way of life. His free and natural mingling among us imbued all daily activities with beauty, richness, and meaning.

For instance, he decreed that the decoration of the theater for the weekly theater-dinner event was one of the duties of the apprentices. This was Mr. Wright's idea to train the youngsters in a sense of design. Each of us would take turns as the chief decorator of the week. The usual would be some foliage of the season spotted around the place in pots. I remember once, when it was my turn at captaincy, I went out with my gang and gathered pine branches by sawing off a substantial number of handsome limbs from a pine tree, trucked them home and hung them off the theater balcony with spot lights to highlight them as if the pine grew there naturally. Because this design constituted a small revolution compared to others, Mr. Wright was pleased with the effect and commented favorably.

For one of the Sunday musicals in the Taliesin living room, I played violin sonatas by Vivaldi with Edgar Tafel at the piano. Afterward, Mr. Wright asked about the composer. When I gave him the name and dates (1660–1743) he commented, "So, Bach did have someone before him to base his work on." He seemed surprised that the genius of Bach did not bloom entirely by itself, that creative leaders preceded him, paving the way. I inferred from his remarks that, with typical self-confidence in his own genius, Mr. Wright believed himself to have started almost from scratch—as all geniuses should.

Mr. Wright loved to draw. When he worked out some architectural idea, he loved to use soft pencils, which he could easily erase and work over; for rendering, a tray of colored pencils was always at his elbow. "The eraser is the most important instrument of the architectural design," he used to say, and he did rub quite a bit when he was designing, sometimes actually going through the tracing paper with the Pink Pearl erasers. Of course, as his ideas developed from moment to moment, his erasers took out what he discarded and the new solutions got drawn over the erasure. This explains why he hated hard pencils.

Edgar Tafel, Yen Liang, and Eugene Masselink.

Edgar Tafel and Yen Liang, 1933.

Bob Goodall from Chicago was an expert draftsman. For working drawings he loved to use hard 4H pencils because they gave him crisp, definitive lines on paper. But Mr. Wright disliked them and forbade their use in his drafting room. When he discovered Bob's possession of them, Mr. Wright gathered all that he could find and threw them into the open fireplace to burn. Bob would, however, buy more on the sly the next time he got into Chicago. It was quite a war.

From time to time Mr. Wright would muse aloud—more to himself than to someone in particular—on thoughts he happened to be intrigued with, while doing something unrelated to what he said. Once, I was close by when he said something like "a circle is an unstable geometric shape unsuitable for architecture." That statement seemed to have implanted in his mind a challenge and perhaps for this reason years later the world witnessed a burst of great building designs featuring the circle: the Guggenheim Museum in New York, the Marin County courthouse in California, the Jester house in California that was never built, Monona Terrace Civic Center in Madison, Wisconsin, and Pittsburgh Point Park.

I returned to China in 1934 by way of Europe, where I stopped to see what architects had been doing in recent years and remained there throughout World War II. At the end of the war, Mr. Wright most kindly wrote with concern, asking me to bring my wife, Dolly, to Taliesin to show her off. And so, taking pity on ourselves, we decided to come over and stay at Taliesin for some months. When we arrived, Mr. Wright said, "Yen! You look like your own grandfather." And to my wife he said, "Why do all Chinese women look like Mme. Chiang Kai-shek?"

During this return stay, I was working at the drawing board in the Hillside drafting room on drawings for the Obler house in California. I was directly behind Mr. Wright's board on which he was designing the preliminaries for a garage project. After a lot of T-square and triangle shuffling and erasing he stood up, looked over the result, and sighed lightly. He shook his head and said to himself— though loud enough for me to hear—"I'm a genius this morning."

KENNETH B. LOCKHART

There are many stories about how clients got to Wright, and one rather interesting story concerns Florida Southern College. In the drafting room, about 1938, Mr. Wright had a call from Dr. Ludd Spivey, president of Florida Southern College, Lakeland, Florida, who later came to see him. We had heard that Spivey had inquired at the Chicago office of an architectural magazine about who was America's finest architect. They had recommended Mr. Wright. Soon, Mr. Wright was off to Florida, and on his return he told us that he had the job. (He added that getting to Florida was awful. The train had broken down about a mile from town, and he had had to walk the railroad ties all the way. Next time he had to go, he would insist on some better way.)

Although Spivey had no funds, Mr. Wright started with the master plan and the Annie Merner Pfeiffer Chapel, for he understood that Mrs. Pfeiffer would pay for it if there were plans to show, and it worked out that way. We got busy with the working drawings; my job was drawing sections, but from there on, I was on other projects, inside and out of the studio.

Kenn Lockhart's story tells of his part in the process. The college went on to be the largest group of Wright buildings anywhere. Visitors come to see them from all over, and the original library has become a Wright museum.

In 1936, after one and one-half years of study at the Minneapolis School of Art, a childhood friend told me about Frank Lloyd Wright and Taliesin. I immediately wrote for information and began searching for steady work to earn the tuition, about $1000. I tried unsuccessfully to work on a freighter out of Los Angeles, and then I tried to go to Alaska via Seattle to work in the platinum mines. Both efforts were foiled by strikes as Harry Bridges organized the longshoremen. When three years had passed, and I hadn't raised the money, I wrote Mr. Wright telling of my predicament, assuring him that I had worked all my life and asking if I could possibly work my way through Taliesin? His reply was "Come and see me."

The first meeting, in July 1939, was in his office off the studio. I was overwhelmed in his presence as he described a work/study plan in which three apprentices would rotate two weeks in and one week out of the kitchen as the cook's assistant. He then said, "You know it takes a long time to be an architect."

"I have my whole life" I replied.

"When can you come."

"A week from today."

Within two days of arrival I was in the kitchen from 5 A.M. until 9 P.M.—out of the kitchen for a week. And then I was made a cook because the other two apprentices didn't show up. Cook duty was three meals a day for a week every four weeks, and we served fifty for breakfast and dinner and eighty people for lunch, because we also fed the laborers working on the buildings. During evenings and weekends I constructed cabinetwork for my room. Hans Koch, an elderly craftsman there, told Mr. Wright about the quality of my carpentry, and, after seeing it, Mr. Wright put me on construction.

My first drafting room assignment in the summer of 1942 was interrupted by what would be the first of many taps on the shoulder by Frank Lloyd Wright saying: "Can we step outside and talk." The first project he proposed was to build a three-tier parking lot for Hillside, the school section of Taliesin. Mr. Wright asked, "You can run a bulldozer can't you?" I said, "Yes."

For two winters during World War II the fellowship did not travel to Taliesin West and the buildings were being vandalized. I asked Mr. Wright if I could go and take care of the place in the winter of 1943 and he said, "I'll think about it." Within a few days he found me, took me to Madison's cycle shop and said "I bought you this motorcycle (a 1932 Harley Davidson with a sidebox) to go to Arizona—you can drive one can't you?" I never had, but the salesman took me for a drive. By that afternoon I was packed and headed for Arizona, arriving two weeks later.

In 1945 he sent my wife and me to the site of the Florida Southern College in Lakeland, Florida. The president, Dr. Ludd Spivey, wanted to start on the administration building (The chapel, library, and three classroom buildings were already built). The previous contractor did not want to continue work, so Dr. Spivey had suggested to Mr. Wright that an apprentice take over, with the salary partially paid by Wright through the college.

I became the contractor in concert with Dr. Spivey and the college business manager. I hired a group of about thirty tradespeople

The Annie Pfeiffer Memorial Chapel of Florida Southern College. Photo by M. Thorn.

and coordinated all the work from my office on campus. College scholarship students had helped make the decorative concrete block for the buildings that were already constructed, but the new students on the G.I. bill did not want this work, so my trainees were black laborers. In addition to building the administration building, I planned and built the parking lot to the west, the wide circular steps on the south side of the water come, and convinced Dr. Spivey, with support from the professor of citrus culture, to change the site from a citrus grove into a campus. We removed scattered parking, planted grass between the trees, completed the connecting covered esplanades between buildings, and started the proposed classroom building east of Dr. Spivey's office. With a hydraulic dredge on a

The Administration Building of Florida Southern College. Photo by M. Thorn.

boat, we built up sand for a proposed swimming pool in Lake Hollingsworth (which was never completed).

During all this time I was in frequent communication with Mr. Wright as questions and problems arose concerning the design and construction. At the end of five and a half years I felt I had fulfilled my obligation to the work and had set up an organization for its continuation. I wanted to return to Taliesin, and Mr. Wright felt I had been away long enough.

For two and a half years during the Korean War Mr. Wright asked me to manage the Taliesin Midway farm and property. I worked with apprentices John Hill, Morton Delson, and Eric Lloyd Wright. The arduous farm work had a side benefit: it provided

Covered Walkways-Esplanades at Florida Southern College. Photo by M. Thorn.

deferment from the draft. The total property in Wisconsin was about 5000 acres, of which we farmed 40 percent. We took care of 45 milk cows, 100 pigs, 25 horses, and 300 chickens (sending cases of eggs to Arizona every two weeks). The Midway buildings were powered by an electric generator, which posed some problems in winters of 54° below zero.

In the mid-1950s, for the second time while I was working in the drafting room, came a tap on the shoulder; "Let's go outside and talk."

Outside, Mr. Wright asked, "How about getting a bunch of stone masons and carpenters and let's go build the restaurant." (He was referring to the Riverview Terrace restaurant on the Wisconsin

River near Taliesin.) Again I acted as the general contractor. For the structure we used trusses Mr. Wright had salvaged from the aircraft carrier Ranger. At one point I ordered 2 × 4 framing lumber for the dining room roof. The wood came full of knots so I consulted Wes Peters, who suggested using 2 × 6s. Later, as Mr. Wright and I were going over the drawings, he mentioned the 2 × 4s. I said, "Mr. Wright, they are 2 × 6s."

"Yes," he said, "I noticed you changed them," and continued the conversation. Normally if someone had made a change without Mr. Wright's approval he would have been very angry. I felt he trusted me and my abilities. Although the restaurant project took me away from drafting room work, I never felt victimized, because the projects were always interesting, and we had a close communication in the process.

After Mr. Wright's death, realizing I had not gained as much design experience as others, I announced I wanted to write specifications for the Taliesin Architects organization, despite opposition from some members of the group.

Over a thirty-year period I wrote about 450 project manuals as director of quality assurance, winning ten national Construction Specification Institute awards for those specifications and ultimately becoming a fellow of the Institute.

I continue to help apprentices learn specification writing in conjunction with architectural projects of Taliesin Architects. It is more than fifty years since I first arrived at Taliesin, and I am happy to still be a member of the Taliesin family.

CARTER H. MANNY, JR.

Carter's background is in architecture, and he was an apprentice at Taliesin for a short while. He became a partner in a large Chicago architectural firm and is presently the director of the Chicago-based Graham Foundation.

A POSTWAR APPRENTICESHIP

By the time World War II was over, it was too late to go back to the Harvard Graduate School of Design, where I had completed one stimulating year with Philip Johnson as a classmate and friend. In order for the year not to be a complete loss, I thought about trying to spend some time with Frank Lloyd Wright, whose work I especially admired. I had grown up in Michigan City, Indiana where Wright's son John and daughter Catherine lived. They were friends of my parents, and I suppose this may have influenced my idea of going to Taliesin. And so I wrote a letter to Wright in Spring Green and got a brief note back from Gene Masselink inviting me for a weekend. This was in November 1945.

There were several highlights of this brief visit: a stimulating cocktail hour with Mr. and Mrs. Wright and other weekend guests in the loggia—that wonderfully complex space off the great Taliesin living room—then dinner in the playhouse at Hillside with the entire Fellowship. The quality of light in the playhouse, which came from plywood light fixtures and bathed the room in a soft glow, was captivating. A movie followed dinner—I recall it was *State Fair*—which put everyone in a festive mood and served as my introduction to Wright's great passion for Hollywood films.

Finally, my interview took place the following morning after Sunday breakfast with the Fellowship. I wonder now how I ever made it into this group, for in talking to Mr. Wright I grew more and more discouraged. He seemed negative about me. He pronounced my hair too short ("We need hair around our ears"); he advised me to throw away my glasses and strengthen my eyes with

Bates exercises; and he evaluated my Harvard background as a liability that would be difficult to overcome. But the most crushing blow came when he informed me that he would only accept apprentices for a minimum of one year.

Happily, after reading the appeal I included in my thank you note for the weekend, he relented and I received a cryptic note. "All right Carter Manny, since you are in earnest, come along. $100 a month. We'll call you a professor. Sincerely, F.L.W." Needless to say, I was overjoyed and joined the Fellowship at Taliesin West soon after its annual winter trek from Wisconsin to Arizona.

When I arrived, work was already in progress rebuilding Taliesin. Things had been neglected during the War when the apprentices were gone. (Most, following Wright's injunction, were conscientious objectors, and several had difficult experiences.) But now with the return of former apprentices and the addition of many new ones—curiously, they were mostly veterans on the G.I. Bill—the Fellowship numbered around sixty, including a sprinkling of wives and children.

There was a buzz of activity. At Taliesin West the great girders which spanned the drafting room and the garden room of the Wright's quarters were straightened and reinforced with new members and new snowy white canvas was stretched and put in place. How magnificent the effect when these translucent roofs were once again put in place. A host of smaller jobs also needed doing: a new cabinet in the apprentices' dining room, a new door to the Wright's quarters, etc., etc. My skills with hammer and saw were apparently noticed, and I was soon assigned mainly to these smaller projects, which I enjoyed carrying out largely on my own.

Some of the experienced apprentices supervised the renovation work, but others were busy at drafting boards that were set up in a finished corner of the drafting room. They were working on projects for various clients. The research tower for Johnson Wax was the big project of the moment. Wright's engineer from Chicago and Johnson's staff architect were there for consultation.

Once for a few days I was asked to do some minor drafting for a commercial laundry project in Milwaukee and another time I was invited to help with a model of the Loeb house, which was being readied for an exhibition at the Museum of Modern Art; but for the most part my days were occupied with hammer and saw and a can of thinned out Cherokee red paint that I used for staining redwood carpentry work.

Our day began about 6 A.M. Breakfast with the other apprentices was at 7, followed by a half hour of choral practice under the guidance of Svetlana, Mrs. Wright's daughter by an earlier marriage. Svetlana was married to Wes Peters, who, like Gene Masselink, was one of the original apprentices dating back to 1932 and 1933, respectively. "Svet," as we called Svetlana, was a great favorite with everyone and I greatly enjoyed the time with her every morning and the new experience of singing works by Bach, Palestrina, and Cesar Franck, which we subsequently sang for guests on Sunday evenings.

The day's work began about 8:30, as I recall, stopped for an hour and a half at noon for lunch and a brief rest in our rooms, then resumed until about 5. Dinner was at 6, and evenings were free. During the evening some of us would drive to Phoenix for a beer or a movie, but usually we saved Phoenix for Wednesdays when we had both afternoon and evening off.

I spent most of my free time around Taliesin reading in my room, or listening to the great Scott hi-fi in the drafting room, or in bull sessions on politics and architecture—in our rooms before a little smoking fire during the cold nights of January and February and outside under the stars as the evenings warmed. As nights grew warmer, I also enjoyed moving my sleeping bag out of my cozy room and sleeping under the stars on one of the chaises in the great apprentice courtyard. In any event, I soon wearied of the architectural bull sessions because it was quickly evident that admiration expressed for architecture other than Mr. Wright's was treated as heresy or breach of loyalty by the older apprentices. My favorite evening pastime was listening to the Scott. Sitting in the still unfinished drafting room, looking out across the vast expanse of desert as twilight faded and twinkling lights came on from settlements that were thirty or forty miles away, while the Scott gave forth with the Bach rendition of the opening of Brandenburg No. 4, is a recollection that still brings a tingle to my spine.

Daily work routines were interrupted for a week at scheduled intervals for "K.P." duty. This involved helping the chef, one of three experienced apprentices who had a flair for cooking. The cooks rotated assignments; one week on and two weeks off. In addition to general kitchen clean-up, after each meal, kitchen helpers did errands in Scottsdale, buried garbage, and gathered grapefruit from an orchard near Camelback, which belonged to friends of Mr. and Mrs. Wright. We gathered grapefruit by the jeep-load, sometimes more than once a week. One of the most pleasant features of Taliesin West was the many large bowls made from harrow discs purchased at Sears, painted Cherokee red and heaped high with grapefruit. The yellow fruit provided a perfect decorative accent for white canvas, orange desert stone and redwood, which was the scheme of Taliesin West, but, beyond decoration, the grapefruit was an important part of our diet and a great thirst quencher during the heat of the day. Coarse dark bread made from whole grain flour shipped from Chicago was another staple.

On one of my kitchen stints I was burying the garbage a few hundred yards behind the camp when Mr. Wright showed up. He was a little upset that the garbage dump was that close to living quarters, but did not seem to blame me since the dump had obviously been started before my turn. The incident actually turned out well for me since it was one of the few times I was alone with Wright, and I was pleased that he seemed to want to talk to me as we walked back to the compound. He had only recently returned from a trip to New York where he had seen Philip Johnson at the Museum of Modern Art and, knowing that I had been Philip's classmate at Harvard before the War and heavily influenced by him, he lectured me in what he considered the negative architecture of Mies, which he knew Johnson espoused and from which he wanted to sway me.

In addition to K.P. duty, every apprentice was assigned an area of the camp for weekly clean-up on Saturday afternoon prior to the arrival of weekend guests. I was fortunate in my assignment, for I drew the great apprentice courtyard. I had a strong affinity for this large expanse of gravel from the first time I walked across it to my room and this was long before I experienced the deep pleasure of Ryoanji. On my first Saturday afternoon I was given a small garden rake and told to rake the courtyard. I slaved for over two hours, and barely finished in time to shower and dress for dinner. By the time I finished there were so many footprints in the gravel that my work was barely noticeable. The next week I found a branch from a paloverde tree that had been discarded after serving as decoration in the theatre. It made a perfect giant rake for the courtyard gravel. Pulling it, I could make a swatch for furrows six or more feet across instead of fifteen inches with the garden rake, and the furrows were deeper and more continuous. I could cover the entire courtyard in a matter of minutes and found the results so good that I raked sever-

Carter Manny raking the gravel in the great courtyard of Taliesin West with a paloverde branch, April 1946.

al times each weekend and still consumed less time than I did that first Saturday afternoon.

This task gave me great satisfaction, and I was pleased when others, including Mr. Wright, noticed, although I had mixed feelings about his remark that gravel raking might well be the best thing I would ever do! I took this comment for another little dig at Harvard, but perhaps he knew Japan so well that he was thinking of another time and another calling. At any rate, I found him basically kind, despite a barbed comment now and then.

I have mentioned earlier that I paid $100 per month. It seems unbelievably little today, but it was a tidy sum thirty-five years ago. However, a couple of incidents illustrate Wright's ambivalence toward money. I had been at Taliesin nearly three months when he came over to me one day and pulled a crumpled piece of paper from his pocket and handed it to me. It was my first check, which he had been carrying around for three months. He said he wanted to shop in Phoenix that day and would I mind writing him a new check. Most of the time, money seemed to mean very little to him, yet I recall that during the cocktail hour during my weekend visit to Taliesin East back in November he boasted of having earned a million dollars in fees.

I have already mentioned how Wright loved a movie. He also loved a party. Perhaps it was because he inevitably became the center of attention—as a storyteller, teacher, actor or debater. Whether it was Saturday nights in the theatre, at dinners, during supper Sunday night in the garden room, during a mid-week gathering on the terrace overlooking pool and desert, or during a picnic in the mountains, or when a guest was present who was just as famous as he was, it was Mr. Wright on whom all attention focused and he never disappointed.

His presence always seemed theatrical compared with every surrounding, as though he were guided by some great silent director. I remember one time in the garden room after Sunday supper, as dishes were being removed and just before music was to begin— Iovanna to play the harp, Hiram to sing a baritone solo and the chorus to conclude with Franck—Wright went over to the piano and with one hand like the clapper of a great bell struck a series of heroic chords. You could tell he was drawn to the instrument like iron filings to a magnet. Then came the remark, which I took to be as much lament as boast: "If I had followed music and not architecture, I could have surpassed Beethoven."

Frank Lloyd Wright in the drafting room at Taliesin West, April 1946 (frame from a 16-mm color film made by Carter Manny).

That he was the essence of genius such as few are given became even more clear to me early one morning near the end of my stay. Breakfast had just concluded when Wright came from his private quarters, a sheaf of drawings in his hand, and called for three of his most trusted aides to follow to the drafting room. There was a feeling of expectancy in the air. Something important was about to take place. Chorus rehearsal was quickly cancelled and we followed to the drafting room and gathered around the table where Wright was issuing instructions. My eyes boggled as he went over three drawings, each for a separate house project, all produced, he said, since he woke at 4 A.M. and could sleep no longer. The drawings were in colored pencil, drawn with T-square and triangle for the most part, but done in part free hand. On each sheet plan, section and elevation were superimposed on top of one another forming wondrous abstractions, but actually concisely depicting multiple aspects of each conception. After a brief explanation, each drawing was turned over to a senior apprentice whose task would be to adapt a module to the conceptual design and prepare separate conventional drawings for plan sections and elevations for Mr. Wright's further scrutiny.

I was astounded by this experience. Imagine, three designs in roughly three and a half hours. This was a virtuoso performance.

BYRON ("BOB") MOSHER

Byron Keeler Mosher was born and raised in Bay City, Michigan. He graduated from the University of Michigan in architecture in the Spring of 1932. Mosher heard about Wright's school from another student, who was to go to Taliesin. Mosher applied and was accepted as Robert Mosher—he had changed his name after having been kidded during his youth about the name "Byron." After World War II, Bob worked for the Fred Harvey chain designing hotels. He then joined other firms and eventually landed in Marbella, Spain, employed by Norman Bel Geddes, for rather high salary. When Geddes didn't meet his financial obligations, Bob began a practice of his own. He architected many residences, including his own, and a school in North Africa.

In May 1992, I had a call from Bob's friend in Marbella, Spain, telling me of his demise the evening before. Bob had worked all day coloring drawings he had made for a new project. About dusk, friends dropped by to visit; they gathered around a coffee table to have a drink. Bob took one sip, his glass fell out of his hand, his heart failed, and within minutes he was dead.

On October 23, 1932, I arrived at Taliesin, elated to be there. I had known about it only from a few articles and photographs. Mr. Wright greeted me warmly and welcomed me as a charter member of the Fellowship. He said he understood that I had just graduated from the University of Michigan and suggested that I forget everything that those professors at Ann Arbor had taught me! I had the right answer because I merely said, "Mr. Wright, that won't be difficult at all because I was the worst—you could say the lousiest—student in the whole university." The maestro answered very briefly in one of the favorite expressions he used whenever we did anything he approved of: "Bobby, that counts you one." That began my great and wonderful decade under my esteemed master at Taliesin in Wisconsin and later Taliesin West in Arizona.

During the first two cold winters we worked mostly on the Taliesin and Hillside buildings, and sometimes in the studio, copy-

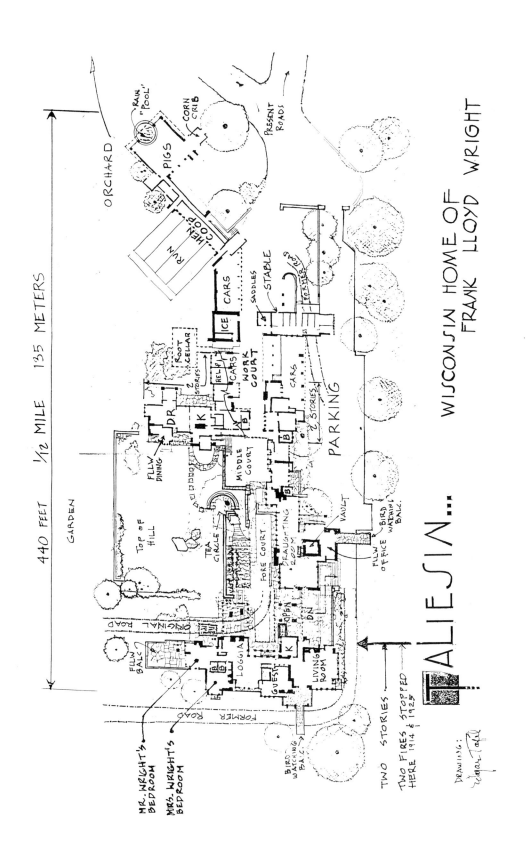

440 FEET   1/12 MILE   135 METERS

ORCHARD

RAIN "POOL"
PIGS
CORN CRIB
HEN COOP
RUN
PRESENT ROADS

GARDEN

CARS
ICE
SADDLES
STABLE
FORMER (HJ)

ROOT CELLAR
STORES
HELP?
CARS
WORK COURT
B
CARS

DR
K
B
MIDDLE COURT
B
VAULT
2 STORIES
PARKING

FLLW DINING
BEDROOM
TOP OF HILL
TEA CIRCLE
FORE COURT
DRAUGHTING ROOM
B
FLLW OFFICE
BIRD WATCHING BALC.

ORIGINAL ROAD

FLLW BALC?
B
LOGGIA
GUEST
OPEN
K
DN
LIVING ROOM

FORMER ROAD

BIRD WATCHING BALC.

MR. WRIGHT'S BEDROOM
MRS. WRIGHT'S BEDROOM

TWO STORIES

TWO FIRES STOPPED HERE 1914 & 1925

TALIESIN...

WISCONSIN HOME OF
FRANK LLOYD WRIGHT

DRAWING:

147

ing plans from Wright's previous buildings. We worked under the leadership of Henry Klumb, who had been a senior at Taliesin for some time. Mr. Wright would come through the studio, make suggestions, and talk about his experiences during the days when those buildings were built.

The third fall we all went to Arizona to work on plans for a model city that would later go to Radio City in New York for a month's exhibition. Wright was considered by some to be the only architect in America who had developed a plan for the whole nation. He called it "Broadacres," and it was a decentralization of the modern city "where the city was everywhere but nowhere."

Four of us took the model from Arizona to New York. Edgar Tafel and I took turns driving the truck, while Robert Bishop and Edgar Kaufmann, Jr., following in an auto, would help set up the model and then return to their own lives. (I have always suspected that one of the reasons Edgar Tafel was chosen was because his folks lived in New York and we could stay with them rather than run up a hotel bill.)

Mr. Wright was there for the opening and stayed on for several weeks. Edgar and I attended the models, explained the concept, and introduced likely clients to Mr. Wright. One day a student from Yale asked if I would come up to the campus and talk to students about Mr. Wright and Taliesin. I went up one day—without telling Mr. Wright—had a good time, and was given a small honorarium. When I returned to the exhibit at Rockefeller Center I looked through the slot of the closed door, saw the familiar figure with beret, cap, and cane and thought, "Oh, boy, I'm in trouble because I'm late."

"Where have you been, Bobby?" he asked. "I knew I shouldn't have left you alone in this evil city. You're always getting into trouble. Now give me an account."

I told him, "I went up to Yale to deliver a lecture on what you've been telling us: how to become architects." Of course, he didn't believe me and said with a smile, "You can fabricate tales like no one I've ever heard. Now tell me the truth—where were you?" I told him about Yale and said that they had even paid me for my efforts. Then I made the mistake of pulling a fresh twenty dollar bill from my pocket and saying, "Here's what they gave me."

Well, that changed his tune immediately. "Now let's you and I take a stroll up Fifth Avenue," he said. We walked through the Rockefeller Center lobby, where he pointed out the location of

Frank Lloyd Wright, Bob Mosher, Edgar Tafel, and Wes Peters.

what were once the murals by the Mexican Diego Rivera, but had been painted over because he was a communist. When we got to Fifth Avenue, we crossed the street and went into Saks Fifth Avenue, where I noticed he no longer was wearing a beret. He said, "I forgot something," and walked me to the men's counter on the ground floor. He asked if they had any French berets. The clerk recognized him and said, "No, we don't, Mr. Wright, but we have some lovely caps from Scotland," and pulled out a dozen of them. Mr. Wright said, "Well, they won't do, really. I've got to have a beret."

Frank Lloyd Wright and Bob Mosher.

Then he tried on the most expensive cap, took it off, and ripped off the visor. The clerk was going berserk, but I just watched with great glee. Mr. Wright replaced the cap on his white hair and said, "All right, now we can go for a stroll along the avenue." But, as usual, he didn't have any money so I had to pay up, and that's where my twenty bucks went.

Now, let's jump to about a year later—1936—to "Fallingwater," the country house for E. J. Kaufmann, owner of a department store in Pittsburgh. We had completed the schematics for the house at Taliesin, went to Arizona that winter to make the construction drawings, and in the spring returned to Wisconsin. From there, three of us (Edgar Tafel, Manuel Sandoval, and myself) drove to Pittsburgh with Mr. Wright. We dropped off Manuel, who would do the carpentry and cabinet work for Mr. Kaufmann's office in the family store.* We continued to Bear Run, 60 miles south, where I was told to stay to supervise construction of "Fallingwater." Edgar

*Which Edgar Jr. gave to the Victorian and Albert Museum, and is there now.

was to drive Mr. Wright back to Wisconsin. I had no idea I was about to have the privilege of spending one of the most exciting years of my young life gaining experience that would hold me in good stead for decades to follow.

We hiked through the heavy woods along the torrential stream, Bear Run, to the spot where it formed a roaring waterfall below a huge boulder jutting out from the north bank of the stream. We stood on a bridge spanning the stream, facing the top of the waterfall. The maestro said, "I'm leaving you here. Do you have any questions?" "Yes, sir, I do." I was familiar with the plans for the

Bob Mosher and Frank Lloyd Wright

house because we had drawn them up in Arizona. But I was puzzled about something and asked, "Can you tell me how to locate the exact datum (level) of the first floor?"

"That's a good question, Bobby." he said. "Now go across the stream and climb up on that boulder."

The boulder was over eighteen feet above the bed of the stream, and it took a lot of effort to get up there, but luckily a couple of small saplings growing out of crevices in the rock gave me some handholds. I finally stood at the top of the boulder. The maestro yelled loudly from the other side of the Run: "All right, Bobby, you've answered your own question." I was a little perplexed at first, but I looked down at my feet atop that great rock and yelled, "Mr. Wright, is this it?"

"That's it. Now goodbye and good luck and don't pull too many mistakes." They drove off, and I stayed on

The maestro had planned to shave off the top of the boulder, but later Mr. Kaufmann said, "No way, I want that boulder to stay just as it is." He explained that he used to go and sit there and cogitate as the water fell below. So the boulder stayed, the house was built on top of the boulder, and the rest, as they say, is history. I supervised the building as it neared the top, Edgar took over from me for a couple of months, then I returned for its completion.

Later, I returned to the Fellowship, and enjoyed life in the country and our communal life, with its advantages and disadvantages. In Arizona I remember that, once in a while, some of us would steal off to town for a change of pace and some relaxation. One day I received a postcard of a local Spanish scene with a message scrawled in childish script: "Dear Bob, Your laundry is ready to be picked up. Please bring your own starch," signed, "Love and kisses, Ginger." Immediately I recognized the fine, mischievous hand of Edgar Tafel, but apparently one of Taliesin's spies had shown the card to Mrs. Wright before I got it. She called me on the carpet, saying she did not know what the boys did in town, but she certainly hoped we would not bring back any germs.

We had many interesting visitors at both Taliesins. One was Henry-Russell Hitchcock, who stayed for some time, preparing his book *In the Nature of Materials*. He and Mr. Wright got along well, and, for about a week, Edgar and I worked with the two of them, bringing out drawings from the files while they discussed them. Sometimes Mr. Wright changed the dates on the drawings to confuse Hitchcock, winking at us as he played his little tricks. During this time, it was our custom—on Mr. Wright's birthday—for each of us to make a gift of a drawing or a sketch or a poem, and deposit it in a beautifully designed box. One day Hitchcock, alone, went through the drawings in the box, thinking they were Mr. Wright's work. He pulled out one I had done and said to Mr. Wright, "I have discovered something: your project for a hotel suspended over the Grand Canyon. Tell me, when did you design this?" The maestro took out a pencil, put a date on it and said he had forgotten all about it. Then, with another of his conspiratorial winks to us, he added a red square, which he initialed "FLLW." Hitchcock never knew!

After I became a senior apprentice I was given a very important assignment in Arizona. The Pauson sisters, Rose and Gertrude, members of a distinguished San Francisco family, had spent winters at the Biltmore Hotel in Phoenix, a building in which Mr. Wright had design input. The Pausons had come to know the Wrights and were often guests at the desert camp. They purchased a hilltop site in the desert and selected Mr. Wright as their architect. When the next spring came, I was chosen to supervise construction of the house. I had already worked on the plans for this massive house of desert stone and rough California redwood, and was familiar with these materials, having worked with them years earlier when we were building the camp in Arizona, Taliesin West. The Pauson construction went well and everyone was happy with it.

Original sketch of the Pauson House, that **Mosher** *did under Wright's direction.*

In 1941, along came Pearl Harbor, and our world changed. I married, left Taliesin for good, and landed in northern Arizona as coordinator of construction for a government ordnance depot. Some time later my wife and I took a trip to Phoenix and we drove out early one morning to the Pauson house—I was eager to show her "my work." As we approached, I was completely astounded. The great stone walls were there, but what in hell had happened to the rest of it? Burned to the ground. In fact, it was still smoldering! The floor was so hot you could not possibly enter where the living room had been, but I found a rake and pulled out several antique Ming sculptures, melted to mush by the fire. We found out later that the house had been rented to tenants who had had a party the night before the fire. Probably started by a cigarette, the hand-woven draperies of the living-room windows had caught fire and went unnoticed until it was too late. The house was never rebuilt; its stone carcass remains on the hilltop.

After half a century I look back and reminisce with tremendous delight at that marvelous, youthful period of what seem like medieval days of being apprentice to a great maestro. I recall it all with a great sense of appreciation, and for the good fortune of being a charter member of the Fellowship. Mr. Wright always treated me like a gentleman and often called me "Little Sunshine." Maybe I was cheerful and enthusiastic; he always made me feel important in working for and with him.

Pauson House, Phoenix, Arizona, after the fire.

BYRON ("BOB") MOSHER

I still have a letter written nearly twenty years after I left Taliesin, addressed to me in Spain: "Dear Bobus: We were all glad to hear you are well and happy and, as always, hard at work with enthusiasm. Enthusiasm, Bobby, is your long suit, don't lose it. Affection, Frank Lloyd Wright. July 30, 1957."

Maybe that makes up for the twenty bucks, and then some.

WILLIAM WESLEY PETERS

On arriving at Taliesin in the fall of 1932, one of the first people I met was Wes—he was everywhere, doing everything, and involved with cheer and humor. We soon found much common ground, working together and humorizing together. Wes's father owned and edited the Indiana Evansville Press, *and Wes related newspaper stories he remembered from far back in his childhood. He was 6'4" tall, robust, and could command yet be gentle and cooperative.*

Before our arrival, there were three "draftsmen": the architect Henry Klumb and his wife, who had come from Germany in 1927; Rudolph Mock, a Swiss architect; and Robert Goodall, a Chicago draftsman. These three men were mainly in the drafting room/studio, and they were part of the first year's efforts to make things operate like a school. Mondays, Wednesdays, and Fridays, Mr. Wright would have half of the apprentices in and around the drafting room, working on redrawing projects he had designed and/or built years before. The other three days, the other half of the fellowship would be in the studio, doing the same. This soon led to a certain grandiose confusion, especially when Mr. Wright would walk in and take some of us out to haul stone, sand, gravel or wood.

At that time, Wes edited a biweekly pin-up paper entitled Taliesin Times, *to which many of us contributed. This would be put together during the evenings or Sundays. When I arrived, there was a piece about two men from New York City who had begun the Museum of Modern Art and had come to visit Taliesin and obtain architectural wisdom. Recording their stay, Wes wrote, "Mr. Philip Johnson wore lavender trousers, white shoes, and a pale green shirt, and Mr. Henry-Russell Hitchcock wore light blue shoes, white trousers, and a pink shirt."*

Mr. Wright's secretary, Karl Jensen, had arrived from Denmark not long before we had, and was taken by the cause of Organic Architecture. He emulated Wright's attire: walking cane, long hair, and besides that, put talcum powder on his face when dating in town. He certainly was bait for us American "school kids," and we would play tricks on him, such as placing a board over his fireplace flue during a cocktail gathering he hosted, thus smoking out his guests. He kept his cane next to his typewriter, pulling it out to impress visitors, certainly not to impress us apprentices. One day, whilst Karl was at lunch, Wes and I removed the handle, from a push broom, inserted Karl's cane into the brush, and nailed it securely. Later, when Karl grabbed the cane, we in the drafting room heard a bang—the brush held firmly, and Karl took it down to his room, and never acknowledged the incident. We didn't see the cane again either. Mr. Wright enjoyed hearing about these events. Wes' poem about Karl was

> *Karl Jensen came from far away*
> *He crossed the broad Atlantic.*
> *He learned to quote what Frank Wright wrote*
> *But quoth it inorganic.*

However, Wes was also seriously concerned with architecture, and when Fallingwater and then the Johnson Building and house came along, his work covered the basic engineering and its relationship to the actual building process. Mendal Glickman, an adult engineer, was with these projects as well, and he and Wes worked together quietly and consistently, although Wes was there one hundred percent of the time. During the two years that I lived mostly at Fallingwater and the Racine projects, working on the preparation of construction drawings and on-site supervision, Wes and I were constantly solving building problems. We were often motivated to do the "inorganic," in which problems were solved with added columns and beams, without Mr. Wright's knowledge or approval.

After I left in 1941, Wes continued to be project architect on many of Wright's designs, and later his own, and these buildings stand as testimony to his abilities. In the spring of 1991, Wes and I were in touch regarding the completion of the interviews. We were to get together and review his architectural career with Mr. Wright and his personal life in general. In July, I telephoned him in Wisconsin, only to hear that he was rapidly fading in a Madison hospital, and within a few days, he passed away. Soon afterward, I joined many of his friends in the church he designed in Spring Green for a memorial service.

Following are two pieces that Wes and I worked on together, the last during a weekend at Taliesin West in 1990.

I

I grew up in Evansville, Indiana, and spent a year at Evansville College, where I got good grades but was always fighting against the academic way of teaching architecture. In 1930 I moved on to MIT. Toward the end of my second year there I saw a notice on a bulletin board announcing that Frank Lloyd Wright was opening an architecture school in Wisconsin. I had already read Wright's Princeton Lectures and his autobiography, which had then recently been published. A school run by Mr. Wright sounded very exciting to me, but when I asked several of my professors what they thought about my going to study with Wright, they said things like, "Oh, don't touch that stuff," or "Wright is just a joker."

But another professor, an old New Englander who had built houses that were not the usual Georgian colonial but great, big houses with huge central fireplaces and wide wooden walls and overhangs, said, "Well, you've always been a bit of a rebellious type, I think you might find something there."

When I got home to Evansville in June I found that my parents were driving my sister to the University of Wisconsin so I went along to have a look at what kind of school Mr. Wright was setting up. From Madison I took a bus to Spring Green, some forty miles, and when I got to Taliesin I saw a lot of signs that said "No Trespassing." They scared me off. I kept walking until I came upon a farmhouse nearby. As I remember, it was a Sunday, and the farm family was out on the front porch in their shirt sleeves. I told them I was looking for Taliesin and they said "Oh, don't pay any attention to those keep-off signs. Just go right on up."

The first person I met when I got there was Mr. Wright's secretary, Karl Jensen, who told me Mr. Wright wouldn't be available until later. So I walked all around the neighboring farms. When I got back to Taliesin I was sent to the drafting room to meet Mr. Wright. At the very first instant he made a tremendous impression on me. Although I am more than a head taller than he was, I got the feeling then—and I've always had it—that he looked tall. Later on he used to tease me and say, "Sit down, Wes, you're spoiling the scale of the room."

From the beginning I had the feeling that Mr. Wright was like a constant stream pouring forth vitality and life. I saw him as the emblem of a creative spirit. I had never met anyone like him.

WILLIAM WESLEY PETERS

As we sat facing each other across a drafting table, he talked for half an hour about his plans to rebuild and expand Hillside, a school adjacent to the Taliesin acreage, and which his aunts had run years before. He wanted to shape it into a new kind of fellowship for architects. He said the buildings were in very bad condition, but he had grand plans. He made it sound so wonderful that I made up my mind right there, that very minute. I wasn't going back to MIT. My credits at MIT were in good standing and I was expected there in the fall. But now I knew it was not for me. I would join Mr. Wright's school. I wanted to be part of the creative spirit I felt in him.

My father would have paid the $675 for tuition, room, and board, but I wanted to pay it myself. I had saved just about that much from working one summer on a highway gang and another summer at a club where I'd maintained four tennis courts. Without hesitating I pulled out my checkbook and wrote a check for the full $675. Mr. Wright really beamed at that and said, "Well, you're the first person to really sign up." Then he walked to the back of the drafting room where there was a whole stack of the German 1910 portfolios. He picked up two (two made a set), signed them and gave them to me. I still have them.

That same day I headed back to Evansville and stayed there until August, then, I drove to Wisconsin in my father's car, a coupe with a rumble seat. That first evening Mr. Wright greeted me and introduced me to Mrs. Wright. I stayed in a room with a fireplace down below the Wrights' quarters.

The next day Mr. Wright took me over to Hillside and we started tearing shingles off the old buildings, where many men were working. Mr. Wright had offered them room, board, and $2.00 an hour and they were happy to get it in that year of deep depression. Two relatives of a draftsman were doing the cooking in the old laundry building. They were wonderful cooks, but we students had to help them and for us that was a terrible job. Kitchen assignments lasted two weeks, and you had to get up about 3 A.M. to chop wood for the two wood-burning ranges.

Mr. Wright had had some big trees cut down on neighboring farms, and we felled more trees and sawed them into lumber at a sawmill on the side of the hill. We did all sorts of things on the job. It was fortunate that I had taken some extra courses in structural engineering at MIT; what I had learned was very helpful in rebuilding Hillside and in many other projects.

Wes Peters and Frank Lloyd Wright.

As the time passed, apprentices began to arrive from all around the country. Several were pretty good carpenters, one was a graduate of Swarthmore (Robert Bishop) and older than the rest of us. I liked them all; they were bright and some were funny. I particularly remember Yen Liang. He drove up from Chicago in a Stutz Blackhawk. It had a rumble seat in the back, and it had a great big sphinx's head. I don't know why it was called a Blackhawk, but it was a terrific old car. The very day Yen arrived they said to him, "Well, Yen, we have to go up to Edda Parsons' in Dodgeville to get some groceries, and we don't have a free car. Would you mind driving up?" Three of us went there in his car, up the steep gravel road, sixteen miles to Dodgeville. Yen was going at a real clip. He hit the first hill beyond Wyoming Valley, which is very steep, and has a sharp curve at the end of the road. He had to brake suddenly, and we hit the gravel turn so hard that the huge monster of a car spun around completely, and faced the direction it was coming from. We were shaken but okay. On the way back one of us asked Yen if he'd been driving long. He said he had learned that day: he'd bought the car in Chicago that morning and figured how to run it on the way up. It's a wonder we survived. (Yen became my roommate. He slept with his eyes open—it was terrifying.)

Well, we did survive. I stayed all the winter of 1932 and 1933. In 1933 I was involved in all the buying of materials, etc., and that year I told Mr. Wright that, eventually, I would like to be married. I told him I hoped one day to marry Svetlana, who was Mrs. Wright's daughter by a previous marriage. Svetlana (we all called her Svet) was 16 and I was 21. Svet often rode with me in the truck when I went to haul the wood we needed to keep the fires going. At first we talked and kidded around, but gradually we fell in love. We knew we were too young to be married, but I wanted Mr. Wright to know that we were in love and wanted to marry.

Mr. Wright had always been so friendly to me, I felt it was only right to be honest with him. But when I told him, he immediately assumed Svet was pregnant. He was sure I had seduced her. He became very angry and said I had betrayed him. That was not the case at all. I tried to explain that nothing like that had gone on between us, but he wouldn't listen. He was both furious and hurt; he was very fond of Svet and didn't want to lose her.

Mr. Wright sent a letter to my father in which he said that I had disappointed and betrayed him and acted under false pretenses. It was a very angry letter. I didn't know about it until 1935 when

Wes Peters with Olgivanna Wright's daughter, Svetlana.

my father died and I found the letter and my father's reply. My father wrote, "Dear Mr. Wright, I do not know you, but you've written me things about my son that I simply cannot accept. My son has faults, but they are not the faults of dishonesty or deceit." He went on to say that he knew I had a tremendous admiration for Mr. Wright and he denied that I could have done the things of which Mr. Wright accused me.

About two weeks later Mr. Wright sent a second letter to my father in which he said, "I wrote you a bad letter and you wrote me a good one." He wrote that he'd looked up my father in *Who's Who* and found he had led the fight against the Ku Klux Klan in Indiana. He was very impressed by this.

Mr. Wright and my father never met, which I think was too bad. Unfortunately, Wright had a way of writing letters in anger and haste. Later, Mrs. Wright was able to keep him from mailing those sorts of letters. In general, though, his letters were the epitome of positive and beautiful thinking.

Initially, Mrs. Wright had encouraged me to take her daughter along in the truck. She had made a point of getting us together. But now both she and Mr. Wright took a very strong view against Svet and me. But both Svet and I stood up to both of them because, as I've said, we had done nothing wrong.

Svet and I decided we had to leave Taliesin altogether. I drove her to Chicago, where she stayed with Mrs. Cree, who was a violinist with the Chicago Symphony Orchestra, and her daughter Margaret, who later became a stellar cellist. I stayed with the Crees that first night, then I went home to Indiana. Svet's arrangement was that she would cook breakfast for the Crees and clean the house and in return she would get a small stipend and Mrs. Cree would give her violin lessons. Svet was already doing well on the piano and while she was with the Crees she made tremendous progress on the violin.

Meanwhile, in Evansville, my father owned a lot in the city and asked if I wanted to build a house on it. I built a $3,000 house of solid oak that is still there. I built several more houses and worked on a modification of my father's newspaper plant. Every month I drove to Chicago to see Svetlana. That went on for two years. It was a very strange time in our lives. Then in 1935 a lot of things happened: that year I took the qualifying architectural examination in Indiana—it was a fierce exam—and got my license; my father died that summer; and soon thereafter Svet and I got married.

Now the situation was different, and we felt we could return to Taliesin. We went back, a little hesitantly because we weren't sure how we would be received; but it turned out that everyone there was overjoyed. They gave us a big welcome, and I took my place again in the Fellowship.

Svet and I had two sons. In 1946 she was driving across the valley at Spring Green with our two sons in the car. She must have been distracted momentarily—she drove off the road and into a pond. She and one of our sons were killed. Our other son, Brandoch, survived. The loss was tragic for me and my surviving son but it was also felt deeply by both Mr. and Mrs. Wright, as well as the whole Fellowship.

Many people have asked me about Gurdjieff, the Russian philosopher/guru Mrs. Wright had brought to Taliesin. Oddly enough, I never met Gurdjieff. I saw him from a distance, holding forth, but that was about all. Mr. Wright asked me once why I wasn't going ahead with some project that Gurdjieff had proposed. I said, "Mr. Wright, I regard you as my master, not Mr. Gurdjieff. You are the star I am following." Mr. Wright was pleased with that, and I never heard anything more about Gurdjieff.

II

By this time Mr. Wright was getting some important projects.

As the Johnson Wax administration building in Racine was being built, occasionally Mr. Wright would go down to the site in the morning, and then drive back at night. We would almost always stop into Karl Ratzsch's, which is a famous German restaurant in Milwaukee. It was run by the Ratzsches, and they were really on the job all the time. Mrs. Ratzsch would get out and help set the tables and supervise all the waitresses, and Mr. Ratzsch was in there all the time, too, like the real landlord. They came to know Mr. Wright and me very well. Then the war came, and I didn't go down there for maybe three or four years.

Sometime after the war, Alvar Aalto was coming to this country and he wrote to ask if he could see Mr. Wright at Taliesin in Wisconsin. Mr. Wright invited him to come up there and stay several days. Aalto was a very jovial fellow—whatever his architectural capabilities. At that time he was well on his way to becoming an alcoholic. Mr. Wright decided to send him down to see the Johnson Wax building, and he had me drive Aalto down. We went down early in the morning and took in some of the buildings on the north shore of Chicago. This was no easy undertaking for every time we'd get going on the highway Aalto would decide it was time to stop for some coffee, which meant that he really wanted a drink. This happened several times. It was a rather pleasant trip as far as that was concerned. We finally got to the Johnson Wax building and "Wingspread." This was a late fall day, very chilly, and by that time it was late in the afternoon. And I suddenly had the idea that it would be nice to go and have dinner at Karl Ratzsch's. We never used to have to make reservations there. So we drove up to Milwaukee and went into the German restaurant. It was late in the evening. We came up into the entryway and saw a huge line of people. I thought what a terrible thing. Here I have this foreign guest, and I had told him how good the restaurant was, and here we couldn't possibly get into it. I didn't know what to do. Then suddenly I saw Mrs. Ratzsch standing far away at the other end of the line. There must have been ten or fifteen people in that little narrow entryway waiting for tables. Mrs. Ratzsch saw me. She hadn't seen me for, oh, maybe four years. She walked up and said, "Mr. Peters, your table is ready now. Is Mr. Wright with you?" (My God—this is the kind of thing that really endears you to an innkeeper.) She led us into the restaurant, to our table, and she sat down with us. She said that she supposed I would like to have a plank of whitefish. Lake Superior whitefish was always Mr. Wright's favorite, and it is what he would always order. After four or five years' absence, I was really impressed, even if Alvar Aalto wasn't—by that time he didn't know what was happening. That was a really wonderful situation.

* * *

I brought the first peacocks to Taliesin, and Mr. Wright loved them. We had about seven or eight peacocks around Taliesin. Later, I took them over to my farm where I raised them—I eventually had twenty or more. We not only had peacocks, but at one time we had two pairs of swans on the creek down below. And we had goats for a long, long time. Svet milked goats every day for seven or eight years. Goats are great pets. They're probably the most intelligent farm animals after pigs. Once somebody gave two Russian wolfhounds to Mr. Wright's son, Lloyd, and Lloyd gave them to Mr. Wright. They were called Sasha and Duchan. They were pure Russian wolfhounds with the very narrow long heads, with narrow skulls and no brains. They were real killers. They bothered the sheep and other animals, so Mr. Wright made a big, high cage to keep them in at Taliesin. (They had nearly killed my little scotty dog.) One day they escaped and began running over the hill toward Hillside. I started rushing after them. In the valley we had a bunch of milk goats tethered. But the goats weren't scared at all. They put their heads down to let the dogs know they would fight. They were more than the wolfhounds wanted to tackle. The wolfhounds ran over the hill. Where the garden is now at Taliesin, at that time we kept a flock of about fifty sheep. By the time I could run after them, the dogs were rounding up the sheep and had already killed about ten or fifteen sheep. Mr. Wright was upset, and we got rid of the wolfhounds shortly after that.

We also had a great big macaw named Lulu, and it belonged to Svet. Taliesin West was alive with birds: parrots; a number of birds trained for falconry, including a golden eagle; and a Mexican eagle that was really quite a character. Mexican eagles are actually closer to vultures than eagles. They walk more than they fly. This one would sit up at the top of the living room or out on the guest deck. Mrs. Wright also had a tame goose named Aesop. This goose would walk around everywhere. Nobody was ever sure of its gender, but we assumed it was a gander until one day Aesop laid an egg—inexplicably! The Mexican eagle was about half the size of Aesop, and he would constantly taunt the goose by flying down and landing on Aesop's back and holding on with his claws. The goose would go crazy trying to get away, and then the eagle would fly up to the roof again. The Mexican eagle was just doing it as a prank! The golden eagle we had was a truly beautiful bird. It was the biggest golden eagle I have ever seen, about 29 pounds, which is tremendous. It must have been a female, because among birds of prey the females are considerably larger than the males. Actually, I don't know how Mr. Wright endured all those things around there.

*　*　*

The brothers Ed and Duke Carmody were workmen at Taliesin in Wisconsin. They didn't speak to each other. Ed had been a hired man for James Lloyd Jones back in the days when James Lloyd Jones was farming over 3000 acres. Ed literally drank Sterno when he couldn't get whiskey. (Later in his life he gave up whiskey—and Sterno—and didn't drink anything but beer.) Ed continued to be a wonderful worker and very steady up until the time he died. The other brother was Clarence Carmody, and he was also a terrific worker.

[**Editor's note:** *One day Mr. Wright was in the drafting room drawing, and Ed Carmody came in. He came in through the door on the other side, and he must have been twenty feet away from Mr. Wright. Mr. Wright kept drawing, but he could smell this whiff of alcohol. Mr. Wright said, "Ed, what do you want?" Ed said, "I want some money." Mr. Wright said, "What for? You're already drunk." Ed said, "I want to get drunker." Mr. Wright reached into his pocket and handed over several dollar bills.*]

* * *

Local Alan Brunker, the quarry man, was also a prospector at one time. Before Alan Brunker died, we went up to his house several times. He lived up in Ridgeway. Mr. Wright and Gene Masselink and I went to his funeral. Alan was a marvelous guy. He had been a lead prospector. About a month before he died, he called me and said that he wanted me to go with him someplace because he wanted to show me something. We went up to a farm that Marshall Erdman owns now. Alan said that when they were cutting this road through there, he saw that there was this big lead vein running through it. He showed me where it was. He dug around a bit and sure enough he got down to this layer of rock, and he shook a piece out and told me that it was rich lead ore. He said that he had always wanted to come up and do this, but he was telling me about it—"You can make your fortune here." I thanked him very much, and shortly after that he died. I was up there a few years ago and I could still remember where the lead vein was. But I don't know how good it is. There is still a lot of lead left in the mines up by Dodgeville.

The house that Svet and I owned adjacent to Taliesin used to be an old James Lloyd Jones house. It was built in 1854. Once when we were doing a remodelling we found a whole bunch of papers in its walls. We also found two old shot bags in the shot tower, and two ladies' purses made out of shot tower bags. And we found a book of records that belonged to the man who was living in that farmhouse. He was the head of the shot tower operation. This book was full of receipts showing how much he paid for everything. He had 18 or 20 mules and oxen pulling wagons full of lead down to the shot tower, then after the shot was made it would be loaded right onto the river boats. These records go clear back to the

1850s when the shot tower was built. It's amazing how little it cost to have these 18 or 20 mules and oxen hauling these huge wagons. The whole process must have taken a couple of days.

*[**Editor's note:** Stuffy Vale's tavern was about halfway between the bridge and Helena. Stuffy had a cheese factory in the valley, but he sold it when processed cheese came along. Then he built himself a tavern. The apprentices used to go over there for drinks.]*

Stuffy's tavern was a really nice place. After the war, Mr. Wright bought the tavern when Stuffy wanted to retire, much to the consternation of its patrons. We transferred the papers right there in Spring Green, at the bank. We filed the actual deed in Dodgeville. We were having a picnic over there, and Mr. Wright said "Well, I've decided we'll have a big bonfire. We'll go burn down the tavern." The tavern was already empty. Everybody sort of protested to Mr. Wright that it would be better to try to sell its materials. But it probably wasn't all that valuable. Mr. Wright had us go down there with the picnic and burn the tavern down— something you wouldn't be allowed to do nowadays. We put kerosene about, and it made a terrific fire. *[**Editor's note:** Mr. Wright directed John Aramantides, violinist, to be there with his violin, and he played while Stuffy's burned.]* A lot of people stopped to look. A lot of the old patrons were literally shocked by this event, as though somebody had burned down the family church or something. It was too bad in a way. It was a nice place, although it certainly was a pretty cheesy looking place.

*[**Editor's note:** It was too bad when Stuffy Vale abandoned the cheese factory, too. It was one of the few places you could take visitors to see—drive them down into the valley, sort of on the way to the chapel. And you'd stop in there, and Stuffy was very nice, and you'd see him raking the cheese and making it.]*

In and around the valley there used to be ten or fifteen cheese factories. They all folded. Most of them folded during the war because big outfits like Carnation came in and made deals with the farmers who served the factories. The big companies would pick up milk right at the farms, so the farmers were selling to them rather than hauling their milk to the cheese factories. Also, the government made it very tough on cheese manufacturers by making them keep such elaborate books. Most of these factories were one-man or one-family operations. They couldn't do the work plus keep up all the paperwork, so they went out of business.

A certain amount of shopping was down at Edda Parson's grocery store up at Dodgeville. They extended credit to Mr. Wright. Edda Parsons was really a marvelous woman. She died just a few years ago. She and her husband operated the store there, and the store was still there even after they both died. Edda promised to give me the National cash register that was there, and she would have, too, except that she forgot about it. Somebody probably got a fortune for it—a magnificent old National cash register.

She was a wonderful woman. Mr. Wright never had any money, and she once advanced him three or four thousand dollars in food and supplies. We all went up there for years to buy everything. Whenever Mr. Wright got any money, he'd make a beeline up to Dodgeville. She trusted him, and most of the other people around there would not. People would come to her and ask her about it, and she'd say "I never lost a cent on Frank Lloyd Wright and I don't intend to."

[*Editor's note:* *There was a time when some sort of fire took place in the store and all the crackers got burned. She gave them to Mr. Wright at a cut rate. And we had those crackers for months. They were these sweet vanilla crackers—and burned. God were they awful! After every meal each apprentice would pick up a half-dozen cookies, eat at one and then throw the rest in the garbage.*]

* * *

I had dinner several times with Harry Guggenheim and Elisha Patterson Guggenheim, who was the wife of the owner of *The Chicago Tribune* and *The New York Daily News*. Dinners were always very formal affairs at their apartment in New York. After the meal the men would retire to the billiard room and the ladies would go wherever they went. The men would smoke cigars. It was very much eighteenth century. Harry Guggenheim wasn't as horrible in some respects as Solomon.

In the middle 1950s Robert Moses indicated he could be of some help to Mr. Wright in getting the building permit for the Guggenheim Museum. Actually, Moses wasn't really of very much help, although he claimed he was. It was a terrible thing, getting the permits. An engineer—Dr. Feldman—was very helpful. Not the calculations he made, but the fact that he put his name on everything. I made all the calculations, and he made them all over again. Then, after George Cohen had accepted the contract, Mr. Wright decided to make some very serious changes. Mr. Wright changed the whole construction. And we basically had to change the structural calculations for the ramps, and we didn't have much time to do it. The Guggenheim Museum, with its spiral form, was something Mr. Wright was never completely satisfied with, though he struggled for years and years trying to reconcile those spirals with the horizontals.

The reasons I remember why the plan was flopped over is that there was some difference in the availability of the land and also that the original plan had this little theater that was designed for this man who had a projection machine that projected on the dome ceiling. I forget his name, but we always called him Professor So-and-So, and he developed this system of projecting forms and colors from various keyboards. You would sit and play it like an organ and project different types of forms and shapes and colors of a considerable variety. There was some way to control this very huge keyboard. It was quite an interesting idea. I saw a demonstration of it on a small scale, done with the model we have at Taliesin. This model shows the separate domed building. Then this man dropped out of the picture, for some reason or other. Then another piece of land became available. There was also the fact that Mr. Wright wanted to deal with that building differently—you know, one side was against buildings and the other side was against the street.

Mr. Wright talked about putting the building in Central Park. But it was never seriously considered because they had had that site pretty early in the game. It was during the war that the very first sketches were made. When the war was going on they came up with the idea that Mr. Wright design the museum. Mr. Wright made several alternative designs for the Guggenheim Museum. It was the only time in his life that he did this—he didn't believe in it in principle. One design was based on the hexagonal spiral, one was based on the rectilinear spiral, and one was based on the circular spiral.

* * *

When we first got to Scottsdale, it was just a post office, a gas station, a bar, a pool hall, and a grocery store. And the old Scottsdale drug store was down on Main Street. The second year we were there, a fellow was staying with a girl up at the Powderhorn ranch near Taliesin. He was a young fellow who went around dressed like the villain in a cowboy movie. He was always dressed in black—black boots and so forth. One afternoon, he came into Scottsdale and walked into the billiard hall and told the old man who ran the place that he wanted to play pool. He apparently had been drinking rather heavily. He was very belligerent. The old man told him that the pool hall was closed, but the fellow said "It's open now because I want to play pool." The old fellow told him that he couldn't do that. So the young fellow suddenly got furious. He grabbed a billiard cue and knocked the old man down. Then he started jumping up and down on top of him with cowboy boots.

According to a couple of people who were there and saw this happening, somebody went out and called for Marshal Fredericks. Marshal Fredericks was a real old-time western peace officer. They used to call him "The Law." He came down there and told this fellow to desist. But the fellow was furious and he picked up a billiard cue again and charged the marshal, swinging the cue around his head. The marshal yelled for him to stop, then pulled out his gun. The marshal later claimed that he aimed for the fellow's shoulder, but he killed him. Svet and I were down in that Earl's Market when it happened, and we heard this terrible sound—a .45 caliber sounded like a cannon in that little town. Everybody started congregating down there. The girl who was staying with this fellow was in the grocery store at the same time. Some ladies came down and told her what had happened.

Edgar Tafel and I were down the next day when they were having the inquest. They had the inquest downtown, right out in the street. I can remember to this day what Marshal Fredericks said. They asked him to tell his story and he said, "Well, he was a-comin' at me, and I either had to fight or run, and it ain't a-fittin' for the law to run." And the coroner's jury acquitted him right then.

The streets of Scottsdale! About a year or two after that two fellows had a gunfight catty-corner from the Chinese grocery that's still there, a little house down on the corner. The two guys had this gunfight across the street until one of them was killed and the other one was very seriously wounded. There are still some scratches on the side of that Chinese grocery. It was a pretty wild town at that time.

* * *

Wes Peters.

Editor's note: *Years later Wes and Stalin's daughter Svetlana married, they had one child, and later divorced, and she went on to live in Europe. At the end of the above interview, I asked Wes if he would consider resurrecting his marriage. His reply: "I wouldn't make that mistake again!"*

MANSINH RANA

Mansinh Rana, the son of an artist, was born in India. He attended architectural school there and came to Taliesin for four years after World War II. Upon returning home, he became chief architect for the government of India. He now has his own practice and is the Architectural Dean of the new Suchant School of Art and Architecture in New Delhi. His practice encompasses a wide variety of building types.

We met when he was an apprentice at Taliesin, and became fast friends. I visited him in 1969 in Delhi, when he was chief architect for the government of India, and in 1974 he arranged for me to come back, under the auspices of the U.S.I.A. for lectures on Wright in Bombay, Madras, New Delhi, and at the ghastly city of Chandigarh designed by Le Corbusier. If there ever was a prize for a Westerner's inhuman design for India, that is it! Mansinh showed me a park he designed in memory of The Buddha, where he had signs stating "Please walk on the grass."

I was in the western part of India then known as Kathiwar, a small peninsula near Bombay. My father was an art teacher, and on his side of the family we were related to the Princess of Limbdi. When she married the Maharaja of Porbandar, we moved there. The Maharaja was an enlightened king, greatly interested in learning and architecture, and the school in Porbandar where I studied had an excellent headmaster who spoke English like an Englishman. Because I drew well, the Maharaja encouraged me to study architecture.

In 1945, when I was 24 and in the fourth year of my studies of architecture at Bombay, I came across Frank Lloyd Wright's autobiography. From the day I started reading that book I could not put it down until I had completed it. Because the book was considered valuable, it was kept under lock and key in the school library and every time I borrowed it, an attendant dressed in gold livery stood behind me as I read it to make sure I was not tearing out any pages. When I read that Mr. Wright had draftsmen—he called them apprentices—working for him, I wrote to tell him that I was in India getting a Beaux Arts type of formal education, senselessly copying Doric, Ionic, and Corinthian orders, which meant nothing to an Indian. I wrote that I admired his approach to architecture, that I was wasting my time in India, and if I were ever fortunate enough to be at Taliesin, I would consider it a rare privilege to work with him.

World War II was still on, and there was a postal strike in Bombay. Day after day I waited for a reply from Mr. Wright. When I didn't hear, I thought perhaps he was too busy to reply. Or maybe the postal strike was delaying the mail. The strike was so bad that the post office couldn't handle the heaps of mail and on a certain date they were going to burn it. People who wanted to claim their letters were told to go to the general post office and collect what they could.

A friend of mine who was a stamp collector thought this was an excellent opportunity to gather foreign stamps from the heaps of mail. While he was going through the envelopes he found an American stamp and as he took it off he noticed that the letter was addressed to me. You could say that he "pinched" the letter and brought it to me. I still remember my excitement when I saw the red square on the envelope; I knew that the letter was from Taliesin. It said simply, "Dear Mansinh, If you can come on your own steam, we can put you to work. . . . Frank Lloyd Wright."

I would like to say that in almost no time I was on a boat, but the reality was that it took more than a year of correspondence with Gene Masselink, Mr. Wright's secretary, and a great deal of back and forth before I boarded a U.S. hospital ship from Bombay to Colombo, Singapore, Hong Kong, Shanghai, Honolulu, and San Francisco. On that boat there were students, missionaries, Polish Jews who got on in Shanghai, and Chinese soldiers on their way to train in America. My first glimpse of America was the Golden Gate Bridge. I took a train from San Francisco to Phoenix.

I had been told to wait in the lobby of the Westward Ho Hotel for Gene Masselink, who would take me to the camp in Arizona where Mr. Wright and his students were staying. Gene took me by way of the Pauson house near Phoenix, or rather, the ruins of the house, which had been destroyed by a fire. It was my first sight of Mr. Wright's work, and I remember thinking how—uniquely— organic architecture made for great ruins.

Gene told me I would be staying in a tent. I thought that would be nice because in India a tent is large with its own com- mode and comfortable fittings. But Gene showed me to a tiny, 6' by 6' pyramidical tent with a camp bed and sleeping bag. It wasn't what I expected. I didn't know what to do with my suitcases, filled with rather formal suits, and from my first glances around I realized I would have to buy work clothes, which I had never owned in India.

It took me several days to get my bearings. For one thing, I didn't know how to get inside the drafting room. In India doors are doors and windows are windows. But the entrance into the drafting room slanted at such a strange angle that for two or three days I waited until somebody came out or went in and then slipped in while the oddly shaped door was open.

Frank Lloyd Wright much as he must have appeared when Mansinh Rana first encountered him.

Of course, I expected to get to work right away in the drafting room. But it wasn't like that at Taliesin. My first job was helping to build a tower in the court. The concrete work was finished and the wooden forms were being taken down. I was told to pull the nails out of the wood, but I didn't know how to use the hammer they gave me. It had a fork-like thing that wasn't familiar to me. I kept applying the fork to the nail and pulling vertically and not getting anywhere. Wes Peters finally saw my difficulties and said, "I'll show you." He put a little block of wood underneath the hammer, pulled at an angle and said, "See, it comes out this way." It was my first lesson in working on construction.

Mr. Wright did not arrive at Taliesin until the fourth day I was there. I was walking under the trellis in front of the drafting room when I saw him coming out of his office. He was wearing a coat, which was not a cape, but cut full like a cape, and he had a walking stick in his hand. He came directly toward me and looked at me intently as if trying to place me. We stood looking at each other for a little bit and finally I found the courage to say, "Good evening, Mr. Wright, I'm Mansinh."

He said, "Oh, hello, we've been expecting you."

We walked along together. He asked what I had been doing, was I keeping busy. I told him I'd been pulling nails. He said, "Okay, we'll see you around."

That was my first meeting with the master. I was kind of dumbfounded that this man, whom I'd admired so much and put on a pedestal and thought of as someone remote, had stood right in front of me and spoken in such a friendly, informal way. He was a person who would put you at ease. You had come to his home and he was very happy to see you.

One thing I noticed at the beginning was that Mr. Wright spoke the way he wrote. Having read his autobiography, I could connect the spoken and written words. I also noticed that his voice demanded one's attention immediately. Later on I learned it was the voice of a family of teachers and preachers. He talked to engage you and communicate with you.

The only other person I ever heard who spoke like this was Mahatma Gandhi. I had met Gandhi when I was a student before I left India and I'd said to him, "I am going to work in the U.S.," and he said, "Oh, how interesting. You must build a house where the windows will bring in all kinds of ideas. But I don't want you to be blown away by foreign ideas, Western ideas. Our homes should be our own homes." Mr. Wright had the same economy in using words to convey meaning. It was remarkable how much Mr. Wright could put into a word or a sentence.

I met Mrs. Wright several days later. At the time she was full of anguish because her daughter, Svetlana—who was married to Wes Peters—had recently been killed in a car accident. She described to me how it happened and asked if there was any Yoga meditation or exercise that she could do to keep her mind concentrated on Taliesin and the Fellowship. She was still greatly disturbed about Svetlana and cried whenever she spoke of her loss. She also talked to me about Indian philosophers whose works she had read. Mrs. Wright was always very friendly toward me, and the first time I returned to Taliesin some years after I'd left in 1951, she introduced me as "our son who's come back from India."

In Arizona I never got to see much of the drafting room. But when we went to Wisconsin in the spring I finally got to work there. At that time the model and the drawings of the Guggenheim Museum were being made, and the house in Mexico and several others were being planned, and work was underway for a large development in downtown Pittsburgh.

In those years at Taliesin I particularly enjoyed the Saturday evenings when everyone dressed up, the Sunday morning breakfasts, the Sunday dinners in the living room, and the very small, intimate theatre. One Saturday evening, the architect Erich Mendelsohn was our guest. He'd come for the weekend from Berkeley where he was teaching architecture at the University of California. He was a bit late arriving at dinner and when he hurried to get into his seat he hit his knee against a sharp corner of the table. He said

Frank Lloyd Wright with Erich Mendelsohn.

to Mr. Wright, "You and your organic architecture." We all laughed, including Mr. Wright.

We had many distinguished visitors: architects, artists, musicians, politicians. I remember Serge Koussevitsky, conductor of the Boston Symphony; Raymond Lowey, who designed the Coca Cola bottle and the Studebaker; plus James Stewart, a mayor of Bombay, and Philip Johnson. Mr. Wright used to tease Philip about his famous glass house. He'd ask, "How do you use your bathroom, Philip?"

By the winter of 1951 I had been with Mr. Wright for almost four years. I had worked on a wide variety of projects and was allowed to become one of the senior apprentices, but I was itching

Frank Lloyd Wright with Mansinh Rana (far right) and (left to right) Abaywaden (Sri Lanka), Russi Patell (Bombay), and Cheng Pao (China) during planning of the Guggenheim Museum in 1951.

to get back to India and start what Mr. Wright often described as "a hell of my own." While Mr. Wright did not expect us to stay at Taliesin forever, he was never happy when someone came in and said, "Mr. Wright, I'm leaving." Finally, though, the day came when I walked into the drafting room in Wisconsin and said, "Mr. Wright, I've come to say goodbye."

He looked up from his drawing board, put down his glasses and said, "Mansinh, we never say goodbye at Taliesin, we say so long." Then he stood up and said, "You know, Mansinh, we have a rubber band attached to your feet and from time to time we snap you back. So never say goodbye." Then he walked me to the driveway where Wes was waiting in his new Jaguar to drive me to Madison. Wes drove so fast I wasn't even sure I'd make it to Madison, let alone all the way to India. But I waved goodbye to Mr. Wright, and to Mrs. Wright—who had joined him—and I called out, "So long."

In 1959 I had just been married and was working on some large projects for the government of India. I had a little pocket transistor radio and about six o'clock in the evening on the world news

I heard that the famous American architect Frank Lloyd Wright had died. I suddenly felt as if there was a complete blackout. I was stunned. I could not believe it. I thought, how can this be? I rushed to the telegraph office and sent a telegram to Gene Masselink in Arizona to find out if the news report was correct. Sadly, it was.

Ever since I'd left Taliesin in 1951 Mr. Wright had been in my dreams. I would hear him talking at different times. Sometimes he would be in the drafting room, or in the garden, or outdoors where we were grading the roads in Wisconsin. I would see and hear him in the kitchen where he would come in to tell us how to organize things and say, "Oh, what a mess this place is, this is not the way to work."

As a Hindu would say, this was a kind of second life in this one life. In dreams I could always go back to that other universe, to that planet, which was Taliesin. To this day that has not stopped. Suddenly something happens in the sequence of a dream and again I am in the middle of the Fellowship.

The interesting thing about the apprentices who make the best use of their time with Mr. Wright is that he brings out hidden parts of the talent within your own being. The questions he asks help you find out who you are and what you are doing. In my case, he helps me ask: Is the architecture I am doing something for India? What makes it Indian? How is it in the "realm of ideas?"

Now I am not saying I have solved that problem, but I have tried, and in every building that I have done in India I have not tried to copy the Indian form, or its Wright form, but to use the materials and the site and to combine them and find a solution that is essentially Indian. When I did a planetarium in the compound of the house where Nehru lived, I found on the big property of about a dozen acres an old hunting lodge from the fifteenth or sixteenth century, made of rugged stones with small arches and a flat roof. Mrs. Indira Gandhi said to me, "Whatever you do, don't make the planetarium in such a way that it cramps the style of this little building. Don't let it stick out like a sore thumb."

This is what Mr. Wright would have said. This is what he did all his life. Whatever he did belonged to the site, respected its neighbors, the contours of the land, the trees and any buildings standing nearby. This is what I think is essentially the spirit of Mr. Wright's work: not to copy, but to capture the spirit of the time and place.

I remember the box of apprentices' gifts—drawings or poems or paintings—we used to give Mr. Wright on his birthday. Every time he noticed a box into which an apprentice had put something that looked similar to a project we were working on at the time, he would get furious and say, "Why this is like spitting in my coffee." That would give him a chance to relate once more his story of the English butler who hated his master and would, every morning, spit into the coffee he served him.

So many times I think consciously or unconsciously about what Mr. Wright would have said or done in a similar situation, and this dialogue goes on all the time. He really wanted his apprentices to go out and talk about organic architecture and what it stood for and what it did. He didn't want us to repeat what he had done. He did not even want to repeat himself. Whenever he was asked which of his buildings he considered the most beautiful, he would say, "The one on my board right now."

I believe the life at Taliesin literally transforms you into a different avatar, a different realm of ideas, a different way of living, and because of that, I have never felt that I've become old or am repeating myself for lack of ideas.

PAOLO SOLERI

Paolo Soleri was born in Italy and graduated from Torino Polytechnic. After a stay of eighteen months at Taliesin, he left to found two educational organizations—in Scottsdale and Flagstaff, Arizona—for teaching and living architecture. He has published several books on architecture, and his drawings are published and shown widely.

I first met Mr. Wright at Taliesin West in January 1947. I had spent Christmas and New Year's on Ellis Island. I could not understand a word of English, and so for six months I had practically no communication with anyone other than Vern Knutson, who spoke some French. I started out at Taliesin by serving the family breakfast, and I learned some English from that experience. Of my eighteen months at Taliesin, only in the last six months was I able to communicate with ease in English.

I had training in drawing, but I did very little in the drafting room at Taliesin. Mostly I did agriculture, upkeep, and gardening. I was in Wisconsin for one season, where I became very good friends with a fellow apprentice named Mark Mills.

I left Taliesin because I was asked to leave. While I was there I became very excited about the idea of community, and I began to think of what I could do if I went back to Italy to establish something similar to Taliesin. At first Wright seemed very positive about the idea. But then I made the mistake of asking other people if they would like to go with me. I asked Mark Mills, Vern Knutson, and Richard Salter. They were "seniors" in a sense, and I, who was proposing all this, was a "junior." Wright remained positive for a while, and even suggested that we four—Mills, Knutson, Salter, and I—stay together over the summer at Taliesin West.

So we stayed there for the summer of 1948 and did some construction work together. Uncle Waldo (Mrs. Wright's brother) and Aunt Sophie were here, and they spoke Italian and were very friendly with me. But by the end of the summer Mr. Wright asked me and Richard Salter to leave. His letter to us was very nice.

After another year in Scottsdale, I went back to Italy for five years. When I returned to the United States and Scottsdale, I went to visit Taliesin. But I realized it was better for me to stay away. They didn't care to have me around. I thought that since I was living in Scottsdale and we were neighbors, there could be some kind of communication. That feeling wasn't reciprocal. I did get to see Mr. Wright every now and then, and I don't believe they ever saw me as some kind of competition.

I was 25 or 26 when I became an apprentice. My training had already concluded in terms of Italian schooling and university. Though I was extremely excited by Wright's work, I never became a disciple. Our parting was basically a misunderstanding, though, in retrospect, we did have very fundamental differences of opinion. Wright believed in suburbia, and I believed that cities were the basis of civilization. So it is not hard to see why we parted. I also had this very naive notion that I could take a chunk of Taliesin and move it somewhere else.

The language barrier was such that I never really became a part of Taliesin. But Taliesin was a premium experience, and I'm very glad and grateful to have had that experience. As for Mrs. Wright carrying on Taliesin after Mr. Wright's death, it's a sad story. But I don't know if it's an avoidable story. It's part of the human condition.

MARCUS WESTON

Architect Marcus Weston joined the Fellowship in 1938, after growing up in Spring Green. He later married, raised a family, and became an associate in a Madison architectural office that did organic works. He still lives in Spring Green and is an integral part of the Wright legacy.

My life was inextricably tied to Mr. Wright, even before I was born. When he started building the first Taliesin, in 1911, chief carpenter Johnnie Vaughn hired my father, even though he had a broken arm at the time. When I asked my dad what he could do he said, "I couldn't do anything—they just wanted my tools." In 1914 my father and his 13-year-old son, Ernest, rode their bicycles four miles to Taliesin every day to work on the building and grounds. Ernest was one of the four workmen killed in the fire/holocaust by the insane houseworker. I was born five months later, in Spring Green.

I remember a rainy evening in 1925. The fire bell rang quite a long time. My father had been working out of town that day and came home late. Mother gave him supper after which he walked uptown to lodge. A little later I heard someone running on the walk. Then my father came to the door, said there was a fire over at Wright's, and went to his truck and was gone. I didn't know when he came home. The following Sunday, Dad loaded the family in the car, drove over, parked at the foot of the hill, and we walked up.

There were several groups of people around, and a large area of ruins where the fire occurred, with wisps of smoke still rising. There was a man walking about asking people, "How did you get in here?" They would tell him and he would say, "Will you please leave the same way." I was afraid and huddled close to my father. That man came walking by and said to my father, "Hello, Will. This doesn't include you," and went on to ask some others to leave. It was my first experience with the importance of knowing the "(W)right" people. When he had sent most of them away he came and talked with us and asked my father if he'd come back and help rebuild it. Of course, he did.

It didn't take me long to discover that a pretty little girl lived there, and I took advantage of every opportunity to go over and play with her. We covered the whole place, from boating on the pond below the house to catching frogs in the reservoir on the hill above (when the water was low). She grew into a lovely woman and a loyal friend, Svetlana, Mrs. Wright's daughter.

There were several local people, as well as people from other communities, working on the reconstruction. My father would tell us things that happened that he thought amusing or interesting. Mr. Wright often came around the work. One day he was watching a carpenter up on the scaffold driving a nail and he missed the nail leaving the hammer mark in the wood. When he had driven it "home" Mr. Wright asked him why he left his trademark and the carpenter said, "There'll be a damn sight more of them if you stay there and watch me." Mr. Wright just laughed and walked away.

Sometimes there were serious things, like plumbing the studding. If Mr. Wright told you it was plumb you could put your level away and nail it. And there was the workman who said that he was working for the greatest architect in the world, "One look and he's got it all."

Dad also said Mr. Wright would never ask you to do something he would not do himself, and told me about a time when he was working with some men on the hydraulic ram at the dam. The water was drained and Dad was holding a pipe out in the mud when he slipped and fell down. Mr. Wright, watching from the bank, without hesitation walked right in and helped him up.

When Taliesin III was all rebuilt and furnished, Mr. and Mrs. Wright had an open house one evening for all the workmen and their families. Everyone could go everywhere. It was a happy occasion and though I was quite young I still have a picture in my mind of Mr. Wright in his chair in the living room happily talking with us all.

Growing up in Spring Green, I heard much of the gossip about Mr. Wright, although I'm sure some people used restraint in my presence. And there were varying views. One local woman sent Miriam Noel, Wright's second wife, flowers on one of her unsuccessful attempts to gain admittance to Taliesin, while I heard another (and a pillar in her church) describe her as a "She-Devil."

Remembering those times and rereading some news accounts convinces me Mr. Wright was correct when he wrote in his autobiography that the newspapers were exploiting a sick woman. My father always knew when she was coming in plenty of time to pick up a crew to block the gates.

In 1927 my father wanted to build a house. Mr. Wright made available to him all the plans he had done for the redi-cut system that didn't materialize. My father narrowed it down to three and then picked the one best suited to his needs and the site. He modified it somewhat, but stuck pretty close to the original. I recall Mr. and Mrs. Wright coming to see it one day while in construction. They went through the whole house. Mr. Wright was only critical of my father's use of an "open cornice" instead of the closed soffit he always designed, and said therefore that he couldn't claim it was one of his houses.

In 1929, Mr. Wright took his staff to Chandler, Arizona, to work on the San Marcos-in-the-Desert resort hotel project. My mother, father, youngest sister, and I went along . . . my father was to be superintendent of construction on the hotel; my sister was working as secretary to Mr. Wright. We built "Ocatillo," a camp in the desert, for a place to live. Svetlana and I went to school in Chandler. It was a great experience for all of us. After the market crashed, there was no need for a resort hotel, and it was never built.

The Fellowship commenced in 1932. My father was there until Mr. Wright—short of money—was forced to get along without any hired help. In 1938, Mr. Wright wanted my father to come back to work. When he found that my brother and I were working with him he hired all three of us. So we worked there that summer.

That fall we worked on the windmill, Romeo and Juliet, about eighty feet high. We took off the original shingles, renailed the sheathing and recovered it with boards and battens. One day while we were working there we noticed Mr. Wright walking over the hill from Taliesin. I was on the scaffold near the top. The next time I was aware of Mr. Wright he was in the balcony of the tower, and I was amazed that he had climbed the ladder necessary to get there—he was over 70 years old! It was straight up with the pump rod in the middle of it and not easy to climb. After making his inspection and talking with my father he went down and went on, apparently satisfied.

When it came time to go to Arizona in the fall of 1938, Mr. Wright called me and said that some of the boys had said I'd expressed a desire to go with them. (I had.) He said they could use me but there would be no money in it for me, just three months on the desert with the Fellowship. That was satisfactory with me and I went, not knowing I was changing the course of my life—to become an architect.

By the time we returned in the spring I was committed. I stayed on as an apprentice. I think perhaps I enjoyed a "closeness" or a "freedom" with Mr. Wright that was unique among the apprentices. (And perhaps each of them felt they had their own special place with him.) If I had any problem it was easier for me to go to him and discuss it than with another apprentice. He was always very kind and patient.

One time at Taliesin West he was directing some work where I was and he said to me, "Marcus, drive this nail." He was holding it! I thought of all the times I'd hit my thumb, and he said, "You're getting rather careless, aren't you?" "What do you mean?" I said, "What if I miss?" "DRIVE IT!" came the reply. I did, but I've never forgotten it.

And another time Mr. Wright sent four of us over to Los Angeles to do some work on a couple of projects there that hadn't turned out the way he wanted them. One was a little guest house sitting near the peak of a small mountain. We did several things, but this particular morning he came and was walking around the building, and, coming upon a big stone (approximately 3' × 3' × 6') he said, "I wish we could roll this away." I picked up a crowbar and inserted it in a crack and I could move it . . . and Mr. Wright saw it move. So he got all of us there around that rock—we'd pry it up and throw rocks under it. We were at least three hours at this, a good half of the rock was buried. Mr. Wright was in the thick of it, pitching rocks under, directing where to pry next, recalling Archimedes and keeping us entertained with his wit. Finally, we had it just about ready to roll down the mountainside and Mr. Wright was gone. Someone happened to look up—he was looking out of the window in the guest house where he could have a better view of it going down. So we pushed it over and let it roll.

When the Selective Service and Training Act of 1940 was passed I took the position of conscientious objector. Mr. Wright believed in me and supported me through the whole ordeal, including visiting the federal prison, Sandstone Penitentiary, giving a lecture and showing a film for the residents and a personal visit with me. He also brought a copy of his renewed autobiography (just out) for me, which I had to leave for the prison library—he had autographed it, "To Sandstone Library—via Marcus Weston."

Then there was the time when I was in Michigan, on parole at a hospital, and Mr. Wright was coming over to address the Michigan A.I.A. I went to the hotel where the convention was being held and found that he was going to be at a luncheon in about 15 minutes . . . and I could still get a ticket. Everyone was standing at their places around the table when Mr. Wright came in with the president of the Michigan Society. When he saw me he came directly to me, greeted me warmly and then went on to the head of the table—we visited later.

There are two things I must set down, which were typical of the relationship between my father and Mr. Wright. About the mid 1950s my father had a set-back with an old health problem and was hospitalized. When Mr. Wright learned of it he sent him an encouraging letter with a check to help speed his recovery.

On my folks' fifty-ninth wedding anniversary, Mother and Dad decided to go over and visit Mr. and Mrs. Wright. They found him working in the studio at Hillside. In the course of the visit Mr. Wright said, "Will, I'm designing a building a mile high." My father responded, "I want the contract to put the roof on."

When Mr. Wright's body was exhumed some years ago, I was stunned and shocked that it had been done. Spring Green is where the center of his life always was. To this day, it hurts me so deeply I can't return to visit Taliesin.

Wright's Secretary, Eugene Masselink

By the end of the first year of the Fellowship, Mr. Wright's secretary of several years, Karl Jensen, found things much too complex, and it was apparent, with his limited Danish background, that he couldn't cope with the 30 new apprentices, the workmen employed, and the drastic changes that were taking place at Taliesin. Apparently he was unsuitable to needs and made off. He had tried to take on Mr. Wright's mannerisms, quoting him in many unknowing ways.

Wes and I were constantly treating Jensen to practical jokes at his expense. We attached his cane (a Wright mannerism) onto a push broom. We placed a board over his rooftop fireplace flue while he was entertaining the female apprentices. Coincidentally, it was shortly after these events that he left.

After a lecture to students at the University of Ohio in 1933, a recent graduate in the arts, Eugene Masselink, made himself known to Mr. Wright, and came to Taliesin as its secretary. He was there from 1933 until he died in 1962.

Ben Masselink, the author of this section, is the younger brother of Wright's great executive secretary, Eugene, who was born in South Africa. Ben studied in local schools and came to Taliesin for the summers. He is a writer of film scripts in California.

Gene had studied fine arts at Ohio State University, was an excellent painter and artist in all ways, and had a musical background (he was a fine baritone). Gene and I furnished many classical musical performances, with me at the piano. Gene gave his heart and soul, twenty-four hours a day, to the furtherance of Mr. Wright's aims. He was loved by everyone, crossed all forces, laughed to keep us feeling fine, and through all his years later he typed me letters of wit and charm.

GENE

BEN MASSELINK

Now, looking back, I realize that the first time I was actually aware of what my brother had done was the Cherokee red, 1935 Cord convertible sedan, top down, rumbling along the streets of Grand Rapids, Michigan and turning into our driveway. I recognized my brother behind the wheel, but not the older man in the pancake Stetson and fluttering scarf. He could have been the Baron von Richthofen or the Wizard of Oz, or at least the winner of the Indy 500. I ran to get my friends. By the time we got back, Gene and his passenger had disappeared inside the house. We gathered at a respectful distance around the car, all eyes, not speaking, and then fled at the first noise inside the house. Around the corner and out of earshot we began shouting: "Wow! That hood! Ever see anything longer! . . . That chrome! . . . Those bumpers! . . . That's real leather on those seats . . . That dashboard. . . . It'll go a hundred and twenty! . . ."

Ah, the glamour of it all. For me at 15, it was the car. The man in flowing cape who got out of it dazzled and frightened me, as I think he did my dad and mother too. But my mother loved the glamour. She loved to insert the teaser in any conversation with her friends, "Gene says that Frank Lloyd Wright says. . . ." And the mouths would properly drop open.

Gene had driven Mr. Wright in that open Cord down the rolling green hills of Wisconsin and along the sweeping outer drive of Chicago and through the smoky war of Gary, Indiana, and up along the huge, blue lake through Benton Harbor and Saugatuck, Gene's old art school, and on into Grand Rapids to see the dentist, who was my dad. Mr. Wright wanted every tooth in his mouth pulled, which could compare to storming the Great Wall of China single-handed, and in one sitting, and then to be fitted for false. This greatly impressed my dad, as this was never done; it was too hard on the patient. Usually one or two teeth were pulled at a time, four at the most, but Mr. Wright insisted, and so my dad pulled them as if he were plucking corn off a cob. Mr. Wright never flinched, but treated it all as casually as if he'd come to have a hair trim.

While all this was going on, Gene took me for a ride in the Cord. Grinning at me, he must have driven past Central High School a hundred times, just what I wanted, and at first I just sat there stony, like I didn't know where I was, with the kids hollering at me, and then I jumped up and yelled and hollered back at them. Gene drove past June's house, a girl I hadn't dared to speak to yet, and all around town with me now in the back seat waving like Lindy just flown the Atlantic. That was the beginning of Frank Lloyd Wright and the Fellowship for me. Not the Imperial Hotel or "Fallingwater," but that red, 1935 Cord, top down, driving the streets of my hometown.

For Gene, it all began two years before that, in 1933. That was his last year at the University of Ohio, and he had just won first prize in a Washington, D.C. art exhibit for a large oil painting called "The Bathers." He had been asked to do two murals for the Chicago World's Fair, when Mr. Wright spoke at the university and Gene was smitten. He followed Mr. Wright out of Columbus, Ohio and to Spring Green, Wisconsin, the way children followed Pied Piper.

The first year I went to Taliesin, Spring Green, to spend the summer was 1938. I hid a lot. It would be called low profile now, and mine was as low as a mole's. I did a lot of crouching behind bushes, ducking behind walls and Japanese screens, darting through doors and just plain, flat out running every time Mr. or Mrs. Wright would appear. I was terrified. Gene tried to set me at ease. They would not bite, he told me. But I had no proof of that. Many apprentices were frightened. At the first sight or sound of Mr. Wright they would all huddle together like spooked cows in a meadow while I sprinted for the Iowa state line. I remember one noon I stopped by Gene's office before lunch. I had been working in the wheat fields and I was all sweaty and grimy. Suddenly Mr. Wright appeared from behind the Japanese screen that partitioned off his office. He wore a tweed suit, shoes so tiny and perfect that they were the kind mannequins wore, two shirts, and a scarf. He eyed me. "Who are you?" he asked, before I could bolt. I grinned. Gene was trying to explain who I was, but he was nervous too. "He usually runs," Gene said. Mr. Wright grunted and tossed a scrap of foolscap onto Gene's desk and stalked out. On it was the first drawing of the mushroom pillars for the Johnson Wax Building.

Eugene Masselink, Ben Masselink, Frank Lloyd Wright, apprentice Benedict, and Wes Peters.

With a nine-year age difference, Gene and I were friends first and brothers second. I never really knew him when I was growing up. I was only nine years old when he moved out of the house to go away to Ohio to college, and then with his art schools during the summers, we saw little of each other, so I didn't really get to know him until that summer of 1938 at Taliesin when I was eighteen and he was twenty-seven. Twenty-seven was an ancient age to me then. Anyone over twenty-one was a cackling old timer. Gene was a friend, and we stayed friends. It was the best way for brothers to be. It was that fine feeling of release and relief and warmth you get when you finally realize that your mother and father are just people.

At Taliesin, Gene, as Mr. Wright's secretary, was an inside man, while Wes Peters was an outside man. Gene was the coordinator, the harmonizer. He didn't actually give up his painting, but he had very little time for it. For me it was outside. I liked working out in the sun at Taliesin, both East and West, and counted myself as one of Wes's gang, and proud of it. We worked the fields, and we built walls, and nailed shingles on endless roofs, me and Edgar and Benny and Fred, and the rest of us outlaws, who seldom answered

Above and facing page: Frank Lloyd Wright during a picnic at Taliesin around 1939.

the tea bell at four. That wasn't for us, and when we would return to hearth and home, we would crash through the drafting room like bulls, while the pale inside men looked up from their tables in alarm.

I always felt that Gene paved the way for me and had been doing so all my life. Like a husband who is very much in love with his wife, who is perhaps a little goofy, Gene, I imagined, would come first into the room to prepare everyone. "In a minute Ben will arrive," Gene would tell them. "He will cluck like a chicken and hop up and down like a frog and say outlandish things, but it's okay—it's just his way. Be kind." I do know that the girls I went with after I introduced them to Gene—who looked just like Lord Byron—would say, "How come I'm not going out with your brother?"

One day Gene asked if I would like to drive to Chicago with him and Mr. Wright. I was torn in two. I wanted to go to Chicago, but I was still terrified of Mr. Wright. And to be that close? For all that way? But the vision of the bars on Rush Street was stronger, and so I crept in the back seat of the Cord and under the rug like a scared cat. I don't think Mr. Wright ever noticed me that whole trip. Off we flew. Mr. Wright liked to go fast. We did.

Somewhere along the outer drive Mr. Wright commanded Gene to stop at a Lincoln agency, and we parked and went inside. I stayed the proper five paces behind, like a jester or Japanese wife. Wearing cape and scarf and porkpie hat, Mr. Wright swept into the agency like King George in mufti (or, it would be more accurate to say, King George swept into the agency like Frank Lloyd Wright) and started thumping the tires with his hickory staff. This was no ordinary day in the Lincoln agency. This was the day the first Lincoln Continentals appeared on the showroom floors—the most beautiful cars ever made in America, long and sleek and classic. A salesman glided over to us. Mr. Wright waved his staff. "I want two," he told the salesman, "That one," he pointed to the sedan, "And this one." He tapped the convertible's top. "But I will design my own top—so rip this one off." He thumped it hard. "And I want both cars painted Cherokee red. Gene here will give you a color swatch." And Mr. Wright turned and marched to the door, where he turned back to the salesman who was still standing there frozen, mouth open. "And," Mr. Wright added, "I don't intend to pay for them." We left. The following week Wes and another man went down to pick up the Lincolns.

What parties and picnics! Some of us inside men would ride off early Sunday morning to some remote part of Wisconsin and dig great pits and build fires in them and bury corn in mud, and then later the whole entourage would arrive in the Cherokee cars, people running ahead of the Wrights, scattering sheepskins and plump pillows for them to sit on.

One birthday of Mr. Wright's, apprentices brought handmade gifts, chairs, and model houses and renderings and plans, and then out of sight there was sudden gunfire, a lot of white smoke and shouting, and we looked up the river and there came a regular Spanish galleon, a pirate ship flying the skull and cross bones. And then Wes, as Blackbeard, the bloodthirsty, hopped ashore waving cutlass, in eye patch, and laid a treasure chest at Mr. Wright's feet.

In the fall of 1940 I joined the caravan from Spring Green to Scottsdale, Arizona. It was a circus, all cars Cherokee red, the Lincoln Continental in the lead, Ford following, tiny Bantams, Wes's Duesenberg, all of us heading south out of the snow and down into the rainy warmth of East Texas and across to the west, sometimes sleeping on the side of the road, sometimes ten to a motel room, and people gaping at us as we trailed by. Finally, we drove into Scottsdale, which was just one gas station then, nothing else, and on across the desert—no roads—to Taliesin West, that white canvas mirage up against the sloping desert. Sleeping outside under the stars on cots, close by cactus, every morning there would be a surprise under my cot—once a gila monster, and once me, who had missed the cot the night before.

That Christmas it rained, and it rained. Apprentice Rowan Maiden had gone into Phoenix that afternoon in the station wagon to pick up my mother and father, who had come down for that Christmas. Right after Rowan left Taliesin it started to rain. But we could tell by the storm clouds in the north that it had been raining up there in the mountains for some time. Rowan and my mother and father didn't arrive by nightfall. The night was dark and cold. Suddenly thunder and lightning, and then the deluge. Mr. Wright stormed about like King Lear. The desert was awash and Gene was first out to look for them. Driving off in the Ford it was like he was setting out into a stormy sea at night in a dinghy. Bone dry just four hours before, the desert washes were now raging rivers, uprooting cactus, boulders bounding on their bottoms with the hollow rumble of bowling balls.

We waited an hour. No Gene. No Rowan. No Mom and Dad. Wes set out in the Duesenberg after Gene, who was after Rowan, who was after Mom and Dad. We waited another half hour. The washes were roaring with flood water. John Lautner and I took the big truck to go after Wes, Gene, Rowan, and Mom and Dad. I promptly drove the truck in a wash. John and I started to walk back in the mud, and were swept away in a wash.

Dawn. And the rain was over. And every car was stuck in the desert. Mom and Dad had spent the night sitting on the top of the black seat in the station wagon, which was stuck in the middle of a wash. The Christmas presents had been washed away, perhaps into Mexico.

But no one was hurt. It was a grand adventure. Slowly we started to dig out all the cars and trucks. Fifteen of them. Like the captain of a ship, Mr. Wright saved his Lincoln Continental until last. We all dug around the wheels and the frame. We dug and pushed and dug. Somehow Mr. Wright must have known the exact moment that the rear tires rested on bed rock. We didn't know. He waved us all off, and commanded Gene to get in the car and behind the wheel.

"Start the car!" Mr. Wright ordered. Gene did. "Put the gears in first." Gene did. "Slowly let out your clutch." Gene did. And Mr. Wright just barely touched the left tail light with the tip of his staff and the car rose from the mud like one of the great dinosaurs. We cheered.

Gene was always running. Not the way I ran, to hide. He ran for just the opposite reason, to serve, to help, to become involved. I ran away. Gene ran toward. Gene broke his hip running from Hillside to the main house at Taliesin, Spring Green. It was at night. Like a horse, he stepped into a gopher hole and went down. How he ever dragged himself to the house, I don't know. He was taken to the hospital in Dodgeville. A new ball and socket were eventually put into his hip. But it was never right. One leg was about a half inch shorter than the other. It always hurt him, but you never knew it. He never flinched or winced; he never even limped. He covered the limp somehow, but it was a strain on him for many years, strain that finally broke his heart.

Gene died in 1962. And when he died, no one knew what to do, who to call, what arrangements should be made. Gene had always done these things.

Acquaintances

Of the thousands of people who would never forget him, two are recorded here. People who met him, or were brought in to his presence, fell into two classes—those who were impressed and liked him and his style and those who hated him from the start—there seemed to be no in betweens.

From 1893 through the present, most American academia fell automatically into the second category. Wright—to them—was the enemy. He believed in the individual, Democracy, creativity, and in architecture he wouldn't preach from one momentary cult to another.

Within the profession, there was both jealousy and hate, and during the time I worked in the Chicago offices, he was referred to as "Frank Lloyd Wrong."

EDWARD STANTON

Edward Stanton studied journalism at Northwestern University as well as moonlighting as a jazz musician. He began his career at Women's Wear Daily *in New York City, and is now the president of a large public relations firm.*

It all started on a cruise ship to Bermuda, many years ago, either 1951 or 1952, when I met a man who would be instrumental in helping me to meet one of the greatest creative geniuses of all time.

I was dining with several strangers as we sailed out of New York, and I invited a man sitting alone at the next table to join us. He, Edgar Tafel, was an architect and a disciple of Frank Lloyd Wright, which really impressed me, a journalist for a trade paper in New York with a rather inexplicable interest in architecture, particularly contemporary. As a college student at Northwestern University in Evanston, Illinois, I was greatly impressed by the Chicago houses Wright had done in the early twentieth century. Wright and his work fascinated me.

Back in New York some months later, Tafel and I lunched together. I had been named editor of the Store Operations section of *Women's Wear Daily*, which meant that I was responsible for a daily section of about five pages with a fine crew of reporters covering a variety of subjects of interest to retail management—branch store planning and construction, credit and control, display, and interior design.

"Edgar, do you think I can get to meet Frank Lloyd Wright? I'd love to do a piece on him for the magazine." Edgar laughed. "You're kidding. That's a fashion paper. Why Wright? What's the connection?" "I'd love to get his views on department stores and on department store architecture," I answered. He pondered a moment. "I'll find out when he'll be in town. He stays at the Plaza. The rest will be up to you, but don't, for the life of me, tell him I let you know his whereabouts."

It was unexpectedly easy getting a date with the Great Man for an interview at the Plaza. Edgar gave me the poop, I phoned, and surprisingly, Wright invited me the next day to breakfast with him at his suite at the Plaza.

I had been preparing to see him for months. I read and reread his autobiography; I talked to other architects about his work, his style and his personality; I talked to Edgar about the years when he had worked under Wright's tutelage at Taliesin and about the innovative Johnson Wax headquarters building in Racine, Wisconsin. I was ready. So, with some trepidation and a great deal of excitement, I knocked on the door of Wright's suite at the Plaza. The Master himself opened the door and greeted me. He was 84 years old, well tailored—high starched collar and stick pin—with a shock of wavy, white hair. It was May 27, 1953, and my memory tells me the interview lasted about an hour.

It was obvious from the start that Wright knew how to make an interview sing. Almost everything out of his mouth was quotable. His eyes were laughing and dancing as my pencil raced to keep up with the lines he was feeding me. He was having fun!

Several times, as I asked a question, Wright would rise from the table, leave the part of the suite where we were having breakfast, and walk into another room. Strange, I thought, but I waited patiently for his return moments later. He always came back to the subject of the question without missing a beat.

At one point, a woman came in from the bedroom, kissed him on the forehead and said, "goodbye, I'm going shopping." Wright muttered something to his youngish wife about my questions to him on Fifth Avenue. She gave a casual nod and left.

The interview finished, we shook hands and I thanked him. I raced for a taxi back to the third-floor news room at *Women's Wear*, shouting to the managing editor, Earl Elhart, as I passed his desk that I had a great feature piece on Frank Lloyd Wright. Elhart was surprised and pleased. I quickly wrote the feature and turned it in. It appeared on page one, on May 28, shown on opposite page.

So from a holiday in Bermuda came a rare opportunity to meet and interview one of the greatest architects of this century; an opportunity, too, to listen to his views and set them down in a newspaper far removed from architecture, but closely linked, nonetheless, to the modes, tastes, and trendsetters of our generation.

Big Town a Ghost Town

It's Wise to Decentralize, City Is Finished—Wright

BY ED STANTON

Take the word of the eminent architect, Frank Lloyd Wright—the Big City department store is on the way out, along with the Big City.

Taking its place will be the one-stop shopping centers in uncongested areas, with plenty of parking space for the convenience of the shopper.

Mr. Wright, interviewed here yesterday at his Hotel Plaza suite, likes the current decentralization movement of people, and of business. The 84-year-old world-famous personality, with the wavy white mane and twinkling eyes, maintains the sub-division is the thing of the present, and of the future.

"Then you believe that the Macy's and the Marshall Field's of the downtown city areas will move out of the big cities?" Mr. Wright was asked.

"They are already moving out," he replied. "Field's is in Evanston, Oak Park, now planning in Skokie. Macy's has new branches in the country. Look at Los Angeles. There they have tried to hold customers to the Old Town, but now everyone goes to the Miracle Mile. No one goes to the Old Town anymore."

The decentralization, Mr. Wright contends, "is damaging to the vested interests, but it is beneficial to the other vested interests—the people."

"The vested interests want their big city skyscrapers to remain. But we're building an 18-story skyscraper in Bartlesville, Okla., a town of 27,000, and this will be a combination of residences and business. You will see others, similar to this, all over the country in the future," he continued.

Explaining his reason for suggesting that the Big City is through, Mr. Wright claimed that "all major cities are hangovers from feudal times."

"Then," he said, "they were useful in providing a higher culture for the people. Now, the bigger the city, the lower the grade of culture."

"The big thing is that you reach a point of diminishing returns in the Big City. Now we must sub-divide, then sub-divide some more."

Parking Space Problem.

What happens, Mr. Wright was asked, when the new regional shopping centers are built and soon afterward they find they have not created sufficient parking space?

"That in itself is proof of the need for more shopping centers," he replied.

Mr. Wright showed annoyance with architecture of habit and business by habit. While admitting that architects are doing "considerable" today in creating pleasant stores in which to shop, he noted that "it is difficult to find the kind of architect who thinks for himself."

"Some do good work today, but there are not many free and independent thinkers among the architects. The reason? The big shot —the man with the money—is usually very shy and he himself is an habituate.

"There is nothing as timid as $1 million except 2 million. That's an old expression of mine that Alexander Woollcott picked up and quoted, but it's my creation," he reminded.

"It takes great strength of character not to be an habituate," he continued. "Standardization is the rise of mediocrity and that is the trouble with our democracy. We will become a 'moboracy' by the rise of mediocrity.

But we can stop this threat by stopping the trend to quantity and insisting on quality."

He admitted that it is most difficult to get people to change their thinking. "It's as difficult as taking the curl out of a dog's tail," he said. "In fact, it is said that the wearing away of stone is faster and easier than the breaking of human habit."

What does he think of the supermarket design and will this form of self selection or self service be adaptable to other forms of merchandising?

"Anything that cuts down on labor would be a saving on behalf of the people, but there is a limit to which this can be carried out," he admitted.

Departmentalization Necessary.

He does believe, however, that departmentalization within a store is most necessary, "so that the customer won't be looking for a toy elephant among the china ware." The thing to do is to make it easy for the customer to get to the store and to find what she wants.

Mr. Wright is here this week from Taliesin, his Spring Green, Wis., home, to receive the Gold Medal Award of the National Institute of Arts and Letters from the American Academy of Arts & Letters. In conjunction with the award, presented yesterday, he is opening a one-month exhibit at the academy, 633 West 155th Street, today.

"It is a typical grouping of my work from the time I began until now. I think you'll find it interesting," he commented. The exhibit, which will be open until June 28, includes a model of the Bartlesville skyscraper—a sheltered glass tower building—being built for the Harold C. Price Co.

ANDY ROONEY

Andy Rooney is a well-known columnist and an author/writer for CBS television. He has a regular spot on the popular "60 Minutes" program, before which he worked as a writer and creative person living in upstate New York.

I was working as a writer for one of those CBS morning television shows in about 1956 or 1957 whose principal was Will Rogers, Jr. We did a lot of interviews, and Frank Lloyd Wright agreed to come to our studio, which occupied a big section of Grand Central Terminal on the third floor parallel with 42nd Street. There are tennis courts there now. We had offices in the Greybar Building and walked from them, across the glass catwalks, to the studio.

I was commissioned to pick up Wright at the Plaza. I was greeted at the door of his suite by a young man—a strange one if my memory is right—and shortly thereafter by his wife. I'll never forget the living room because it had a huge oriental rug that went up and over almost everything in the room—chairs, sofas, etc.

Wright was reasonably affable, and we went down to where there was a limousine waiting. Wright grumbled about everything during the drive from the Plaza to the Vanderbilt Avenue side of Grand Central. He detested New York. I agreed with him about some things, but I love New York and especially Grand Central.

There was access by elevator from the west side to our studio but I decided to force a tour on him. I took him down the marble steps off Vanderbilt and walked him kittycorner, past the clock, to the elevators in a little cubicle on the north side near the stairway that goes to the lower level. Those elevators went when they tore down the terminal buildings.

I recall clearly that he stopped and looked back across the grand room before we got on the elevator. The sun's rays were slanting down toward the information booth from the windows above where the Kodak picture is now. "It is a grand building, isn't it?" he said, almost apologetically, and I accepted this as a retraction for all the terrible things he'd been saying about everything else.

We went to the third floor on the elevator and started across the catwalk. It's one of the great sights in New York for me. Thousands of purposeful people going their own directions and with doors and stairs and levels enough for all of them in Grand Central. Midway across, Wright stopped and neither of us said anything. He must have stood there for more than five minutes, and I didn't speak because I knew nothing I had to say could match what he was thinking. I finally had to tell him we were due very shortly in the studio, and he reluctantly finished his crossing of the catwalk.

The whole incident gave me a great feeling because I thought I'd had some effect on Frank Lloyd Wright's opinion of my city and I know he could never think completely negatively about it again after his visit to Grand Central.

That's my Frank Lloyd Wright story.

An Evening at the New School for Social Research, 1980

In 1929 Frederick Gutheim, a student from the Experimental College at the University of Wisconsin, was visiting Wright at Taliesin as part of his studies. During their conversation, Wright received a telephone call and asked the student to wait for him in the drafting room. After the phone call, Wright entered the room and exclaimed that he had been invited by Princeton University to give a series of lectures on modern architecture. These lectures were later published by Princeton University Press, with a Wright drawing on the cover and many black and white drawings inside done specifically for this book by Wright's staff.

Gutheim went on to a successful literary career, as a planner, and compiled *Frank Lloyd Wright on Architecture* (1941), among other books. He has taught extensively.

Fifty years after the lectures Gutheim, recalling the incident, went to Princeton and reviewed its archives. He found an interesting background to the talks, which were part of the cultural series financed by Otto Kahn. Gutheim discovered that the architecture department had originally invited the Dutch architect J.J.P. Oud to speak. At the last moment Oud had become ill, and had written to Princeton that he could not come. He suggested that they invite Wright to speak in his stead. (Oud had written a Wright article for the Dutch publication of a Wright book.) Of course, in the late 1920s the academia of the Ivy League wanted nothing to do with Wright and his "organic style," but Oud's suggestion had swayed them—temporarily.

After reviewing the archives, Gutheim suggested it might be appropriate to have the school reexamination of Wright at Princeton, commemorating 50 years since the original lectures, and they did. Gutheim was the only Wright-phile to speak at the all-day affair; the others were teachers, critics, and architects who had never known Wright. He had me invited to attend. The sessions were conducted mostly by architects who neither had read Wright's work nor seen his buildings, and I squirmed the entire day.

Soon thereafter, I organized a gathering entitled "An Evening with Frank Lloyd Wright" at the New School for Social Research in New York, a venue where Wright had spoken before and had described in his autobiography. Only people who knew Wright were invited to speak, and we filled the same auditorium Wright had filled some fifty years before. His granddaughter, Anne Baxter, would have introduced the affair, but was called away at the last minute to act in a play in Canada. Instead, I had her introduction recorded on tape and played for the audience. Her contribution is a transcription of the tape of that introduction.

Included here from that evening's presentation are contributions by four men who had known Wright in various ways. The first is by Marshall Erdman, a design build contractor who built Wright's Unitarian Church in Madison, Wisconsin, as well as several of Wright's prefabricated buildings. He now has a highly successful design/build firm in Madison, Wisconsin that constructs over $100 million a year. He is a generous supporter of Taliesin. Second are Frederick Gutheim's notes for his talk that evening. Next, George Nelson, an architect who had worked with Wright on both the 1938 and 1948 issues of the magazine *Architectural Forum*. Finally, Henry-Russell Hitchcock, a professor of history, offers his memories. He has written many books on Wright and, along with Philip Johnson, initiated the Museum of Modern Art in New York. I introduced the speakers.

An evening with people who knew Wright was a most unusual event; unfortunately, none of the local schools of architecture made a point of introducing it to their students.

THE NEW SCHOOL ASSOCIATES

present

A FRANK LLOYD WRIGHT EVENING

COORDINATOR:

EDGAR TAFEL

Practicing New York Architect, Designer of Church House at corner of Fifth Avenue and 12th Street. Faculty member of the New School and Parson's School of Design. World Lecturer. Apprentice to Frank Lloyd Wright for nine years. Author of "Apprentice to Genius: Years with Frank Lloyd Wright."

PARTICIPANTS:

ANNE BAXTER

Actress. author, granddaughter of Frank Lloyd Wright.

MARSHALL ERDMAN

Builder of Frank Lloyd Wright's Unitarian Church. President of Marshall Erdman Associates, design and building specialists.

FREDRICK GUTHEIM

Distinguished planning consultant. Author of many writings on Frank Lloyd Wright.

HENRY-RUSSELL HITCHCOCK

Architectural Historian Co-Founder of Museum of Modern Art, Professor of Fine Arts at New York University and Wesleyan.

GEORGE NELSON

Designer, architect, teacher, writer. Winner of many awards, including the Rome Prize in Architecture. Lecturer at Harvard and Columbia. Author of "Problems of Design" and "George Nelson on Design." Fellow of AIA and IDSA.

There will be other invited guests who knew Frank Lloyd Wright.

New School Auditorium	66 West 12th Street	New York, N.Y. 10011
Monday, November 10, 1980	8:00–10:00 P.M.	Admission: $7.00

Co-Chairmen: RUTH HERWITZ and GWEN WILLIAMS

— —

Tickets on sale in the hall on 4th floor (opposite elevator) or in room 408.
Please make an early reservation by returning this form to:

"A Frank Lloyd Wright Evening"
The New School Associates
66 West 12th Street
New York, N.Y. 10011

I We enclose check in the amount of $_____ for _____ tickets at $7 each for this event on Monday, November 10, 1980. Make checks payable to The New School.

Name:_____   Telephone:_____

Address:_____

For further information telephone 212-741-5687

ANNE BAXTER

INTRODUCTION

This is Anne Baxter. I was to have joined you this evening as one of Mr. Wright's granddaughters but I have an excellent reason for not being here—in a funny way, a reason he would have approved of: work. I'm going to rehearse and perform a new Norwegian play in the wilds of Alberta, Canada.

I receive as much joy from my work as grandfather received from his so I think he would have understood, although I am extremely sorry not to be with you.

Why don't we start with this room, with where you are and what happened in it 50 years ago. There is no one better to talk about what happened to him than grandfather himself.

So I thought I'd read from his autobiography, about the New School for Social Research in New York City.

The following evening—Thursday—I was posted to speak on twentieth century architecture at the New School of Social Research on Twelfth Street, Dr. Alvin Johnson presiding.

Henry Churchill introduced me in a very satisfactory auditorium designed by big hearted Jo Urban. Jo designed the building for the New School and I could not refrain from saying complimentary things about it. It seemed so remarkable it should be there in New York at all. Jo Urban is one Viennese gift to the country that has not gone wrong. Jo's touch is as Mozartian as his character is Falstaffian. He is responsible for a more lyrical beauty in our world of decoration than anyone I know. He was in Europe so I couldn't get him up on the stage to keep me company. But there was no room for him. The stage was filled. As I came in the front door, Doctor Johnson was turning several hundred away, asking them to come again some other time. It hurt me that anyone should really want to hear a serious lecture on architecture and not be able to get in to hear it.

Several appealed directly to me to let them in and I took them in with me.

Not willing to trust to extemporizing, I had carefully prepared a lecture on twentieth century architecture for this occasion. To treat the subject adequately with best thought where real issues are at stake, a well-studied written discourse that may be read will always be best.

Since you have had no discourse from me on modern architecture as a whole, it is perhaps time to sum up in different terms my best thought on the subject matter of this book. Inasmuch as this lecture is a unit, I might take it out and make it a separate booklet. So this "lecture," too, may be "skipped." But since it contains, compact, the essence of work and life as philosophy of form, line, material and symbol—here is the unit in itself.*

Why I can't resist telling you or revealing what happened very often with grandfather? He contradicted himself royally many times and it affected my life at one point since I had heard him speak for two hours at a time, three hours at a time without notes and I thanked him with amazement, astonishment and I said, "Oh my word grandfather, you don't have a note" and he said in stentorian tones, "Anne, if you don't know your subject, don't get on your feet."

Of course I never did read a piece of paper after that and had to memorize everything. And here he is telling me the opposite. I think it's awfully funny and very like him.

*Reprinted from *An Autobiography*, by Frank Lloyd Wright. Copyright 1932 by Longmans, Green and Co., New York.

MARSHALL ERDMAN

THE FIRST UNITARIAN CHURCH

I was not Frank Lloyd Wright's first choice in the summer of 1948 to build the First Unitarian Church in Madison, Wisconsin. He had tried the Turner Construction Company, Fuller, and a few others but none of them were interested in building a little country church for $75,000. I, on the other hand, was ignorant of building costs, naive, and a great worshipper of Mr. Wright. So when he asked me if I wanted to become famous, I jumped.

Mr. Wright assured me that $75,000 was ample to build the small church and added, "If you do a good job, there might possibly be $5000 left for you as a reward for a job well done." About nine months later, Mr. Wright, just back from Taliesin West, came to look over the job. He found that the church was about seventy-five percent complete, the money was all gone, my truck, which the congregation had used to haul stone to build the church, was all gone, and so were my knuckles and fingers—and the church, as I said, still was not done. He told his secretary, Gene Masselink, to arrange a quick executive meeting at Taliesin and he wanted me there as well.

I arrived, after forty miles, to find Wes Peters and Gene standing near Mr. Wright's office with their heads down. Gene said, "Mr. Wright wants to talk to you." I went in and Mr. Wright was sitting at his drafting table and said, "Marshall, now I know I shouldn't have let you have that job. I thought you were smart and young and brave and imaginative and could do a great job. But I see you let me down and you let the congregation down. What are you going to do about it?"

Well, I had spent not only all of the congregation's money, but I'd spent all of the money I had at that time, too. The $5000 I was supposed to get as a fee was gone—I had contributed it already. Remembering the still unplastered ceiling, I offered that I might be able to borrow some money. "That would be a good idea," Mr.

Wright replied. So I promised him that I would raise $15,000 and I left in tears.

In the other room, Gene and Wes came over and they each put a hand on me. Gene said, "Marshall, welcome to the club."

Raising the money was a very difficult job, but I was successful. The church got finished, and Mr. Wright ended up becoming like a father to me. I think perhaps he felt that he had imposed on me a little, but I must admit I didn't mind. He told me that he would make me whatever I was to become, and he did. When we finished the church, people from all over the world called to ask if they could come see it. It took me about five years to recover financially from that great experience.

Had I followed Mr. Wright's design for the church perhaps I would have met his $75,000 budget for he planned to build it out of tooth-picks—he didn't want to use anything bigger than a two by four for the whole building. He wanted a very simple country church and wanted only very light materials. When we built the trusses for the church I suggested that we should use two by sixes, to which he responded, "What the hell do you know, baby?" So we built the first truss with two by fours, but when we picked it up with the crane, it broke in half. After this, when Mr. Wright was not around, I used two by sixes, and I took quite a beating on it.

An even more serious problem existed with the design of the prow: it was lacking the proper structural elements to hold up the glass panels. I consulted with Wes Peters and we decided we'd put in some very thin quarter-inch steel plates between these two-by-twelve oars and the glass panels. When Mr. Wright saw the plates he had a fit and yelled, "Who told you to put those in? Take them out." "Mr. Wright," I responded, "if I take them out the whole thing will fall down." He said he did not care and that we should get stronger glass. After I was finished with the church, Mr. Wright brought in his apprentices and they took out the steel plates. They have since been put back, of course, because if one plate of glass had broken, the entire thing would have tumbled down.

The other quirk about the church is the entrance, which is only 5' 10", low enough for most people to hit their heads upon entering. I asked Mr. Wright if we could lower the step, and he responded, "No, let people bow when they enter my church."

Frank Lloyd Wright and Marshall Erdman.

* * *

Unity Church, Madison, Wisconsin.

Unity Church Sanctuary.

In 1954, I was designing houses that my company was prefab-ricating. One day Mr. Wright stopped by my office and said, "Marshall, I hear you're doing prefabricated houses. I want to see them." I was delighted. He looked them over very carefully, walked back twirling his cane in the usual way, and said, "Marshall, I think you'll really go broke this time."

I thought quickly and said, "Mr. Wright, you could save me by designing one." He said he'd have a go at it, and that's how I got to build the first Frank Lloyd Wright prefabricated house.

When it became known that Mr. Wright had designed one of these structures, a lot of people became very interested and we began getting mail from all over. I got a phone call from a man named Jim Price, who was the president of National Homes, which at the time was the country's largest manufacturer of prefab houses. He had never heard of me and he said, "Marshall, how much did you have to pay Mr. Wright to design this house? Several years ago I went to Mr. Wright and I offered him $100,000 to design a house for us that we could manufacture. All I wanted to do was just one house. How much did you pay him?" When I told him I had paid nothing, he was dumbfounded. I told him that his problem was that he had only wanted to build one house.

House and Home, a Luce publication, offered to do a piece on them—Mr. Wright knew how to get publicity. The house was fin-ished on the outside, but not on the inside, because Mr. Wright had not yet picked out the knobs for the cabinets. I got an urgent wire from New York saying, "We're going to photograph the house in two weeks. It must be finished." I ran out to Taliesin and I told Mr. Wright about the wire and pressed him to make decisions on the trim, the cabinetry and so on. He replied, "Don't get excited. Let them do one story on the outside and then a second on the inside."

Mr. Wright's idea of saving money on these houses was to leave out the frame and put the glass right into the stone. Though we used the simplest, most basic material on the first house, Masonite tiling, he made it appear to be such a massive and flowing house, simply by inserting a redwood fastening into the Masonite.

On the second house, Mr. Wright insisted that the stone be laid the way it was found in the quarry, that is, on its natural bed. We had a stone mason named Dick Johnson, who was from Granite City, Wisconsin, and who was well known as a temperamental stone-cutter, but who was very good. He was about 65 or 70 years old when he agreed to do this job. One day Mr. Wright came out and watched him. Johnson was very skillful, and he would fool you by taking a flat stone, putting it on edge, and cutting it in such a way that it would look like a thick stone from the quarry. Mr. Wright caught him doing this and said, "Dick, you're doing it wrong. This isn't the way to cut stone." Dick turned around—he'd had a few drinks before breakfast—and said, "Frank, do you know that I've been cutting stone for almost fifty years?" Mr. Wright looked at him and said, "You know what the trouble with you is Dick? You've been cutting stone too damn long. You ought to quit."

[**Editor's note:** *Marshall's talk was entirely extemporaneous—no notes.*]

FREDERICK GUTHEIM

RECOLLECTIONS

At Taliesin recollections of Frank Lloyd Wright have been institutionalized. In them a saintly figure has emerged, that of the architect, by whose rule as well as whose personality, buildings are designed and life is ordered as when he was alive. In these academic surroundings, and facing the inevitable character of this evening's reminiscences, we might commence by remembering that anecdotes have no standing in the world of scholarship. They are seldom confirmed. Too often they have been attributed to some other personality. They prove nothing.

But they do entertain.

Before we yield to the inevitable, a few facts are in order.

Speaking as an historian, we have only begun to tap the rich vein of Wright's life and his architecture as it leads to interpretation of such themes as the American family or the city. The Wright family in Oak Park in the 1890s was a Victorian family. The parental authority was illustrated in the formal dining room (a part of the house Wright was later to claim, correctly, that he killed). It has been said that the tall-backed dining chairs were designed for bishops to sit in. Gathered there daily, the family group was unmistakable authoritarian. Certainly these chairs with their slatted backs were as Victorian as the earlier Windsor chairs were the taste of the middle class Philadelphia in 1725.

The incorrigible individualist, Wright gave no quarter in competition with other architects. He was disloyal and unfaithful to Sullivan, and returned to him only when Sullivan was on his deathbed. He could not overcome his fundamental reservation, and in what he announced as a biography, spent most of his effort in self-projection. We have the candid Bendiner as witness to Wright's ignorance that Sullivan had ever worked in Philadelphia for Frank Furness, the first important American figure in the art nouveau. His penchant for rewriting history has been documented by Robert

Twombly. This is not just indifference to dates and facts—including the date of his own birth—but systematic falsification to make a point or overcome an opponent. But, as Alan Gowans has described it, this was characteristic of the times and of the other rebels in architecture battling with the establishment. Many passages of Wright's (as also Sullivan) are incomprehensible and show no evidence of being looked at once the pen had left the page. Gowans quotes the review of *Genius and the Mobocracy* (the original title of this purported biography of Sullivan was "I Was a Pencil in His Hand"): "—push bottom power," plush bottom power, could be push botton power. Why not? All gagism (ours). Bewildered, the reader flounders along with his Boswell, looking in vain for Johnson, and wonders sometimes whether Boswell is Johnson, or Johnson is Boswell. Assive of reader. It will appear strange to posterity as to mobocracy (ours) that so lucid a mind (his), the master of so organic an approach to modern building, could produce so unorganic a discourse, or is it that he who, in construction, is so conscious of wood is, in writing, mesmerized by trees. Lieber Meister deserved better treatment. Sad, resurrected (not really, Giedion did a good job) only to be reinterred in morass of pseudo quasi philosophy. Can't help lovin' that man. Which? Why?" (*Journal of the RAIC*, XXVI (1949) p. 314 by Eric P. Arthur.)

Frank Lloyd Wright

Perhaps Wright's individualism was most visibly expressed in his attire. From earliest days he was marked by his self-designed clothes—flowing ties, loose shirts. This was all part and parcel of the artistic style of the time. But for Wright it continued for another couple of generations after the *art nouveau*, as the photographs of Pete Guerrero document the carefully designed tweeds, capes and knickerbockers. But if this was a gesture of freedom, why did Wright continue to wear those Dr. Munyon collars?

While some of his quotable efforts show signs of earlier work, many were improvised. One of these was a comment to the actor, Charles Laughton, who admired Taliesin West, "I have given Arizona a voice." Another was produced when touring Houston before receiving the AIA Gold Medal. Passing the then new Shamrock Hotel he said, "I can see the sham—but where's the rock?"

It requires an effort to appreciate Wright's age. Robert Clark has pointed out in terms of his architectural contemporaries, he belonged to the age of Joseph Olbrich (1867–1908), the generation before Gropius, Mies, and Le Corbusier. He should have been a Victorian; but he did not belong to that culture. To me he was detached from any chronological definition; he stood alone. But that means he found it easy to relate to contemporaries as he found them at any point in time. It was one reason for his success with the young—of any time.

Much of his personality comes through in his writing—his puns, his exaggerations, his repetitions for emphasis. A lover of music and poetry, he weighed these values with the literal meaning of words.

Oskar Stonorov believed Wright was a follower of the hydrotherapy mystic, Father Kniepp, and walked barefoot every morning on the walled enclosure of carefully rolled turf, wet with Arizona dew, thus protected from wind-blown cactus.

I should not leave the impression of perfection. He used people unmercifully. He justified this by saying they needed to protect themselves. His practical jokes were frequently cruel and heedless. He was grasping. Most of his famous fights with his workers were over money matters, and most commonly his draftsmen left because they could not live on what he paid them—particularly after they had married.

While Gimbel's exhibition was being prepared, Stonorov was a frequent visitor at Taliesin. A sculptor who had worked with Maillol, and a facile portraitist, he commenced a portrait head of Wright in clay. Of course Wright had ideas about this, and so it appears did Mrs. Wright. Stonorov went to his work one morning and discovered that ahead of him the Wrights had transformed his work into their own caricature, thus ending that enterprise. Instead of which we have the highly varnished idealization of Heloise Swaback, one of the Taliesin apprentices.

David Gebhart describes Wright as the only architect who achieved the popular status and recognition of a movie star. Taxi drivers recognized him. People pressed for his autograph. He was spoken to in public places. The runner-up would be Stanford White. Not even Gary Cooper could make Ayn Rand's *Fountainhead* a good movie. Wright responded to this recognition, played up to it. He made his Stetson a "pork-pie" hat, a trademark. He architecturalized it by explaining it was a cantilever.

America's greatest architectural humorist, Al Bendiner, in a *Harper's* article, described how Wright got his gold medal from the Philadelphia chapter of the AIA. Wright appeared swathed in a white cashmere scarf—over which he hung his gold medal from the Royal Institute of British Architects. Bendiner supplies further

Frank Lloyd Wright

details. His mane of white hair was rinsed blue and appeared almost a halo.

While helping Wright into his coat Bendiner noticed it was of the lightest weight pure cashmere. He remarked to Wright that few architects could afford such a coat. Wright explained it was a gift from Kaufmann, president of Gimbels, the Philadelphia department store. He had admired it while passing through the store and Kaufmann presented it to him.

Coats played some significant part in Wright's giving and getting. I remember a meeting at the publishers, Duell, Sloan and Pearce, where we concluded the contracts that resulted in that trilogy of Wright books, the amplified version of *An Autobiography*, my version of *Frank Lloyd Wright on Architecture*, and Henry-Russell Hitchcock's *In the Nature of Materials*. In an expansive mood after this business was accomplished, Wright appraised Hitchcock and said, "Russell, you look pretty seedy. Let me buy you a coat." So we marched up Madison Avenue to Abercrombie's and Wright bought Hitchcock an overcoat.

He was a spur-of-the-moment consumer. I had picked him up at the Plaza for a short walk, and wanting to show him something he would take pleasure in, I introduced him to Bonnier's, then but newly arrived on the New York scene. He was delighted with everything, and for a moment I was afraid he would take the entire store home with him. He settled for a beautifully shaped and glazed bowl. But then, characteristically, he ordered 120 of them—and asked for a discount.

It would be worth a term paper to discover where Wright stayed when he gave those lectures at the Metropolitan Museum of Art or at the openings at the Museum of Modern Art. But with the Guggenheim, he always stayed at the Plaza—where Solomon Guggenheim stayed, of course. It was a professional sacrifice to occupy Room 223. I had breakfast with him on several occasions, looking across at Central Park, and the complaints were endless—including the rancid butter.

In the book that gives us the best domestic portrait, by his sister Maginel Wright Barney, *The Valley of the God-Almighty Joneses*, there is a memorable description of how she smuggled into Wright's suite some simple baked potatoes and a part of a baked ham—and they were eaten, skins and all, by these simple Wisconsin gluttons.

But my favorite story from "Little Sis:" she wrote, "I was in the drafting room at Taliesin, marvelling at all his projects; at the inventive joy that seemed so inexhaustible. 'Frank,' I said, as we walked up the hill garden, 'How do you do it? How do you think of it all?' 'I can't get it out fast enough,' he said. And another time, when someone asked him much the same question, he answered: 'Why, I just shake the buildings out of my sleeve.'"

HENRY-RUSSELL HITCHCOCK

MY MEMORIES OF WRIGHT

It's hard for me to remember when I first visited Taliesin, but I think it was in the late 1920s. At any rate, all told, my acquaintance with Mr. Wright must have extended over some thirty years. There are two difficulties for me in reminiscing about Mr. Wright. One is that my acquaintance with him was very intermittent. Only one period lasted for any time in which we actually worked together—the book called *In the Nature of Materials*. That I will return to later. The other difficulty is that over the last forty years I have read a great deal about Mr. Wright. I have read descriptions of him in different periods of his life, accounts of his relationships to different clients, such as the fascinating book on "Fallingwater" which will shortly, I hope, be bound together with the book on the Hanna house.* All of these descriptions and accounts merge, or become diluted or strengthened as the case may be, by personal memories. My personal memories tend to take the form of vignettes, or what I wish might be actual slides to project. They are stills, curiously enough, since Mr. Wright was not a very still man. But the pictures that survive in my mind are mostly the pictures that all of you I am sure have from portraits such as we've seen tonight.

I think that one gets the correct impression that Mr. Wright was an actor—that Mr. Wright was not only a great man, he was determined to behave and look like a great man. That somewhat oversized head and face—oversized in relation to the rest of his body—seemed to expand when he was present and occupy all the space around. And of course everyone knows that Mr. Wright dressed in a very special fashion. Some people say he continued to dress as though it were the 1890s. But I don't think anyone has ever dressed quite as he did. His clothes were special. I don't know

*The two books referred to are *Frank Lloyd Wright's Fallingwater: The House and Its History*, by Donald Hoffmann. New York: Dover Publications, 1978; and *Frank Lloyd Wright's Hanna House* by Paul R. and Jean S. Hanna. Cambridge, MA: M.I.T. Press, 1981. They have not been bound together.

where they all came from, but those very strange hats were specially produced by a French hatter in the Place Vendôme. Since Wright was rarely ever in his life in Paris, I don't know how this connection was established. But of course those broad-brimmed hats were not at all in the Texas manner—they were the French hatter's idea of what a Western hat should be. I think one has to remember this about Mr. Wright because it explains various aspects of his career. I don't mean to say that these juxtapositions I'm remembering were staged, except in the sense that Mr. Wright's entire life was staged. It was intended for an audience. It was, above all, a projection of personality, it was a very considerable part of the impression that he made on people.

I remember once being in Taliesin with my mother; at the time I was working with Mr. Wright on *In the Nature of Materials*. I had been in Taliesin before, often the only guest, and I had been very aware of Mr. Wright. It could hardly have been otherwise. His tables had only one head—no head other than where he sat. Well, all of a sudden, it was as if a beam of radiation hit me and then turned at ninety degrees onto my mother. I could almost feel it turn off of me. And my mother said she felt it was quite turned on her.

Henry-Russell Hitchcock and Frank Lloyd Wright.

The magnetism—there are other names for it, especially for politicians—was I think an important part of Mr. Wright.

I don't think such terms as "sincere" had any meaning in his case. He was always acting the part of a great man, and the audience could be, as in the case of the dinner table, one person, one guest, or it could be, and often was, a large public gathering. And, of course, he gave of himself on such occasions, even in his later years.

Another vignette: I was teaching at Smith College and we wanted Mr. Wright to come and lecture to us, but he was too expensive. Mount Holyoke, another college across the river, had more money for lecturers, and so they were able to pay the $1000 fee that Mr. Wright demanded for a lecture—the same fee for which they had booked three whole Sitwells! Edith Sitwell, you know, would come to the rostrum, see a microphone, and brush it aside, and nobody would hear another word. But Mr. Wright knew how to use microphones, and did. I remember him in that hall at Mount Holyoke: this beautiful phenomenon in the somewhat darkened room, the face gradually becoming larger and larger until it encompassed the entire environment. Mr. Wright not only gave the lecture for which he was paid, but spent hours with students afterward that evening, and came back and went to classes all the next morning. He certainly was worth his fee.

Then there was another amusing episode. When it came time for him to leave it was discovered that he had come alone, there was no one to look out for him, and he had no return railroad ticket. And he didn't have any money on him either. You can't go to a railroad station and ask them to take a half-dollar check. However, the necessary funds were dug up. But it was characteristic of that princely attitude, as one understands that royalty never have any money in their pockets. They always have somebody with them with the pocket money.

Mr. Wright never had any money with him. I remember the time when we were starting to do *In the Nature of Materials*, for which he hired me, I was his employee. He thought I needed a winter overcoat, and this was going to be over and above what I was being paid. So we went to Abercrombie's and we picked out an overcoat and he approved of it, and then out came his checkbook. But the salesman had never seen Mr. Wright, never heard of Mr. Wright, and he was being asked to take a personal check out of the blue. Well, Mr. Wright got away with it. He insisted on seeing higher and higher officers in the company until they took his check.

The illustrations for *In the Nature of Materials* were not so much of a problem. Difficult as it is to get Wright plans to publish today, for this book, of course, any plans that we wanted were redrawn in proper scale, at Taliesin. But the pages were designed according to a special formula that Mr. Wright devised, in which a square was placed over another square in an asymmetric position. All the cuts of the illustrations, the halftones, the plans, and even the captions, were to be fitted into this pattern. You were to use the lines that this pattern established. This meant that there was a harmony of proportions throughout. There was a design relationship between facing pages, and yet it never repeated, because you could choose this line one time, and then that line, or you could choose the side of one square one time and the next page you'd choose the side of the other square. Well, it was a hell of a job. But perhaps the most difficult aspect of it was that captions were considered, designwise, as merely gray patches, and therefore the size of a caption was determined not by what you had to put in it, but by what space you needed to fill out the pattern. So, some captions would be no more than four words, and other captions might go up to a quarter of a page. The quarter-page ones were after all the kind of cutting that one does for any sort of writing. But those single-line captions had to be letter-counted, you see, because they had to come out just the right length.

Well, as I wrote in the introduction to the reprint of *In the Nature of Materials*, I really feel that this book was one of Mr. Wright's books—one of Mr. Wright's most interesting books. And it certainly was a great privilege for me to work with him so closely on this portion of a career notable for its writing as well as for its physical architectural production.

GEORGE NELSON

George Nelson, F.A.I.A. had been a brilliant architectural student. He won a Beaux Arts scholarship to go to Europe and refused it, and without any work for young architects during the Depression, he gained employment as a writer on the staff of Architectural Forum. In preparation of the 1938 Forum issue on Wright, Nelson and art director Paul Grotz were sent to Taliesin to work with Wright on the issue. My job was to show them the countryside and take care of their possible needs. That first meeting developed into a long-lasting friendship. Later, George published several of my articles from India while I was stationed there during World War II. The following talk was given without notes as it was delivered.

Nelson's recollection of how Wright obtained the Johnson Wax commission is not correct, even if he remembered Wright's description.

MAKING BRIDGES

I was not an apprentice—I guess Mr. Wright had a copyright on that term. I was sort of a staff member at *Architectural Forum* when Howard Myers, our boss and the publisher, somehow came up with the idea that it was time to do an issue on Frank Lloyd Wright. Mr. Wright's name was known to me, but not much else about him. I knew that he had been involved in some unforgivably scandalous behavior. The worst sin an architect can commit is to run off with the client's wife, and Mr. Wright had done that. So, suddenly I had this job, and our boss sent Paul Grotz and me. Paul was designing the magazine, laying it out every month, and acting as a kind of wonderful, invisible editor. I wrote stuff, as the youngest employee naturally would, with the superior ranks editing what the young ones wrote—a very fair division of labor as I think back. Anyway, suddenly in the middle of winter we found ourselves in the Wisconsin house, Taliesin. There were icicles going from the roof overhangs right down into the snow. I had never seen anything like this. I'd seen ice on colonial houses and icicles stop long before they hit the ground, but Mr. Wright had designed his house so that the icicles would really bridge the gap—and don't think we weren't impressed by this! What is architecture except making bridges between one thing and another? I had just never heard of icicles being used this way before.

Neither Paul nor I realized that we were in for an unforgettable experience. It was the most godawful time we ever had! Paul thought that he was supposed to lay out the magazine and design it, but not so. Somehow Mr. Wright took it away from him, page by page. I thought I was supposed to write it, which turned out to be a complete misconception. Mr. Wright wrote everything. The only thing I can say in Mr. Wright's favor is that it really did turn out better than if Paul and I had done it. But we were never quite the same afterward.

At that time, if I have my dates right, the Johnson projects, the "Wingspread" house, and the Johnson Wax building were in progress. I remember a meeting with the client. Paul and I weren't allowed anywhere near this meeting. But we could hear the loud voices raised on the client's side, and afterward Mr. Wright came out and saw us sitting wherever we were sitting—I guess it was in the big living room—and said that the client was unhappy. And we said, "How can that be, Mr. Wright?" He said that the building was going over budget. I said, "By the way, I don't want to get personal, but how did you get that job anyway?" He said, "Now, that's very interesting." He said that they had some architect somewhere, maybe a Racine architect, who made a design for the building. "Somebody in the Johnson company said, 'You know, we have an architect up at Spring Green, and he used to be quite well known, when he was behaving himself. Why don't we show him the plans, the drawings, and get his opinion, get a criticism from him?'" So the Johnson company did that, and waited with bated breath. Wright said to us, "It wasn't a bad building, really. It was a one-story thing, and it had these flat arches on this front, and, you know, if you accept this sort of pseudoclassical approach to a building, there was nothing wrong with it"—that knife going in there. So they asked him for a criticism, and he said that was really fine and that "This is supposed to be a mausoleum, I believe." I said, "What happened then?" He said, "Well, they asked me to design the building, and that was, as it turned out, a good idea."

Frank Lloyd Wright on site during construction of the Johnson Wax building.

● An authentic original in the world's modern architecture. The new headquarters office of
S. C. Johnson & Son, Inc., Makers of Johnson's Wax, Racine, Wis. Designed by Frank Lloyd Wright.

Postcard of the completed Johnson Wax building.

There was trouble with the client, apparently because the building kept going over budget. When he came out from this meeting, where voices had been raised somewhat, he said to us, "You know, they really don't understand this building at all." He said, "They're acting as if this were a normal office building and you calculate this the way you would a normal office building. But they have forgotten what they told me initially, which was that this was a memorial to Grandpa, the founder of this great industrial enterprise, and you don't build memorials with the same materials, or the same spirit, or the same budget, you know, as you do speculative office buildings." He said, "One of these days, they're going to be sorry." And I said, "Why is that?" He said, "Because when you go up to the building you're going to see lines of buses that have just disgorged tourists from all over the country to come and see this building." And, you know, oddly enough I went back about 25 years later and what do you think I saw? A long line of tourist buses. He was absolutely right about the whole thing.

Howard Myers, our boss and publisher and very much a man of himself, and Mr. Wright loved each other. Mr. Wright loved Howard Myers because Howard Myers was doing very nice things for him, and bringing him back into the limelight, which he richly deserved. Howard Myers loved Mr. Wright because he loved real people and was particularly fond of geniuses; and since the supply of geniuses is limited, he would sort of go off the deep end when he encountered a real one. So Paul and I basked in this warm light of approval, since we were Howard Myers's boys, as it were, coming out bringing gifts, or whatever, to the genius. And everything worked quite well, except that Mr. Wright was not exactly a man who moved at an even pace. One day—I don't remember the incident that caused it—I was suddenly accused of being a traitor to some cause or belief, and it had something to do with another magazine. I have no recollection of what it was all about, except that I was not only innocent, I was ignorant of the whole thing. Nonetheless, Mr. Wright persisted in viewing me with great suspicion and disfavor, which struck me, for some reason, as funny. I don't know why I wasn't crushed, but I really liked him quite well, and I didn't mind the odd behavior that was manifested from time to time. In any case, for two or three days, none of the apprentices would speak to Paul or me, or look at either one of us, because, you know, for a man who believed in a democratic ideal, Mr. Wright ran Taliesin like a marine boot camp spiritually. And those kids were absolutely scared witless, if not of Mr. Wright, then of Mrs. Wright, who, in my book, was always the scarier of the two. But then, on the second or third day, something happened to clear up this strange case of unplanned treason, and Mr. Wright ran into me in the drafting room and said, "George, I understand the situation was not this way, but that way—is that so?" And I said, "Well, yes, that's how I think it was." He said, "In that case, I forgive you." You know, I still ended up in the wrong, but I got forgiven.

At some point in our relationship, which went on for quite a few years, we were introduced to the desert camp, Taliesin West, which was another absolutely shattering experience. I'd never had any idea that architecture could be like that. It was incredibly beautiful. The fact that it leaked and so on was really not a big thing, because in the desert, water is very welcome, even if it comes through the ceiling. One of our visits took place just before Thanksgiving, when the desert is very beautiful and all that, except that if it does rain during the year, it tends to rain just before Thanksgiving. And there were three consecutive weekends of cloudbursts. When it rains in the desert, it's just like the drought—I mean it's worse. Thanksgiving came, and there were plans to have the Thanksgiving dinner in such and such a place—I think it was in the old drafting room. The apprentices were there all night setting up the dishes, the tables, the napkins, and the decorations, when water began coming through the canvas roof. No roof except, say, one inch of solid stainless steel, could have resisted that water the way it was coming down. So it began coming through the canvas and then found its way around—sort of a small-scale "Fallingwater." It started going down the wires and then it rolled over these green shades that were over the drafting table, and within minutes the whole room, which was a big one, had these circular rings of water coming down. At this point, the apprentices decided that this was not going to be a good place to have dinner. The only things we were sure were not going to get wet were the turkeys, which were sealed in ovens that were two or three inches thick.

Well, one place led to another until, finally, rather late in the day, Mr. Wright decided to have the dinner in the theatre, which was a solid concrete pillbox and which stayed dry. It was like that forest in *Macbeth*—you know, the whole forest moves into the theatre. In no time at all the turkeys and all the stuff were coming out of the oven, and Mr. Wright viewed the work of his loyal followers with what, I must say, was a very benign expression. Then he stood up at the head of the table—I don't know where that was, except that it was wherever he was. And he said, "You see, George," addressing us because Paul Grotz and I were the foreigners, the visitors who had to be impressed, "once again we have snatched victory from the jaws of defeat." And there was no doubt about it. He had done, they had done, exactly that.

During that rainy season we went to a house near the Arizona Biltmore that Mr. Wright had done for a couple of sisters named Pauson. It was a kind of Usonian house, although just before it was built he had made some very powerful pronouncements to the effect that the line of the desert was a jagged line. But when he got to the Pauson house he forgot his pronouncements, because the house was a little too small, perhaps, for jagged lines. It worked fine on the desert camp, and it was marvelous the way he would turn completely around, you know, and do exactly what he said you shouldn't do. It was part of what you ended up liking best about him, because he was what you might call an extremely human kind of man, and I don't think he could have done the kinds of buildings he did without being that way.

Anyway, we went to the Pauson house, and it was a story of unmitigated disaster. First the water had come down through the roof. Then the Japanese houseman had rushed up and got a big tub, and he had torn the shower curtain off the shower, and the four occupants of the house held the shower curtain, while they channeled these torrents of water into the tub. Then somebody would rush out onto the terrace and throw out the water. Then, about the time it looked like everything was under control, the clapboard siding began to let water through, which is something I would have thought was a physical impossibility. But by golly it came through. So, as Mr. Wright and I got there, the sisters and the houseman were very tired. And the story was related by the sisters, taking turns; the Japanese houseman had nothing to say about it at all.

It was really a disaster story from the beginning to the end, and Mr. Wright listened very, very sympathetically, and the sisters, seeing that he was looking very sympathetic, sort of embellished the story and brought in more and more detail of what happened on that dreadful day. Finally, Mr. Wright, apparently responding to an internal clock, realized that he had something to do down at the lumber yard in Phoenix. He said, "Rose, a dreadful experience for you girls. Thank God it was no worse." And he put on his porkpie hat and said "George, let's go." And, indeed, we left. They were

Frank Lloyd Wright at Taliesin West in 1936. This photo was taken by Edgar Tafel. When Tafel presented a copy to Mr. Wright, he tore it up, commenting that it was a horrible picture, which made him look like a mouse.

scared to stop him, but then what would they have stopped him for? They'd told him the whole story.

I'll finish this piece with two brief stories. One has to do with Louis Sullivan. Mr. Wright told it to me on one of my visits. See, once the *Architectural Forum* and Mr. Wright developed this relationship, Paul Grotz and I developed these urgent needs to go to either Wisconsin or the desert camp because there was some newsworthy thing that was about to break, and our boss was very kind and would let us off to chase whatever will-o'-the-wisp we had spotted.

The Louis Sullivan story has to do with a time when Mr. Wright, as he described it himself, was Mr. Sullivan's pencil. Mr.

Wright was the draftsman, the designer, in Sullivan's Chicago office. One night he was working quite late because there was a deadline, and he had gotten the drawings to the point where he wanted them and, suddenly, around 10 or 11 o'clock, he heard the outer door to the office open and slam shut. Then some rather unsteady steps came closer and closer to the drafting room, which is where the only light was on. And in came Mr. Sullivan in evening dress, apparently a little the worse for wear, and he plunked himself down on a stool next to Mr. Wright. Sullivan explained what he had been doing that evening, which is he had been to some party or other. Suddenly, out of the blue he said, "Frank, how many women have you had?" Mr. Wright said, "Well, you know, I've never really thought much about this." Mr. Wright told me that of course he knew that Mr. Sullivan had been a great favorite with the ladies, and that he (Wright) had been sort of embarrassed when Sullivan asked him this. But finally, in response to Mr. Sullivan's question, he did a lot of counting—they didn't have pocket calculators then— and he said, "Well, Mr. Sullivan, I don't really know, but between five and six, something like that."

Mr. Wright told me that at that point Mr. Sullivan slapped his thigh so hard he practically fell off the stool, and he said to Mr. Wright, "Why, you poor fool. Do you realize that if you took all the women I have had, Frank, and laid them end to end on the Chicago and North Western railroad line, they would reach all the way from Chicago to Milwaukee?"

I asked Mr. Wright if that was true; did Mr. Sullivan have that much free time, along with drawing all that beautiful ornament? And Mr. Wright said, "Oh, yes, he was inordinately attractive to and attracted by ladies." But he said, "You know, afterward, I was really kind of sorry for Mr. Sullivan."

I said, "Really? After a success story like that?"

Mr. Wright said, "Well, my performance compared to Mr. Sullivan's was hardly worth talking about," but, he said, "I loved all those women, and they loved me, and I don't think Mr. Sullivan could quite have said the same thing."

My last story takes us back to the desert. I was out at Taliesin West and it was late afternoon, and there were no apprentices around. It was winter, approaching sunset. A very long February or March twilight was on the kind of pointed prow that went out into the desert—in those days it really went out into the desert instead of a neighboring subdivision. I heard a door slam and looked, and there was Mr. Wright in his costume, with his cloak and cane, and he clearly had had a very good day. Since I was the only living body in view, he came over to pass the time of day. He talked a little about the weather, and about a couple of other things, and then, suddenly, he said, "George, do you know what architecture is?"

Well, I knew that Mr. Wright couldn't have cared less whether I thought I knew what architecture was, so I said, "Mr. Wright, why don't you tell me?" That was really what he had intended, and he didn't delay an instant.

He waved his cane at a paloverde tree, which is a very lovely, green tree that has needles rather than leaves and at that time of year was covered with beautiful, buttercup-like blossoms. It was an absolutely ravishing sight. He said, "Architecture is like that paloverde tree coming into bloom."

I said, "Is that really what it's like Mr. Wright?"

He said, "Yeah, that's about what it's like," and started to go off twirling his cane, Charlie Chaplin-style, practically.

And I thought, you old blackguard. I'd been following him around for years hoping I would learn his secret. So he tells me architecture is like a paloverde tree! But then Mr. Wright stopped cold. He had another thought. He was about five or six feet away. He turned around and said, "No, that is not really exactly the way it is, George." And I said, "Isn't it, Mr. Wright?" He said, "I think it's more like a boy falling in love with a girl or a girl falling in love with a boy. I think that's more like it." And he went off again with his cane.

And, you know, there have been very few times in my life when I felt this cheated, being this close to a really valuable answer. It took me years to find out all of the things he could have possibly told me that would have been true and good and wise and real. This was it, and it took me ten years.

[**Editor's note:** *George's talk was entirely extemporaneous—no notes.*]

At Taliesin

Those of us who were architecturally oriented will never forget the constant excitement of the drafting (always spelled "draughting" by FLLW) room. Located in the middle of the Taliesin complex, between the help's quarters, kitchen, shops, car stalls, chicken coops, and pig pen, it was the center of circulation, especially in the depths of cold winters, with temperatures going down way below zero and beyond. People would come through, to check on their mail, see Mr. Wright about things, seek people working on the boards, make phone calls, and more.

When clients arrived, soon after being made comfortable, they would be brought to the drafting studio, and Wright would show them about, always introducing those of us who were there. He was always cordial and enticing to the clients. While in the room, we would hear him on the phone, taking incoming calls. In the early days, outgoing calls could only be made if collect. His payment record with the telephone co-op didn't allow credit.

So, there we were in the center of the action. If there was a crisis, there was the place to find bodily help. And, if there was an accident, such as an apprentice falling out of a tree, being hit by a car, or a sawblade, we in the drafting room would be first to hear of it. Mr. Wright had a standing comment about accidents: "Something always happens in the country."

The studio was the place "to hang around." We had no lounge, loggia, or student commons, except our own rooms. So, it would be the studio. "Meet me at the studio . . ." was the term. In the later '30s, when the drafting activities were moved to the new building at Hilllside, there was the place you found people. And, if you wanted to avoid a crisis, that was the place to hide from. One apprentice had selected a room with a large walk-in closet, where he hid out in a crisis, or to duck a possible chore. The following remembrances are from this phase of our existence.

IN THE DRAFTING ROOM

Mr. Wright had an array of friends—and some enemies—among the architectural scene. On returning from New York City to Taliesin one time, he told of meeting again with architect William Lescaze, whom he had met several times before: "This time, Lescaze said, 'Mr. Wright, I have asked you often to lunch with me, and this is the last time I will ask.' I thanked him and said I would remember the invitation, and said goodbye."

On returning from New York another time, he told of having had lunch with his friend, Raymond Hood (one of the architects of Radio City). He told Hood that he liked his McGraw-Hill building on 42nd Street and added, "Ray, you must get great satisfaction having designed that fine structure. Tell me, what do you think about when seeing it each time?" Wright said Hood's answer was, "Frank, every time I think of the building, or look at it, I think of all the shit that goes down the soil lines." And Wright laughed and laughed, and repeated the story often.

* * *

The most exciting residence of the three that Wright designed for "Usonia" at Pleasantville, New York, was the Sol Friedman House. Perched on top of a rocky hill, it was designed so that the masonry foundation would sweep down to a lower area—revealing toward the road a two-story stone wall, all curved, to fit the circular plan of the house.

The house was originally budgeted at $35,000. One day, when the house was framed up and nearing completion—and by now the costs had swollen to over $80,000—Wright and his client were standing in the living room. Friedman had borrowed on his insurances, sold one of his music stores (so the story went) and was almost penniless. Wright put his arm around his client's shoulders and said: "Sol, don't we live in a wonderful country—where a small businessman like yourself can build and own a fine house such as this?"

Homosexual behavior was anathema to Wright; he could never understand it, feel for it, or condone it. On one of our frequent forays, driving him from Taliesin to the Johnson Wax building, then under construction, Wright talked of many things, as he often did—the beauty of Wisconsin red barns, the need for poultry back at the coop, the need for more workmen at Hillside, and other topics. Then he came to the subject of homosexuals, stating that an ex-apprentice was one, he couldn't understand it, and so on. He seemed to be asking my opinion on the subject and I answered, "Mr. Wright, there is no place in the frontier of America for homosexuals." He said, "right," and repeated my statement word for word as if it were his own. Years later he visited another ex-apprentice, also homosexual, in an eastern city. The ex-apprentice had designed his living room in the International Style, with two Mies chairs, etc. When asked by his host what he thought of it, Wright replied, "It is a most appropriate place for artificial insemination."

*   *   *

Mr. Wright would walk into the drafting room, always clearing his throat, often stating "Gute Morgen," and always with something to talk about. He would go to a drafting table, look at a drawing and then pick up a pencil and start to work—adding to or changing whatever work was before him.

*   *   *

In the 1950s one day, Mrs. Wright phoned me to ask if I would pick Mr. Wright up at a doctor's office on 57th Street in Manhattan and lead him back to the Plaza since he was having inner ear trouble. Leading him toward Fifth Avenue, half way there, he lifted his cane, and pointed it at the rear of a scantily clad young lady, and stated, "what a handsome piece of sculpture."

*   *   *

When Henry-Russell Hitchcock was working on the book of Wright's work, *In the Nature of Materials*, Mr. Wright would keep the conversations going, telling stories about the projects. When Hitchcock would state a date for some job Mr. Wright would take issue and often change the date on the drawing.

During this process one day, in an attempt to make conversation, Wright said, "Tell me, Henry-Russell, how is Philip?" referring to

Edgar Tafel at work in the drafting room.

architect Philip Johnson. "Fine, fine," Hitchcock said in his combination New England–British accent. "Do you and Philip differ on design subjects?" asked Mr. Wright. Hitchcock thought for a moment and stated hesitatingly with the taken-on brogue: "Yes, Mr. Wright, we differ. Philip is partial to line and I am partial to surface."

* * *

One day while I was in the drafting room, Mr. Wright came by from his office with a manuscript, stopped at my board, and dropped it in front of me. "Edgar, read this and tell me what it is about. . . ." It was *The Fountainhead* by Ayn Rand.

It was about three inches thick, and I took it to my room. After trying to get into it, it seemed a racy, sexy attempt into making architecture into a fashionable gossip legend with an author's message of some kind. I couldn't get past fifty pages, and with my authority as a senior apprentice, I gave it to a junior apprentice, with words to the effect that Mr. Wright wants this read and wants an opinion. The apprentice some days later said, as he handed it back, "It's a piece of junk." I gave it back to Mr. Wright, and said, "Sir, it's a piece of junk."

Mr. Wright later designed a house for Ms. Rand that wasn't built. She had patterned the legend after him, and later it made a piece of junk movie.

GOOD CLEAN FUN[1]

the front page

mourning edition

taliesin's nose knows

*   *   *   *

Met mme d-kn-t-l[2] who have been
studying art while slumming in
the hinterland have returned to
see paris but not die. famous
as they were, as the man (sic)
who brought picasso (pronounced
picasso) to taliesin this paper
suh will not consider it news
until somebody brings taliesin
to picasso. Kindly omit flowers

i am still doing business just as
honest as I been since 1908. watches,
diamonds, no trumps, old information.
j.w. zangl,[3] jeweller and obstetrician

honest abe dombar[4] rang the bell again
last night. waiting outside for the
springgreen stage, casting the
dombar on everything as susual: I
see we finally got some window
shades in this barracks, he
snivelled, pointing at the italian
exhibit or mr mussolini's folly

j w zangl's message to taliesin:
I see in the near future a customer
approaching. . . before god, he
shall not perish from the earth. . .

have some wheatina bettina between
da weina we meana Fatima.

social item by the ferret, social
editor of good clean fun

a cute man
who refused to admit that his name
is budshaw[5] is visiting taliesin
today. he denied everything.

i have it; see me. j w zangl. spring
green's leading and only jeweler,
also harness and picture framing
neatly done.

bettina, helena[6] lies somewhere betweena
arena, springgreens, galena, and the
perfect apprentice.

the back page

comics: W W (moby dick)[7] Peters
impersonating lady godiva on
the way back from the livery
stable. (sluggish livery)
editorial: "the time is (has)
come, the walrus said, to speak
of other things . . ."

Fourteen
thousand years ago confucius said
this and it is just as true today.
What do we know of the hanseatic
league? What do we know of incomplete
metabolism of glucose? Of ontogeny,
recapitulating philogeny? Of the
libido of the condemned felon who
may find himself willy nilly in
jail? This countwy is all wong.

questions and answers dep't:
— *q*, how many wrigkles in a prune?
— *a*, send a stamped self addressed
     envelope to your congressman
     and the answer will be sent
     you in a plain wrapper.

swords, ploughshares, and midwest
securities shares, see zangl the
god damned optimist and optician

the pests corner.
             o, wud some
power the giftie'd gie us
             to see oorsel's
as ithers see us. . . .

Will some
kind reader furnish information
that will enable me to track down
this old literary landmark?

J. Cass II[8]
Dear Mr Cass: the poem you
enquire about is called Polonius'
advice to Laertes and you can find
it in any phone bood. just walk
upstairs and ask for tony. but
shucks, i can complete it for you
myself right here and now. it goes:
A thing of beauty is a boy forever,
o slender and subtle dolores, our
lady of brain. It is from the Pirates
of Yen's[9] pants by j w zangl, the
giddy ass. yours affectionately
             J Cass IIa[8]

the boys for the last time have
transgressed the bounds, it is
alleged of human manmnnn etaoin shrdlu
shrdlushrdlu it is alleged

---

[1]Was posted on the bulletin board in the Drafting Room in fall, 1932.
[2]An apprentice, William Deknatel.
[3]J. W. Zangl had a jewelry store in Spring Green;
had ads in local paper personal column each week.
[4]Abe Dombar, an apprentice from Cincinnati.
[5]"Budshaw" was apprentice Irving Shaw, nicknamed Bud.

[6]Helena, former town near Taliesin.
[7]Moby Dick was one of the first sound films.
[8]J. Cass II and J. Cass IIa are imaginary names for an
apprentice who was tracking down information on the
former local town named Helena.
[9]Yen Liang, apprentice.

THE JOHNSON WAX BUILDING

Occasionally, when looking at published drawings of Wright's, I come across the drawings that I made of the Johnson Wax project. I recall its inception, how it was carried out, and what it took on Wright's part as well as the Fellowship's.

I drove Mr. Wright down to Racine to meet with Mr. Johnson, which started with a luncheon at the Johnson residence on Main Street. The three of us lunched together in the dining room, Johnson holding forth on the history of the company and the nature of it, what he saw in its future, and what part the new building would play. He wanted Wright to meet with both the highest level of executives and also the department heads. And he said strongly: "I want you to ask questions of the department heads, listen to them, but don't pay much attention to them, for they won't be here when the new building is completed."

All of this was done that afternoon. We got back into the car and drove back to Madison and Spring Green by a different route from the way we came, for Mr. Wright never wanted to make the same trip the same way, always wanting change.

The very next day, Mr. Wright and several of us who hung around the drafting room watched him as he started out. He brought out the plans for a building for a newspaper plant (the Capital Journal building, Salem, Oregon), done many years before (1931), which had mushroom columns throughout the main space. We had brought from Racine, a plot plan, with indications of set-back requirements from the streets. Immediately he took his idea of the mushroom (concrete) column, placed them on 20-foot centers both ways, found the "extra" space to the lot lines was some 14 feet, and he was off—the big workspace, the two central "cores" (having air conditioning breathers in them he dubbed them "nostrils"), about which were the main winding stairs, later to become stone. He then described how, as he drew, the "service" entrance was on the left, where mail arrived and mail and messages to the factory went out. He arranged a business flow.

S. C. Johnson and Son Co., administration building, Racine, Wisconsin, 1936.

Then arranging the mezzanine, all around the outer walls, deep enough between the ceiling below and the mezzanine floor level to accompany warm air heat or air conditioning, or just fresh air. He drew the three-story entrance, with executive offices coming off at 45 degrees, the forms ending in circles, and the president's office there was in the middle—"in command"—with its fireplace, the only one in the building. (Later at "Wingspread," Johnson's house, the center "core" of the 40 × 60-foot living room would have five fireplaces, one of which was on the balcony.)

Where to put toilets in this huge space? Simple: circular stairs down in two areas, making it a basement. Workers wouldn't be obliged to walk endless corridors in front of each other to go to the lavatories.

The entry to the building was in the rear, with spaces for executive and visitors parking.

We were off drawing! Divided among us were those who did elevations, others who did plans, sections, and details—always details—where the heating and air conditioning ducts went—in order to make the presentation complete and clear. These were no ordinary pretty drawings to show the client; these were realities.

Mr. Wright directed, always, the basic design, with pencils in his own hand. We were four or five of us working, and he would move quickly from one table to another. During the afternoon and evening (for we worked day and night), he would walk over to the fireplace, lie down on his back on the bench to rest, and fall asleep for 15 or 20 minutes, then awaken, startled, browse back to a table where he had left an idea, and continue drawing—and changing! Change seemed to be a word for "refinement." Too often changes upset each drawing, for if it was a change in plan, we would have to correct those changes in elevations and sections. But the central idea prevailed.

Fireplace in the drafting room. The portrait is of Mr. Wright's mother. The bench at right was Wright's resting place.

Mr. Wright must have had a target date for completion of this drawing stage to present to Johnson. Several days before this date, I had completed the cut-away perspective (shown on page 243). This drawing shows how the exterior expresses the interior, where the principal stairs and breathers come through. It was a tedious job, taking about three days to complete, always with his viewing and changing. Coming back to my table the next morning, I found that the table lamp's electric bulb filament had broken. The broken hot wire had fallen on the T-square, triangle and paper, and had burned the whole drawing, along with paper items. Upon seeing it, Mr. Wright took charge, treated it with his usual saying: "Something always happens in the country," and I was directed to redo the drawing, taking another couple of days.

One night at about 10 o'clock, just before all the drawings were completed, Mr. Wright went into the vault, and came out with four Japanese prints, one for each of us, and placed them on our respective tables, saying they were gifts showing his appreciation of our efforts. He then walked to the door, and turned around as he always did, and warmly said, "Good night." We all looked at each other, collected our prints, and turned off the lights as we went to our rooms. I still have this thin, long print, where I see it every day at home. It gives me a wonderful feeling of being mine—an accomplishment.

Japanese print by Toyuhiro presented to Edgar Tafel by Frank Lloyd Wright on completion of the Johnson Wax building drawings.

Edgar Tafel in 1989. Photo credit: Rick Glintentkamp.

With another day's work and the drawings completed and wrapped up, Mr. Wright told me to get the car: "Ed-gerr (as he always pronounced it), get the car; we are off to Racine!" He had a target date, and target hour to arrive. Three hours later, arriving at the agreed moment and place, I took the drawings under my arm and followed Mr. Wright to the door, where he took the drawings under *his* arm, saying "The architect carries his own drawings."

His presentation was astounding and unforgettable. He took his audience to him and his labors. He was designing for them and their requirements. His voice was certain and imploring. The Unitarian minister in him sallied forth creatively. All of us there would go on to live greater glories. He gained absolute approvals, and we headed home to continue the work.

Back at Taliesin, construction documents were begun at once. Added to the program were a gymnasium, the bridge from the executive floor, and a special "waxing" garage at the main level.

Construction soon began, even before a building permit was obtained. I was sent to "Fallingwater" for about two months, to top off the floors and get fireplaces and interior spaces constructed, while Bob Mosher traveled to Racine supervising the foundations. At one point, Mr. Johnson told Mosher that he wanted a sign on the main street saying the name of the company, and Mosher stated that Mr. Wright didn't think it necessary, saying "The Washington Monument doesn't have a sign, does it?"

Across the street from the Johnson building construction, an office was set up for the contractor, behind which was a "draughting room" (Mr. Wright's spelling) behind which was my abode for almost two years. It was a simple room and bath, with a slight refrigerator plus a portable two-burner electric stove. Upstairs was an occupied apartment, which occasionally poured bathroom leakage onto the drawing tables. No fires. Often, as problems on site arose, I would make the solution drawing, take it across the street to the superintendent, and the job continued uninterrupted. Not even record drawings were kept—the building was and is the record.

Along came the Johnson house, "Wingspread," and the same contractor and same arrangements continued simultaneously. My supervising took me to glass, brick, door, and millwork makers. Hundreds of my letters from those jobs, and theirs, are in the Getty files.

When the Administration Building was completed, the Johnson people had a grand opening occasion. Nobody asked me to attend: maybe it didn't occur to anyone, or maybe Mr. Wright would have been asked to credit his supervisor. He never wanted to give acknowledgment to his staff; it just wasn't his style or desire. By then I was exhausted—years of trips, hundreds of telephone calls and letters and shop drawings galore—I wanted away. Away meant Wright had me construction managing houses in various directions—more endless miles of auto travel. But, it was exciting, I was in charge, and the designs got built.

VISITORS

During the early years of the Fellowship at Taliesin, Mr. Wright often would invite friends to come and visit. Among the many who came were Alexander Woolcott, Rockwell Kent, and Carl Sandburg. Some came for overnight visits, others longer, and always there was an event held in the living room to which we apprentices were invited to meet the guests and hear their banter with Mr. Wright.

In one instance, well-known concert singer Sophie Breslau was brought up for a daytime visit; she had performed the evening before at the University of Madison. She sang for us in the living room without accompaniment. Mr. Wright asked for more and more. Her voice was strong and pervasive. It filled the entire room, adding beauty and romance. The situation enthralled Mr. Wright, who was completely enveloped, charmed, and a bit smitten as well. When he asked if she wouldn't stay over for an early train the next day, she said she had to be in Chicago that evening to take her train back to New York.

The arrangement was that she would board a train at Spring Green, change at Madison, and arrive in Chicago to transfer to the New York train. Mr. Wright ordered Gene to bring the car around. Gene later recounted the events that occurred:

Mr. Wright rode with Breslau in the back seat while Gene drove. During the ride to town, Mr. Wright slowed the pace to a crawl to show her historic places and tell of his forefathers. Having waited until the last moment before leaving Taliesin, and having dawdled along the way, they arrived in town just as the train was departing. Mr. Wright directed Gene to call Taliesin and tell them they were on their way to Madison. Along the way they stopped here and there, Mr. Wright assuring Miss Breslau they would make the train. However, on arriving at Madison, they found the train in motion, en route to Chicago. Gene called Taliesin again, saying they were off to Chicago and would call later. On the way to Chicago, Mr. Wright talked with Breslau, recalling music, beauty, creativity, and such, for that was almost a three-hour trip.

It was later learned that meanwhile, at Taliesin—after the call from Madison—Mrs. Wright apparently in a jealous fury, summoned one of her lady helpers to remove her clothing from her bedroom to a spare room upstairs. However, soon, Gene called from Chicago, saying she had made the New York train and they were on their way back. Apparently, at this point, Mrs. Wright called the same lady and had her clothes returned to her own bedroom.

FIRED!

People often ask if I was ever "fired" by Mr. Wright. Of course I was—several times. The first, in 1932, occurred during the first year of the Fellowship. I was fired along with several others. Earlier, we had harvested grapes, and wine was made. One Sunday night in the living room with guest Rockwell Kent, the renowned artist, our home-grown wine was offered. We had no wine glasses, most liquids were dealt with in newly bought boardinghouse-like white cups. The wine, like the coffee, went into those cups.

After dinner, Mr. Wright gave an uplifting talk, quoting several of his literary masters. I played piano pieces, the chorus sang, and, finally, we all bade each other good night. When I stepped outside I saw several apprentices running on top of the roofs, others were singing loudly and walking toward Hillside, where they were billeted. One, Bob Bishop, later admitted that during the fray he had urinated into the radiator of Mr. Wright's Cord convertible, in order "to save alcohol." Noises were heard all over the place.

The next morning, right after breakfast, Mr. Wright summoned all apprentices to a meeting at one end of the drafting room. He asked how many had partaken of more than one cup of wine—and would we step forward. Most of us stepped forward. Then he asked those who had taken more than two to step forward. Several of us moved forward. Again, he asked if any had taken more than two cups. Four of us stepped forward. He then gave a talk on alcoholism, said it couldn't be acceptable at the Fellowship, and walked toward his office, instructing the four of us to follow. We four watched him get seated facing us. He told us that he had to set an example, and we were invited to pack up and leave. At that moment one of us asked him, "Sir, were any of your clients alcoholics?" Another asked about a certain house, and we soon had him talking about his clients and their histories. Then several minutes later he said, "Boys, go back to work, and don't do it again." And so we did. That was firing number one.

* * *

The next year three of us went to Madison late one afternoon to see Shankar dance. After the concert we went to the deli for snacks, after which we found the car frozen. So we put ourselves up at the local YMCA. Next morning we went back to the deli for breakfast. After that we decided to take a tour of Wright's houses in Madison, of which there were only two. We located them, introduced ourselves to the owners, and got in. At lunchtime we delied again, then set off to Taliesin, arriving midafternoon.

On our arrival we were summoned into Mr. Wright's office and given a stern lecture. We should have called and informed him. He was responsible for us to our families. He told us to pack and leave right away. He would not stand for our actions and had to set an example.

At that moment one of us asked, "Mr. Wright, before we leave, why was the last house named 'The Airplane House?'" At which Wright went into a fury, saying that was not his name for the house, the house had nothing to do with airplanes and its name should be disregarded. Another of us asked how he obtained names or designations for houses. He went into a long dissertation about how every house should have a name, describing its nature and place. Then another of us said we would be sorry to leave him when all we wanted was the experience of seeing his worthy works. At which moment he said, "Boys, don't do it again, and stay." That was number two.

*   *   *

Some time after the aforementioned happenings I was called into Mr. Wright's office. (When someone said he wanted to see you in his office you knew you were in trouble.) On my arrival in his office he said, "Edgar, we have a situation, and I think that you should leave." He didn't say what that situation was or when it happened—only that, under the circumstances, I could no longer continue in the Fellowship. I asked what the circumstances were. He said, "Think about it, and let's talk again in a week or so." I was completely baffled and very disturbed. I asked him what I'd done, but couldn't get an answer. He told me again to "think about it."

A week later I went to his office and raised the question of leaving. (During that week I had worked on as usual.) I sat down and awaited his answer. He said things had not changed, but why not keep working as I had. Some time later he ended with, "Mrs. Wright will get over it in time." He then paid me one of his rare compliments by saying that he felt I was doing well as a senior in the Fellowship. Looking back, I still don't know what I did. Maybe it was that Mrs. Wright had intercepted a letter I had written to someone who had left Taliesin under a dire cloud and consequently earned Mrs. Wright's extreme displeasure. It took a year before she spoke to me—she never said hello or even nodded a salutation. But finally it all returned to the old friendly relationship. That was number three.

*   *   *

After the Johnson house and building were completed, I was in charge of a Usonian house in upstate Wisconsin. In charge meant completing working drawings, selecting the site, meeting with contractors and subcontractors, and staying in that northern Wisconsin town almost every week. During the early design phase both Wes Peters and I noted that steel beams were required as main support over the living room. I asked Mr. Wright about the steel, and he said "absolutely not." He believed strongly that a wooden house should not have steel. Secretly, Wes and I went ahead and had steel inserted.

Later, a similar situation developed in the South when another apprentice was in charge. I warned the apprentice that he had to use steel and not to tell anyone about it. He did not do as I suggested, the roof fell in, the client called Wright, who railed, "Send the boy back." Was I ever scared.

I was told to get out the plans of the similar house where the roof had stood up without steel. At this point I had to confess my action. I was fired right then and there with, "I can take care of my enemies, but I can't trust my friends."

Then he ordered me to bring the car around. I drove the Wrights toward Madison while he railed on in top fury. Soon, seeing a gas station, he directed me to stop close to its toilet—he had to use it fast. While he was out of the car Mrs. Wright asked, "Why did you disobey him?" I told her I saved his reputation in Wisconsin and the other apprentice was losing it in the South. When he returned to the car she patted his thigh, saying in her best Bosnian accent, "Frrank, we must drop the subject, Edgarrr did what he thought was best, etc. etc. . . ." My firing was never mentioned again.

I've often wondered if I'd set a record—fired only four times in nine years.

LEAVING TALIESIN

During the late 1930s, my principal abode was at Taliesin, Wisconsin, since I was working on several of Mr. Wright's projects locally. My doctor was Dr. Nee, in Spring Green. I was often short of salary. Clients paid Mr. Wright $25 per week, from which I was entitled to half, or $12.50. My salary was paid intermittently, to put it kindly, and I owed Dr. Nee $14. I stopped in his office (second floor, opposite the hotel and adjoining the post office), and told him as soon as I got paid I would pay him. And I suggested (facetiously) that possibly he had some architectural work? To my surprise, he said he needed someone to select colors for repainting his house, and would I do it? He told me to choose the paint, consult with his wife, etc.

I contacted his painter—we all knew the painter because his wife was Elsie, who cleaned rooms for apprentices (at 35 cents each) and did our laundry. When the painting job was completed, I went to see Dr. Nee. He told me how happy he was with the result, gave me a check for $25, and waived the amount I owed him. That was my first paid commission.

Around this time, Mr. Wright bought seven Bantam cars. They were small roadsters, and one was designated for my use in work. Soon I found that the car often broke down. It had a gravity water cooling system that didn't work, and often had to abandon the car during my travels. So I found a car at the local Ford dealer—a blue roadster with wire wheels and two spares, one set into each of the front fenders. I went to the Farmers State Bank and borrowed about $100 on the $140 cost. When Mr. Wright saw the car, he became furious—it wasn't his "cherokee red" color. I was perceived as revolting from his given (or lent) course. He insisted that I hide my car from the parking lot. Still, I had to get to his jobs, and later mine; and this little blue Ford worked well for me. Eventually I traded mine for Wes Peter's cherokee red real convertible and Mr. Wright forgave me. Through the Racine connection, I brought in a house of my own to design, and that was the start of leaving Taliesin. Mr. Wright always said we apprentices would "borrow" some coals from his fire, and start a fire of our own, and so I did. When Mr. Wright heard that my client was happy, that the house came under the budget and on time and didn't leak, he stopped all apprentice work, and I had to leave after nine years—leave what I had thought would be the rest of my life.

Sayings and Happenings

In 1946 I sat, apprehensive, for the interview part of the New York license examination. The interview was held in a formal and imposing setting—I was at one end of a long table facing eight judging architects. They passed my application folder ceremoniously among themselves, each either grunting or sniggering—a few smiling—as their eyes fell on a certain folder notation. There seemed to be mystery afoot. When my folder reached the last reviewer and the closest to me, I took a look at it. I noticed a familiar Wright red square on the letter at the top of the group of recommendations. Knowing immediately that it was from Wright and being unable to restrain my curiosity, I asked if I could hear what Wright had written about me. The judge replied in a dour tone, "He says we aren't qualified to judge you." I was allowed to take the examination and I passed.

QUOTABLE QUOTES FROM FRANK LLOYD WRIGHT

"Harvard takes perfectly good plums as students, and makes prunes of them."

"Bureaucrats: they are dead at 30 and buried at 60. They are like custard pies, you can't nail them to a wall."

"The devil you know is better than the devil you don't know."

"Only fools and women criticize unfinished work."

Reviewing another architect's hectic work: "He mistakes nervousness for emotion."

"I wouldn't mind seeing opera die. Ever since I was a boy I have regarded opera as a ponderous anachronism, almost the equivalent of smoking."

After returning from a South American trip with architect Eliel Saareinen: "All I learned from Eliel Saareinen was how to make out an expense account."

"The architect's best working tools are the eraser at the drafting board and the wrecking bar at the site."

"There are tricks in everyone's trade but Dad's—and he drives screws with a hammer."

"What a man does, that he has."

HAPPENINGS

During the Fellowship's second winter in Chandler, Arizona, we worked on plans for Stanley Marcus, the son of the Dallas department store owners of Neiman-Marcus. One day there was a telephone call from Marcus. He was coming to Arizona. Mr. Wright then phoned the then restricted Arizona Biltmore Hotel and got the manager. We heard him request a reservation for his clients. There was a pause, then Mr. Wright said, "He is, but she isn't." The reservation was obtained.

The plans for Marcus never went beyond sketches when Mr. Wright was discharged and a local architect was selected. One day, Marcus sent a note to Mr. Wright along with a newspaper clipping of his proposed house. Mr. Wright sent the following letter:

> Dear Stanley:
> I didn't know you would be satisfied with so little.
> Yours, FLLW.

* * *

One of Wright's great hates was the firm of McKim, Mead and White. To him, they personified the predominant force that held back Organic Architecture, and they fostered the classics and European tradition. Academia and the Eastern forces were wedded to the past.

Partner Stanford White was well known as a ladies' man, and his demise was the result of his being shot at Madison Square Garden in New York (which he designed). The assassin was the husband of a former lady friend, Harry K. Thaw. Often, when anyone brought up the name of McKim, Mead and White, Wright would state emphatically, "Harry K. Thaw killed Stanford White, for the wrong reason."

* * *

Mr. Wright had a keen interest in preserving his own works. I remember one building in particular—German warehouse in Richland Center, a few miles from Spring Green. It had been built around 1914 and had gone through several owners. Some time in the late 1930s, Mr. Wright was selected to alter the building. He proceeded to design the remodeling of the building into a hotel, and I worked with several other apprentices on plans toward that goal. The layout was extremely tight. Each room was designed too small, and Mr. Wright got around that obstacle by having me show the beds as exactly five feet long, thus making the rooms look larger. Fortunately, roomwise, the project never went ahead.

*   *   *

An oft-repeated story concerns Herbert Johnson, owner of a Wright-designed spectacular residence in Racine, Wisconsin. Mr. Johnson is said to have telephoned his architect to say that he had dinner guests and the roof was leaking over the dining table. (This seems an impossibility to me. I supervised the job from footings through roofing. It was a tight roof, with waterproofing and tile above.) Wright's reply was simply, "Hib, move the table." Leaking roofs are not confined to Wright houses. A story goes that a client of Le Corbusier's phoned him in the middle of a rainstorm to report that his living room floor was flooded. He asked Corbu to come over immediately to solve the problem. Arriving, Corbu was asked what to do about the situation. The architect asked for "une pièce de papier," which he took, folded into a little boat, and pushed it into the water.

In the spirit of "when given a lemon, make lemonade," the following story comes to mind. Barcelona architect Gaudi received a call from an irate purchaser of one of his designed apartments. She complained that she could not install her grand piano in her apartment because for the stairs were too narrow. She was a pianist and obviously had a problem. His response was, "Señora, you should purchase a violin."

*   *   *

The third winter at the Fellowship found twenty-five of us headed for Chandler, Arizona. As was Mr. Wright's wont when traveling from one place to another, he would go out of the way to see some earlier completed project so he could see it again and show it to us.

Our first stop was at the Henry Allen house, in Wichita, Kansas, built in the later Prarie type, 1917. This was a short foray—

we went through the house, had tea, and then returned to the caravan to go West. The next house stop was at his cousin's, Richard Lloyd Jones in Tulsa, Oklahoma. The house, built in 1929, was well known to those of us who worked in the drafting room. Mr. Wright had often complained that the Joneses had rejected his first scheme, all on a plan grid of 30 and 60 degrees, like a honeycomb, with no right angles. The house was built using right angles. It consists of an exterior of concrete columns about 20" square, with glass between. Exterior walls as such are used only occasionally.

It was arranged that we all would arrive in time for early dinner, see the house, and camp there in our sleeping bags for the night. After dinner Mrs. Jones took us around in a group, telling about living in the house: its excitement, the flow of spaces, and experiences of each season with light pouring in in different ways. The tour ended in the kitchen, where she made her final pronouncement: "We have two sets of kitchen utensils—one for cooking, of course, and the other to catch the water from the leaks."

*   *   *

By some power of persuasion, Mr. Wright was able to get some lumbermen, idle from work because of the depression, to set up a saw mill just below the Romeo and Juliet water tower at Hillside. We cut enough lumber to build the drafting room in green lumber, literally dripping with sap.

The sight of these men slinging tremendous logs onto the mill and riding the logs toward the buzzing steel saw to turn raw nature's living things into building material was another revelation. With a twist of the wrist, they turned the logs to cut the raw tree trunks into lumber for construction.

Wood at Taliesin is always left with the natural texture and the beauty of the grain showing. No paint or stain is used, only a little oil. With the added surprises of unpredictable markings of the green lumber, another dimension was added to the use of wood. Unsanded, unplaned, and with the saw marks showing, the wood showed a character of rugged sturdiness unequaled in other finishes.

*   *   *

Whenever I drove Mr. Wright to Racine or other Wisconsin places, he would almost always note the charm and grace of the Wisconsin red barns. He would say that the red lead color was great against both the greenery of spring and summer and the winter snows. Then he would talk about how he met Daniel Parker, president of the Parker Pen Co. in Janesville, Wisconsin.

It seems that Parker disliked the constant red barns in his county and offered to pay any farmer the difference in cost of having his barn painted in another color (red lead was cheaper than other paint)—to which Mr. Wright took exception and wrote Parker to that effect. One thing led to another and they became friends.

Early in the Fellowship, we were invited to be guests of the Parkers, and have a tour of the factory. The Parkers provided a picnic lunch, and we were taken through the plant. At the end of the visit the manager told us a story: Recently they had shown a contingent of Boy Scouts through the factory, and a couple of days later discovered that eleven pens were missing. The manager wrote the Scoutmaster about the disappearance. A week or so later the Scoutmaster sent a package to the manager with a note saying he was sorry—the package contained 26 new pens!

* * *

During one summer at Taliesin, Mr. Wright hired a couple for the summer months. He was a school teacher who worked mostly in the garden, and his wife, who was most attractive, was a helper with teas and in the kitchen. Her attractiveness encouraged me to smile at her and talk whenever occasions allowed. We had some conversations—that was all.

One day I was told by another apprentice that Mrs. Wright wanted to see me in the living room. I knew this meant I was in trouble, but I could not think what I had done wrong. When I went to see her, I was informed, after a cool welcome, that it had come to her attention that I was paying attention to the teacher's wife. I was told that I should cease immediately. She said her husband had a fierce and jealous temper, and if he thought I was making advances toward this woman, he would kill me. She further stated that there had already been too much tragedy at Taliesin, more than was needed, and I must stop. No word was said of the safety of my life.

* * *

Mansinh Rana remembers whilst at Taliesin, often the conversation in the dining room would be on the subject of Mrs. Wright, and someone always asked: "Who is she mad at this week?"

*   *   *

Soon after returning from the War, and having started my own practice in New York City, I called the Wrights at the Plaza Hotel, and was invited for tea. After a lovely interlude, Mr. Wright, to fill in conversation, asked me what kinds of work I was doing. I told of several residences, and a restoration/alteration of a Pennsylvania Dutch 1779 farmhouse. I said that the client was a collector of French impressionist paintings, this house would house his collection, and I called it the "O'Henry House" at this point. Mr. Wright asked why, and I said that each month or so, the contractor required payments, and the client would sell a painting, . . . and Mr. Wright said: "And when the house is finished, the client won't have any paintings left?" and we both had deep ye olde drafting room laugh.

Then he said he had a story about Bill Deknatel, another erstwhile apprentice: He ran into Walter Kohler, president of the plumbing fixture company, and Wright told him he had heard that Bill designed his new house, and how does he like it? Kohler said: "Frank, he cantilevered everything." And laughter continued.

*   *   *

Recently, a former employee of mine, Walter Blum, told me that he met Wright many years ago and told him he had worked for Edgar Tafel. Wright said, "I regret that Edgar left the fold." My dictionary states: "Fold, an enclosure for domesticated animals."

*   *   *

When coming into the dining room, at Taliesin, we would go toward the kitchen, where we could see the kitchen through an opening that started at waist high—above which was a saying: "We have poetry like that because of prose like this." Just what it meant was never discussed, except that we know Mr. Wright liked plain farm food best—and that's perhaps what he wanted for us. One would take his plate, fill it with whatever assortment he or she wished. Sometimes we would be handed a plate all ready dished up; one then would hesitate, looking into the dining room, and choose a place most interesting—or, you might take a place away from some who you didn't like, etc., etc.

Apprentices in the dining room at Taliesin. Left to right at rear: John Howe, Noverre Musson, Blain Drake, and Hulda Drake. Front right: Burton Goodrich.

One time I found myself with a group of us talkative types, and somehow, I came about talking of an imaginary encounter between Mrs. Wright and the Spring Green postmistress, Mrs. Smith, who could read lips, couldn't hear, and had a voice that sent each word up to high sounds, or back down into contralto. My interpretation of Mrs. Wright was my usual imitation of her Yugoslavian accent that she never lost—so, everyone was in tears of laughter, my telling the postmistress that I (being Mrs. W.) wanted five two-cent stamps, and when the stamps were delivered, I (being Mrs. Wright) said I wanted three five-cent stamps. Postmistress, being confused, said in up and down voice that she thought she (Mrs. Wright) wanted whatevers, and I did their voices of confusion back and forth. We all thought this of general humor.

About an hour later, one of the apprentices found me at work someplace, told me that Mrs. W. wanted to see me in the living room. That was always a scary moment—if either Mr. or Mrs. W. wanted to see you in the living room—that meant you had done something wrong, you were guilty, and would get a dressing down for some unremembered cause, possibly such as not having your room tidy, or, the like. I went to the room, quietly knocked and entered. She was awaiting me standing up, beckoned for me to be seated, and then said "Edgarrrr (rolling the r). Tell me the, Edgarrr, the story about Mrs. Postmistress and myself, in both our native languages.

I smiled and did the best I could remember. She laughed and laughed, thanked me for the performance, and showed me the door.

*   *   *

When Wes and Mrs. Wright's daughter Svetlana had been away for about six months, Mrs. Wright had me sent for one day, and this time it was a different situation: She reminded me that I had taught Svet piano, that we all were friends, and that she wanted to ask me a favor. Hearing that I was about to go to New York city for a visit, she asked if I wouldn't call Svet, who lived then in Winnetka, and ask her to lunch, and just remind her of our friendship, and tell her that her mother wanted me to tell her "that she loved her." This I did—and the subject was never mentioned again.

*   *   *

Back before that, Piatagorsky, the cellist, was to play in Madison at the stock Pavillion. (There was no other large hall usable for concerts, and we apprentices went there for concerts.) She told me that she would appreciate my taking Svet to the concert, in all secrecy, before which, Svet would have dinner with her father, who was a friend of the cellist, and wanted to visit with his daughter. So, we went, driving the 40 miles to Madison. Svet and her father went off to dinner alone, later. I met them at the box office, we sat together, and after it was over, I drove Svet and myself back—not a word was brought up, except that it was understood I would tell nobody of the meeting event.

Newspaper Articles

From time to time, we apprentices were asked or told to write pieces for the Madison, Wisconsin papers. They could be topics of local color or wider interest—almost always architectural. In general, the purpose of the articles was to acquaint the public with our objectives and to invite them to our theater at Taliesin on Sunday afternoons to see our films.

A total of 285 columns were written by Wright and various apprentices from 1934 to 1938. Reprinted in this section are a number of my pieces from local papers and one by Wright. For the most part, they are self-explanatory.

PALACE OF THE SOVIETS

On reading of the Russian Palace of the Soviets—the proposed building honoring Lenin—I gathered my writing forces. As I wrote, I could hear echoing in my mind Mr. Wright's denunciation of the International Style, and I really put my heart into this essay. Mr. Wright, on reading it in front of me, made a number of corrections, as he often did, but no changes to the substance of the article. The article is reproduced here in its entirety, together with the first and last pages of my longhand text with Mr. Wright's longhand corrections. The article was printed in the University's Cardinal.

In America, under capitalism, the architect has many enemies. First of all, the client himself—and then down the line, such as: the client's many friends and all his relations, the banker of the mortgage holder, building code laws and other code laws—then all the systems of sabotage—the union. And more often than not, even his draughtsman. Any decent correlation between the architect and his work is almost impossible unless the architect is imbued with the spirit that conquers every obstacle. So most architecture is a series of compromises by way of compromising. The plasterer will only plaster as he has done for generations, the carpenter can't read other than 'stock' plans, the engineer can only calculate as he learned at school—the post and lintel—and the steel manufacturers can comfortably make only certain stock products. With these limitations the organic architect begins his work where the eclectic ends. Cost is a subject in itself never entirely satisfactory to anyone concerned.

From the economic structure of Soviet Russia we would expect a different architectural experience. Supposedly, each 'comrade' subjugates his labours to an ideal common to all, and in the case of building he would always be 'with' the project. Then up the line from ditchdigger to draughtsman there would be the common interest, the glorious realisation of a building that is 'of the people and for the people', if not by the people. This building would grow out of the Russian soil, of course, and be a part of Russian life. It would live and breathe Russia. Why not?

Yet, architecturally, Russia has found herself barren. She employed many European architects to build her housing projects, and imitate others.

'Internationalism' was taking Russia over, until it dawned on the simple mind that his cold structuralism expressed little but corner windows, gas pipe railings, two by two balconies, and cardboard effects. The gas pipe column became a religion. When the Palace of the Soviets was to be built, an international competition was held, to which all and sundry architects were invited to enter. The sundry did enter. The results were judged by a Soviet committee, Stalin at the head, and just which course architecture in Russia was to take nobody seemed to know. Evidently they wanted something like something else—like Hamilton's cold columnar—Beaux-Arts—imitation of an imitation. 'Objective', so called, but really a left over from Roman judicial facades, made over to modern skyscraper ambitions. It was 'modern' in this extent only—the capitals were chopped off the columns. So far so good. Hamilton went to Russia and after continued difficulty left the country with the cry of 'cheatism'. This left an opportunity for B. M. Iofan, the Russian second prize winner, to take Hamilton's place in designing the palace. Iofan started out with a project that resembled telescoped series of wedding cakes, also chopping off columns, to be 'modern', nevertheless all in accordance with Vitruvius, Palladio, or Vignola's diminishing 'orders'. But Russia, too, like her capitalist enemy wants something big, perhaps bigger—why not? That much she has learned from capitalism. So the latest drawings for the sold project show a pile of six wedding cakes with a prosaic statue, Lenin, this at least realistic and outrageously bigger than all the bigness as the guiding light or candle to the cake pile. The structure which will be completed in 1937 will be taller than the Empire State building and probably has more chopped off columns than any two buildings in the world, only to arrive at a completely insignificant effect that fails even of bigness. The conflict in scale between pedestal and figure reduces the whole of impotence. The conflict of orders reduces each part to incompetence. No single competence of form or correlation nor any sensible function can be seen anywhere in this so-called palace. The beholder is left to wonder what goes on inside, if anything.

Russia is afflicted with eclecticism in the pre-natal state. She brings forth not even wholesome eclecticism but a bastard even from the bastard.

Palace of the Soviets.

Frank Lloyd Wright's handwritten corrections to the first and last pages of Edgar Tafel's manuscript for this essay.

building, and probably has more ~~columns~~
chopped off columns than any two
buildings in the world only to arrive at a
completely inconspicuous effect that fails even of bigness.

The conflict in scale between pedestal and figure reduces the whole
~~No single~~ competence of form or co-relation nor any sensible
Russia is afflicted with a more
eclecticism in her pre natal state. which
She brings forth not even wholesome eclecticism
a bastard even from the eclectic standpoint
bastard.

Mar 21 - '34

FRANK LLOYD WRIGHT

Frank Lloyd Wright wrote this article about Edgar Tafel, published April 20, 1934.

JOKE-BOY

We have a joke-boy in the Fellowship. He looks shyly at you with cool, pleasant eyes and goes around a good deal with one—Johannes Brahms.

He—the joke-boy—works like this: Ruth, wife of another "Fellow" is dressing in the privacy of her own apartment—getting ready to go to Madison. The boy discovers this when, wanting to locate Brahms or something, he knocks on her door and is told to go away. Soon another knock. Another boy outside wondering why she sent for him—told emphatically to "go away"—a short interval one more boy, solicitous, "Here I am. What is the matter." Ruth exasperated shouts "go away." At regular intervals come more knocks from more boys, one after the other—until Ruth is frantic.

Finally the grave Maestro Brooks himself stands at the door, solicitous. And knocks. The door opens suddenly and his sensibilities are shocked by a berating from Ruth. His solid worth does not deserve it. He is innocent. He is offended. But others are innocent too. All sent on some pretext by Johanne's little pal.

Alfie is a new boy from Brooklyn, inclined to be faithful. The joke-boy introduces him to several of the Fellows after whispered confidences in his ear concerning each.

First, rather dignified Paul, chief of the fortnight, who is giving orders to the boys for two weeks— "Nice fellow but, too bad—delusions of grandeur—likes to give others. Otherwise alright—just pay no attention to him." Imagine the result of that one.

Next Maestro Brooks—"hard of hearing"—Alfie is advised "to shout loud when you hear him"—Alfie does, and the Maestro thinks him a queer if not an idiotic oaf.

Then Nick—big fellow— "looks strong—but has fits—look out for him." And Nick (previously tipped off) drops to the floor when he meets Alfie in a good enough cataleptic fit to scare a good doctor.

Nick's room is next to Alfie's and Alfie is now urged to keep a pail of water in his room and throw it on Nick should Nick have another fit—Nick unaware of these preparations is urged to knock on Alfie's door and throw a fit. Nick's turn to "get it" this time—etc., etc., etc.

The conductor of the Fellowship is not immune—for he found a heart outlined in soap on the glass of the windshield of his Cord car and inside the heart the names "Frank and Olga." And so it good humoredly goes from A to W.

If there were an X-Y-Z our practical joker would go there too—the limit.

Some say he always was like that. Several cures have, more or less cruelly, been proposed. But it seems so much a part of him, so inalienable to his charm of person and manner, that—like Cupid—who wold have him otherwise? So we have decided to leave it all to Johannes Brahms, himself.

FRANK LLOYD WRIGHT

Edgar Tafel, the Joke-Boy, at Taliesin.

WISCONSIN HOME NEWS

APRIL 26, 1934

The Reverend Francis Bloodgood of Madison visited our chapel last Sunday to talk to us. The Episcopalian's text was "The Spirit of God." The young vicar was an impressive figure in his black and white robes and we all liked him immensely. The service was augmented with some of our own music. The Fellowship sang its work song: a Bach Chorale—myself at the piano, Charles Edman leading. Ernest Brooks came alive and surprised everybody by playing—beautifully—a Bach organ prelude and fugue as a voluntary. There is an almost endless amount of fine church music that is available for the more stereotyped and solemn service, even from the few masters such as Handel, Bach, and Palestrino. But we have been trying to have a more varied musical program suited to the spirit of the Chapel gatherings.

We would like to talk about spring, but somehow we seem to get on ice when we do. Spring doesn't care to get around to us here although there is a little green. Billy Bernoudy slips "shorts" on every time the sun threatens to appear, but gets snow on his knees and is now mothering a cold. The other evidences of warm weather are Phil Holliday's onion planting and Jack Howe's seeding and our Gardener moving in. A farmer on the way. Jack has a new baby—a key to the new tool room. He spends half the day losing the child and the other half finding it.

Our old friend of last summer, E. A. Schneider, and his little family are back this year to help manage the truck garden, and Yen Liang is fortright boss. From his padded tractor seat he dictates the destiny of all details the next two weeks. How is sleeping on the tractor, Yen? Yen's chief worry is about his four stellar workers who are away for the time being—Beye Fyfe, Hank Schubert, and Fredandrouge.

The Playhouse program for Sunday is as follows: to wit—"Pandora's Box," a Pabst German film; "old King Cole," a silly symphony, and short subjects. If spring actually comes by Sunday we will serve iced tea, otherwise hot coffee and cake by the fireside are still holding out.

EDGAR TAFEL

Owing to its chief servant being bed ridden, the Fellowship's usual Taliesin Sunday supper hour at home was forgone in order that the members of the Taliesin Fellowship might have a coveted quiet evening each to himself. Or herself.

Whereupon, having attended the Fellowship free cinema entertainment in the afternoon, all but several produced quarters from somewhere, begged rides, and impetuously rode on to the nearby village to the movies.

N. B. The maestro went along too—blowing in the quarter he had been saving against a new pair of pants. Or should have been.

Q. E. D. You may culture the bushman, you may build him at will—

But the scent of the bush (ergo the city) is on him still.

WISCONSIN HOME NEWS

MAY 10, 1934

Some of our most interesting Sunday chapel services have been when our visiting preachers have been omitted. This past Sunday the service was taken over by four of the apprentices, each giving about ten minutes to some phase of life that he felt applied to our work here, from the more spiritual aspect. The meeting was opened with a Bach organ prelude played by Ernest Brooks, and followed by our Fellowship song, everyone singing as if it were the first day of spring. John Lautner was the first to speak, and in John's inimitable way he told of life as simple living by way of the co-operation of intuition and intellect. John was sure of his ground, impressing us all, so that now while he is "Boss," we can argue back on the intuitive basis, as well as the intellectual.

Gene Masselink read some of Robert Frost's poems, and I'm certain that Gene likes Frosting. The Frosting was beautifully done, with clear, clean expression. An intermission with more organ music by the Brooks was followed by Fred Langhorst in a reading of Edward Arlington Robinson, another American poet, of a different school. Robinson is the logician, the intellect, using strong complicated forms to get his point over. Then Karl Jensen read from Nietsche, "Thus spake Zarathustra," the more Germanic fundamental material that has no need to step down to poetry but employs its own form to drive the thought home. To be just a poet is like being just anything. That a man can spend his life writing little impressions or thoughts in a pattern of words is too much like a man sewing cross-stitching on some muslin all his life. There are too many real things to live without reverting to living on fluff. Even French pastry is no diet for a man.

It looks as if we've missed spring this year and jumped blindly from winter into summer. The boys are preparing a tom-tom dance to some God on rain—there must be one, or we would have rain. We are drying up on the hill as the neighbors are in the valleys. If any of our neighbors would like to put on horse feathers or some-

Frank Lloyd Wright with former apprentice Frederick Langhorst visiting Taliesin West in 1938.

thing and join the party in this wild dance we'll be happy to have them. We'll dance around a telephone pole with telephone wires for music somewhere along the road. A quick drying strawberry patch is one of the motives. The two chiefs of the rain dance squad are Paul and Yen, they went to town Saturday and had their heads shaved for the purpose. Now they are preparing the prayers for the crops. Yen looks like Mahatma Ghandi (*sic*), and Paul looks like "hell." Here's to a head of hair.

Catherine the Great, the great production by the English director, Alexander Korda, will be shown at the Taliesin Playhouse next Sunday. With this feature will be the usual Mickie Mouse and other short subjects.

WISCONSIN HOME NEWS

MAY 31, 1934

Philosophy is fun. We, as men using facts of nature as we see fit for our purposes, create systems of philosophy, schools of philosophy, trends of philosophy, and even after it all, a cynical denial of its real use. We fight, quibble, teach it, and most often are quite serious about which school of philosophy we and our friends belong to, or, which is just as bad, we take a slight smattering of what we comprehend from a college course of the latest book of "condensed philosophy." And last Sunday at Taliesin there were evidences that most of us weren't quite sure which philosophical trail we belonged on. Dr. Eliseo Vivas of the University of Wisconsin spoke to us in chapel, giving the general outline of philosophical thought, in such a manner as to inspire us to do some of our own thinking. Therefore his talk was a success. When one can find his own solution to the problem of life that he has set up—then and only then will he achieve mental poise and spiritual repose. We are too often making our questions about the meaning of life so remote from our natural living that there is no answer. But my humble self sees that most truly creative beings aren't particularly worried about cynicism, platonism, humanism, and all the other "isms." The creative person lives in creating. The average philosopher lives in talking about living.

Our picture "Nana" was well attended on Sunday, and its theme song was memorized by Jack Howe, and immortalized. Any visitor to Taliesin should be well prepared to hear the groaning "Kiss me and say goodbye," from any corner window or peony bush. We often wonder if Jack isn't a paroled crooner. Of course we are used to Jack's singing and for publication let's say we love it. But last Sunday three charming young ladies of the Kappa Kappa Gamma Sorority, completely bewildered and crying to Gene for help—they thought the "Kiss me—" song was the last of the "Thundering Herd." Gene sings too. Lovely songs, from Brahms to Vincent Youmens, by way of Grand Rapids. Gene is the fortnightly boss now, and heads the rock breaking squad with more voice than Paul Robeson. Gene receives two letters daily from Madison (news item). We are all jealous.

Mr. Wright and Bud Shaw drove up to Minneapolis where Mr. Wright made further arrangements for the Willey house in the midst of the murder strike taking place in the streets there.

Hank Schubert is back with us, but on crutches for the time being. One for each leg. He thinks that two weeks of rest will find his legs mates once more. Good pals—those legs.

Mrs. Robert Gilham, Mr. Wright's niece, Rosey Posey of New York—child Nikie and nurse have come to Taliesin to spend the summer. Good boy, Nikie.

Our brief series of Hollywood films have come to an end. This week, we are looking forward to seeing a group of very modern experimental films. *The Fall of the House of Usher,* by Dr. Watson; *The Coffin Maker,* by Robert Florey, and *L'Etoile De Mer,* by Man Ray. We are expecting to see a complete departure in film technique that should be refreshing after so much too much Hollywood. With this program will be added some music of our own.

THE JOKE BOY.

AT TALIESIN

DECEMBER 1, 1934

NEW YORK—In this country we generally won't recognize a new form in art until it has been branded by some institution that has a good sounding name. Too often this "new form" has long been dead by the time it gains public view, or else this institution has killed what spark of life the new form may have had. For example: the Museum of Modern Art in New York city, with its architectural department seemingly promoted by Philip Johnson and H. R. Hitchcock Jr., has gained recognition rapidly, through giving the public parlor talk, through some aesthetic whimsy or other in the way of a show, whether it be painting, architecture, or stream-lined mechanics. And now, with the parlor talk growing thin on Picasso and Chirico, the museum turns to "Housing."

* * *

RECALLS SHOW

MOST of us remember the architectural show the museum spon-sored some three years ago. It was a good show, good because, while it cloaked a number of tyros, most of the work exhibited was by a certain high standard of architects. The museum did not need to do anything but cart the drawings, models, and photographs about the country in order to get an audience for the new architec-ture. Fortunately the architecture exhibited was strong enough in purpose to talk for itself, and whether or not the show needed exploitation, it was a good show—rather, most of the work in it was sincere.

The museum now riding on its laurels, thinks the need of housing can be crystallized by a housing show. The exhibit is super-ficially interesting, containing charts, maps, models, photographs, full size rooms, projects, etc. Work from all over the world has been exhibited in such a manner as to startle the visitor. Three floors of it, neatly arranged, with a typical tenement apartment or "Dumbbell" flat thrown in for good measure. Even Macy's has two rooms of modernized furniture to show the low cost of fitting the modernized home. The modernized museum has forgotten nothing "modern" except the purpose of the exhibit.

* * *

ALL of the information at this exhibit is of course easily accessible through already existing channels, to anyone really interested in housing. The government has generously spent sums providing this technical information. What we now need is some direction, or some course of action, to fulfill the need of decent living conditions for the family; not a mere subsistence. Being merely non-committal in this direction, we cannot but feel that the museum is just putting on a type of show that doesn't hurt anybody's feelings. It is so "objective" that it evidently wants nothing said. Nor has it anything to say upon the question involved.

There is only one constructive way toward a genuinely new housing. The people must be shown clearly, concretely with some idea of correlated life, what their own housing conditions could be. We do not want to replace the frowsy old, hand-made slum with another machine-made slum, even if it is more antiseptic. The root of the matter where the people are concerned is not yet reached, by such as this one.—*Edgar A. Tafel.*

* * *

THE PLAYHOUSE

AT the Playhouse this Sunday at 3 p.m. we are showing a new German film entitled, "Nur Am Rhein," or "Only on the Rhine." Remembering "Merry Wives of Vienna," "Congress Dances" and "Liebes Commando," we look forward to another German film with promise of quality. The story is based upon the British occupation of the river Rhine, just after the war.

NEWS NOTES FROM
TALIESIN AT HILLSIDE

DECEMBER 13, 1934

The Taliesin Fellowship spent the larger part of Monday and the very early hours of Tuesday morning traveling through southern Wisconsin and local Iowa in three different groups. The Lautners left early Monday, in search of fine materials for fine clothes, taking in the Baraboo and Reedsburg knitting mills, and returned to Mrs. Nachreiner with fascinating fabrics for fine feathered fashions. Most of the Fellowship was jealous of the conquest so our fine feathered friend and traveler, Cornelia Brierly of Pittsburgh assembled a multitude of twelve fellows to ride out to Dubuque to hear Mr. Wright lecture a congregation of art-clubbers. The crisp farenheit of five didn't faze our frozen fellows and they drove off in the open truck with a loud song and enough ply-wood slabs to keep themselves on the cool side of things. The reports of the lecture are invigorating, as Mr. Wright delivered an inspiring talk to the Iowans. The ride back from Dubuque was cold and it was nearly dawn when the group returned to hot coffee and cold radiators. Three of us went into Madison to hear the Jane Dudley quartet give its first concert in a series of four, at the Delta Gamma house. Not having heard the quartet since its infancy two years ago, the three of us marveled at its technical improvement. The program at times had "tempo trouble," letting a fast movement run away with itself to the point of wonder as to which instrument would get to the end first. Fortunately it was a draw as all came in together. However Jane Dudley has a fine group and music lovers shouldn't miss her concerts. She has promised to give us another concert at the Playhouse this season.

William Bernoudy led chapel services last Sunday and preached on the difficult topic "Purpose." The service was well arranged and Bill quoted from Emerson and Thoreau to substantiate his own views. Next Sunday John Lautner will officiate on the topic of "Energy."

EDGAR TAFEL

The Taliesin Playhouse, now in the midst of the snow covered fields and hills of the country, continues throughout the winter as an automobile objective for Wisconsin people. Each Sunday it presents as usual at three in the afternoon the most excellent films from abroad, occasionally from America, a cup of hot coffee by the roaring fireplace, a home-made cookie or two, and informal discussion and talk afterward. This coming Sunday we are showing for the first time a picture from Italy, "Terra Madre" or "Mother Earth." The film has been rated "five stars" high wherever it has been shown to discriminating audiences.

AT TALIESIN

MAY 25, 1934

WE HAVE borrowed, begged or stolen our traditional culture from Europe almost mercilessly for 200 years. If we had taken it as a spirit, or copied exactly, there would have been some justification. But no. Thomas Jefferson started us off architecturally by dressing us up with 17th century ruffles, our few painters ran to France to live their surface art, yet in music we didn't know which way to turn.

NEED MUSIC

EVIDENTLY the American needs music, needs it badly, but doesn't have the sufficient background to understand its original source. Maybe music is not just a facade, it has many dimensions, and to enjoy it is to "feel" it. To "feel" it is to know every side of it.

We have grown accustomed to Sousa's marches and to the jazz, both of which have their place in our lives. But we need whole wheat bread and beef in our homes, and similarly need a basis of music that is closer to us. The symphony orchestra is still difficult for us to comprehend, and financially prohibitive to have at hand. There is still a better field of music that could be on hand—chamber music.

STATE IS LEADER

Wisconsin has been leading the little theater movements quite well in the past few years. Small groups get together and do creative work which apparently is more entertaining than the Sunday comic strip or a common movie. Wisconsin could foster small musical groups in the same manner. Travelling small orchestras can arouse social interest as done in foreign countries for centuries.

In Cuba Alejandro Caturla with a small orchestra tours his country playing Debussy, Stravinsky, Cowell and other moderns in towns of 200 inhabitants and less. He writes his own transcriptions to fit the needs of the individual orchestra, and plays native compositions in the native settings. We have plenty of pianists and violinists and the schools teach many other instruments.

*   *   *

TRIOS, quartets and quintets could be plentiful in all our small towns. This could be a feature of recreational life. Teaching children the "bandstand music" has the grim aspect of ROTC and war's beating drums. Our band music in most cases has been so sickly that a trained ear becomes nauseated at the thought of listening to a program that beats aimlessly and endlessly. Our schools teach this sort of music year in and year out, and upon graduation the students lose the little amount of interest his teacher has pumped into him to "make a show" for his alma mater.

*   *   *

PROGRAM

I CANNOT imagine anything more invigorating for a Sunday afternoon than sitting in a shaded grove with a picnic lunch and a cold glass of fresh beer, a quartet by Bach man! Then later, compositions of our or Ravel, a trio of Mozart or Townsown, written by native composers of each village. Each person could contribute to the communal life with music or appreciation of it in some way that would make the small town Sunday be a worthwhile experience. Each town could have its "musical grove" for the summer, well shaded from the sun's beat, and far enough from the center of town to make a pleasant drive. Neighboring villages would exchange programs.

*   *   *

At Taliesin we are welcoming groups of musicians to play for and with us. Music is a genial part of our life and we want to extend this in the near future to people in the vicinity. Taliesin is in an ideal situation to create for us all a center of music that is just as much a part of ourselves and our landscape as our buildings.

EDGAR A. TAFEL

EVENTS IN BRIEF

L<small>AST</small> Sunday at Unity chapel Joaquin Ortega, professor of romance languages at the University of Wisconsin, was the speaker. His topic was "The So-called Generations." A generation according to Mr. Ortega is a division of humanity according to age, a new generation coming to the fore every twenty-five years. It is generally conceded that except for precocious youth and sprightly maturity, most of the creative stimulus and formulated ideas of the day are the product of the generation between the ages of twenty-five and fifty.

This guiding generation, said Mr. Ortega, is one that makes history for its time and upon it depends the direction of a people. Each new generation is different, being always a reaction in some degree to the generation immediately preceding it. The present generation, the speaker believes, is one ahead of its time. That is it is one which is dealing with problems so new and so vital that it cannot realize the ultimate character of its actions.

At the Playhouse this Sunday we are showing the popular American film, Nana—with Anna Sten as the star. Our policy of charging 50 cents a head for conducted tours through Taliesin and the new Fellowship buildings will continue through the summer.

WISCONSIN HOME NEWS

JULY 4, 1935

At last we are happy to announce the arrival of a trio at Taliesin: Anton Rovinsky, pianist; Edgar Neukrug, violinist; Youry Bilstin, cellist—all of New York City. Mr. Rovinsky, well known as soloist in orchestras in many large cities, will take charge of our musical activities during the summer. He is bringing some ancient instruments such as the spinet and gamba d'amour, which will be used at our programs at the Playhouse each Sunday.

The Broadacre City model is now set up in Washington's best exhibit hall, the Corcoran Galleries. Mr. Wright and Blaine Drake drove to Pittsburgh, picked the model up there after its visit had been extended from one to two weeks and took it to Washington. Cornelia will be in charge of the model in Washington for the next ten days.

Harold Wescott of Milwaukee, a painter and teacher at the State Teacher's College, has joined the Fellowship for the summer. Jim Thompson has returned from his home in Farmington, Connecticut, after visiting there and attending his sister's wedding. Jim has the rare distinction of driving his car from Arizona to Connecticut without any license plates. He says he had trouble only once, in Pueblo, when the entire city's policy and detective force swooped down on him with guns and demanded to know if he were Public Enemy No. One, the noted Karpis. After extended questioning and long distance telephoning, the police department decided that Jim wasn't much of an outlaw, anyway, and let him go. But on his way out Jim picked up the chief-of-police's gloves instead of his own, and again the harsh words of Pueblo's law were on our Jim.

Fortunately, Taliesin is in an ever state of change. Walls are being extended and new floors are being laid to accommodate our musical friends. We are trying out the new concrete mixer which marks a new day in our building activities.

Last Sunday we returned again to the chapel in the valley. Uncle Enos, Richard and Mary Lloyd Jones, Mr. and Mrs. Porter and Charlie Curtis were our special guests. Don Thompson took charge of the service and delivered a pertinent talk on "Relaxation." Don's conception of relaxation may be condensed into three words: "change of work." To relax from one labor, try another and another. If tired, if the body is drained of its resources, then rest—stretch out and relax completely. Sleep if necessary. But never sit, just for the sake of sitting.

News from Bar Harbor Maine, tells of Marybud and her chow dog flying in a big transport plane along the coast: "Chub-chub" is now big enough to fly alone but his master won't let him.

Excellent entertainment at the Playhouse next Sunday, June 7th. A French comedy, "Prènez Garde à la Peinture," which has been a very great success in the east will be shown. It makes full use of the latent possibilities of the screen and more than justifies its right to be seen on the screen. With this feature will be shown a charming French travelogue: "Cotes Normandie."

EDGAR TAFEL

WISCONSIN HOME NEWS

JULY 25, 1935
TALIESIN WRITES OF WEEK END TRIP

On Thursday last, each apprentice took a bath, shaved and rushed around Taliesin as if his head were cut off, and tried to find the place scheduled for himself in an automobile. The Fellowship was going to Janesville to visit with Mr. and Mrs. George S. Parker. The trip was also the christening of the new station wagon. The day was hot, and for the first time in its life the Fellowship was out en-mass on a new type of activity. It was being entertained. Instead of receiving week-enders it was itself a week-ender. Upon arriving in Janesville, Mr. Parker had a grand dinner spread over the lawn of his country home—Stonehenge, and we divided our time between eating and feeding the Parker's pet monkey, Benito. We made our home at a new camp of Mr. Parker's, about a half mile from Stone-henge. It was a new type of vacation (any "vacation" is new for us except the one we are in every day in nearly every way but this new way). Bunched together in "Camp Cherrio," with our activities reduced to reading magazines seated in soft lounge chairs, the Fellowship grumbled and quarreled. This being together, indulging in several hours of non-activity was a new one on us.

However, I guess it was fun—observing ourselves and others whiling away time reading magazines and sitting—just as we might be in a score of years from now, and then instead of quarreling with the fellows it'll be with our wives—maybe.

The next morning after breakfast we were shown through the Parker Pen Company's factory. We followed the operations of the manufacture of the pen through its five thousand stages. The Ford assembly line idea is used in assembling the pen. They start the bar-rel moving along the assembly line, and each worker adds a part, fitting and polishing all the while, until the pen reaches its final glory labeled, recorded, tested, packed:—it's all done but the selling. Even the selling is accounted for in the recording office, where each retailer has a card, duly punched and kept on file, telling of the quantity and types of pens in his stock. If one found a pen and wanted to trace its owner, it could easily be done by sending the pen number to the factory. Within a half hour the dealer who sold the pen could be sifted from any one of the many dealers, there being thousands spread through sixty-eight countries. The peculiar part of the merchandising of the Parker pen is that half of them are exported. We then went back to dinner and, ready to go home, fizzed out trying to sing our chorale without an accompaniment. We hope the Parkers had a good time, but we don't know.

Don and Mary Thompson left for Washington on the large truck to pick up the Broadacre City models and Cornelia Brierly. Cornelia has been away over a month, in charge of the models in Pittsburgh and Washington. Soon after the return of the models we will set them up at Hillside for exhibition before it goes on tour again. It is estimated that over 125,000 people have seen Broadacres so far, while it has been shown in three major cities, not to mention our own minor Madison. The reaction is almost unlimited in its diversity. Broadacres has been called every name, and classified under every theory of government. Yet, its principle is quite simple—both in words and in model form.

Among our visitors very soon we expect Karl Jensen, Mr. Wright's former secretary. Karl is working for the government in land re-habilitation surveys, and is being sent to various parts of the country to study and tabulate conditions.

Youry Bilstin, Russian and a musical genius distinguished in European concert circles, a true master of the cello and Viol de Gamba, will play with the ensemble for the first time on the Playhouse program next Sunday, July 28th. The three artists, Rovinsky, Bilstin, and Neukrug are working almost constantly on a group of programs of rare music by the great masters. They are making wonderful music afternoons for the public beginning sharp at three o'clock Sunday afternoons.

At three forty-five entertainment a la mode begins. "Escape Me Never," the English film, starring Elizabeth Bergner, will be shown following the recess after the music program. Elizabeth Bergner is one of the greatest of actresses, we said when we saw her in "Catherine the Great." We are looking forward now with high anticipation to seeing her next Sunday in this, her latest film.

EDGAR A. TAFEL

The Aftermath

WRIGHT'S LAST BIRTHDAY

Mr. Wright passed away on April 9, 1959 in Arizona. Soon thereafter, many former apprentices came from all over the country to attend his funeral at Taliesin in Spring Green. The body lay in state in the living room next to his beloved Bechstein piano. The casket was then laid on a horse-drawn hearse, and the large funeral procession followed the carriage across the valley. After a brief Unitarian service, Mr. Wright's body was put to rest in the family graveyard.

Our feelings and thoughts were kept to ourselves as he was laid to rest near the family chapel. He told us often about working on his first Chicago job for the same architect who had designed the chapel and the early buildings for the family-run Hillside Home School. As apprentices we had attended services in the chapel and had sung in the chorus, accompanied by the foot-pumped organ. Mr. Wright had often remarked—with a twinkle—that as a boy he pumped that organ, and that he belonged to only one organization—the Organ Pumper's Guild.

Mr. Wright's birthday, June 8, was always an important occasion for the Fellowship and after his death in 1959 Mrs. Wright decided to continue the tradition. A gathering was held at Taliesin the first birthday after Mr. Wright's demise. Many of the apprentices were invited, along with members of the "first family," his sister, and several public figures such as Adlai Stevenson and Marc Connelly. We all visited together at breakfast, luncheon, and a more formal dinner in the large drafting room at Hillside, which we "first-generation" apprentices had helped build.

On the following day I went into the main house to bid Mrs. Wright farewell and to express gratitude for having been included in the gathering. She asked me to stay a moment as she wished to discuss something that she had been thinking over—namely, the future of the Fellowship. She said she had already talked with Wes Peters and Gene Masselink at length, and they all agreed that there should be a board of directors composed of friends, such as the editor of the *Madison Capital Times*, their local lawyer, and Mr. Wright's good friend, architect Edward Stone. They wondered whether I would consider serving on the board as the representative of former apprentices. After all, Mrs. Wright reasoned, I was practicing in New York City, my work had been well-published, and I could fill a position that would round out the board membership. I thought the offer interesting and asked what exactly my role would be. She answered by suggesting that I stay another day or two, talk with Wes and Gene, meet new apprentices, see the work in the studio, and then talk with her some more.

Over the next two days I met and talked with the apprentices who had joined the Fellowship quite recently and renewed friendships with those I had known before. I had been back to Taliesin several times before, both at Taliesin West and in Wisconsin, and had kept in touch with Mr. Wright. He used to telephone when he was in New York, needing blueprints, or in the case of the Guggenheim, a contractor.

When I spoke with Mrs. Wright again after the first postponement of my departure, I still had questions and some reservations. She told me to take my time and said that it was nice to have me back. She asked if I had met some other people, and before coming up with any firm thoughts on the nature of the Fellowship, she said stay a couple more days, which I did.

After about four days had elapsed since our first talk, Mrs. Wright and I had our last one. . . . I had conceived of the Fellowship as serving as the umbrella for an international association of "organic" architects, with Taliesin as the "home base." I laid out a total program. It would take several years before this new Fellowship would complete any new work, so in the meantime there could be a concerted effort to "woo" a press and keep them informed for later publications. There could be stories about former foreign apprentices, and since they were scattered about the world—India, Egypt, Germany, Hawaii, Iran, Spain, South America, New York, San Francisco, New Orleans, St. Louis, etc.—we could initiate work from all over. Further, I told her we could engage a public relations firm for overall publicity, establish scholarships, and approach foundations and various funds for preservation of many types of Wright's works and Taliesin itself. There could be apprentice recruitment programs and work programs in our various offices. I outlined the possibility of obtaining Federal work—with offices everywhere and four senators from Arizona and Wisconsin as their friends—the future of an Organic Architecture was bright. We could service an American Architecture for America!

Finally we agreed that I would draw up a proposal of the concept and come back with it at a later date for further consideration. I would be both a board member and part of the major practice until things settled down to some form of continuing organization. We had a warm parting; I was kissed on the cheek, and I went off to New York City.

Once home, I was consumed with this great concept, thinking it would have so many important ramifications. After all, Mr. Wright was gone and the Fellowship would have to restructure its administration. My wife listened quietly and patiently to my many thoughts and schemes.

About two days passed, and then came a call from Mrs. Wright. She said "they" had talked it over and it was agreed at Taliesin (whatever that meant) that they would continue their work as they had done in the past, remaining unattached to any outside forces. My wife's response was "Thank God. You can continue your own life." And two days following, a letter came from Mrs. Wright.

Looking back now, I can appreciate that Mrs. Wright had inherited many problems. For one, Wright had created a disorganized financial situation that would take time to sort out. Soon after Wright passed away, a local county judge made a ruling that Taliesin did not qualify as a not-for-profit institution. The buildings for farm were put on tax rolls. This decision signaled the IRS to make its investigation, and their ruling was similar. They assessed a penalty for back taxes of some $700 thousand on the organization, payable at $35,000 per year, for 20 years. This assessment fell to the Fellowship to satisfy. It was a terrible burden, and possibly the initial Wisconsin decision accounted for the hatred Mrs. Wright felt for the state until her death.

After Wright's death, the Fellowship had several important projects to complete, such as the Grady Gammage Memorial Auditorium in Tempe, Arizona, and the Marin County Center in San Rafael, California. Wes Peters directed the construction documents—both projects came in under the allowed budget, and then went into construction. There were also many houses to complete during this period. Later, they encountered some large rejects, including an office building in Louisville, Kentucky and a performing arts building in Sarasota, Florida. Mrs. Wright chose the exterior

June 15, 1959

Dear Edgar,

I felt sad after talking to you on the telephone. I had
a serious discussion with Wes and Gene concerning your
business proposal. We are happy to have you as our friend,
but we think it unwise at this time to consider your association in business with us. However, we want to assure you
of our friendship in view of your having been an apprentice
18 years ago. In the following 18 years of your complete
separation from us, much has taken place in the progress
of the members of the Taliesin Fellowship spiritually,
intellectually and business-wise. Because during these
years you did not participate in the conditions of our work,
we found difficulty in fusing our ideas with yours in regard
to business connections and projects. A unanimous decision
was reached that we return to our friendly relationship
of reminiscences of our mutual past experiences. We would
like you not to undertake any kind of activity in regard to
the Frank Lloyd Wright Foundation such as publicity and
advertisement of any nature. We, the Frank Lloyd Wright
Foundation, will follow the wishes of Mr. Wright as he
stated them in his will.

It will be nice to see you again, and I hope that the next
time you will bring Lucille.

With affection to you both,

TALIESIN

Mrs. Wright's letter to Edgar Tafel.

colors for the latter building, which is known in Sarasota as "The
Purple Cow." Never before had she had input into design; she had
never been involved with the work in the drafting rooms. It was an
ominous development.

Olgivanna Wright came from a privileged background. She
was born in Bosnia, brought up in an upper-middle-class family, and
sent to Moscow for finishing school. She went then to Fontainebleau with the Gurdjieff school called the Institute for the Har-

monious Development of Man. She was involved there with programs in writing, drawing, and gardening. She married another student, they had a child (Svetlana), and in the early 1920s she went to Chicago for a divorce. During this time she met Wright and followed him to Taliesin. They had a child before a divorce could be obtained from his second wife, Miriam Noel; the attendant "scandalous" circumstances were overly documented in the press.

Photo of Olgivanna Lloyd Wright, given to author in 1976 by Mrs. Wright. Photo taken in 1949.

From below.

Courtyard.

Entry: covered area.

Drafting Room.

Workman.

Drafting Room.

Postcards of Taliesin, Spring Green, Wisconsin taken circa 1920, around the time Olgivanna arrived.

They left Taliesin for short periods, but eventually settled down there. By the late 1920s his practice had expanded, but the stock market crash of 1929 killed most works in progress. Then he wrote his autobiography with Olgivanna's help, and the book was published in 1932. Together they conceived the idea of the Fellowship, which was started in the fall of 1932.

The arrival of about thirty apprentices caused many problems of housing, feeding, and programs in general. It was run by trial and error, and amended constantly. In many ways Mrs. Wright was a queen at Taliesin, and her Ottoman background had prepared her for her regal standing. She certainly was not the usual American housewife. Mrs. Wright engaged in manipulating personalities, intrigue, and behind-the-scenes instigation. She selected a chosen few for her followers, and they made up her entourage. Mrs. Wright and I remained friends, and I later visited Taliesin occasionally, maintaining my friendship with her and many apprentices.

My practice had always remained independent from the Fellowship. But in 1974, two projects came to my attention that could involve the Fellowship, thus bringing us together. The first was an auditorium in London at St. Catherine's docks—I met the owners there, and proposed the Taliesin architects (and the Frank Lloyd Wright imprimatur). Wes Peters subsequently made a stop there and made a great impression. Soon Wes and I visited the clients together. We drew up an agreement, but with the impending recession, nothing was done and the project died. A similar situation arose with a performing arts center in Atlantic City. I made the arrangements and introductions. Wes and I made two trips to the city and we "got the job." The schematics were drawn, but eventually the project fell through. Although Mrs. Wright had rejected a "business association" between Taliesin and me, I presented opportunities to the Fellowship in pursuit of an Organic Architecture that might benefit all of us. Perhaps she would not reject a worthy program, I reasoned, and so far she had not.

My first book, *Apprentice to Genius*, appeared in 1979, and Mrs. Wright wrote a charming letter thanking me for its existence. Soon after, however, her attorney demanded from the publisher $10,000 for alleged infringements of copyrights. The suit was settled a year later for $400. A direct word was never spoken from her to me about it.

ALWAYS WANTING TO HELP

I was always wanting to help. Through a family connection I was involved with the Hammer Galleries, and I often discussed with representatives of the galleries some kind of exhibit of the Wright drawings. At one point Victor Hammer, who headed the galleries, examined with me the possibilities of exhibits. He and I developed what we thought would be an excellent proposal to present to the Fellowship. I then went to Arizona to talk to Mrs. Wright about it. I followed the usual procedure: I asked the person-in-waiting for an appointment, it was set, and I went to her living room. We went through greetings and general catching up on topics.

Then I told of the program that could be. The Hammer Galleries would arrange for exhibitions of drawings in Iran and then Moscow, ending at their gallery on 57th Street in New York. A companion book would be published. The Hammers and their Moscow connections would open doors for possible architectural work in the then Soviet Union. At this point Mrs. Wright called someone and directed that a meeting be held with the Fellowship board in the private dining room. Within ten minutes, there we were— Mrs. Wright and myself, along with about a half dozen of the senior Fellowship people.

Mrs. Wright asked me to reiterate my proposal, which I did, adding that Occidental Petroleum (which was associated with the galleries through Armand Hammer, who was president and head of Occidental), was also a heavy owner in Ramada hotels outside of the United States and that, too, might be an avenue through which work could be established. At that moment, Mrs. Wright exclaimed in her pure Bosnian accent, "Rahmaaadah, Rahmaadah, low clahss, low clahss. John [one of the board members], what do you think of it?" He agreed with her. One after another she asked the same question and got the same response. Turning to me she said, "See, Edgar, we agree, and so would have no association with this program." She rose, the others followed, and that was the end of that. My dreams of a worldwide practice for the Fellowship and of Olgivanna being in Russia with the Hammer group all faded immediately.

DEJA VU

It is 1972. I have returned from Spain, having visited Bob Mosher in Marbella, and I am at Taliesin West. Saturday night dress is formal. As a guest I am seated at Mrs. Wright's round table, which seats about a dozen. During dinner, one of the apprentices asks me, when there is a lull in the conversation, what was it like visiting Bob—what was he doing, and so on. Everyone looked up and I explained that Bob was very busy designing houses for important people from around the world. I related that I had gone with Bob to a site that was to have a Mosher house. Bob met the contractor there, who asked where to start the house. Bob picked up a stone, threw it to a place 20 feet away and said "there." I related another story from my visit with Bob: We drove to a wonderful location overlooking what Bob called "Mere Nostrom," and he took me through a framed-up house, describing all the elements, and we proceeded inside. It seemed to me that the entrance was in the wrong place, the kitchen too far and small, the master bedroom not large enough, the interior bridge spindly, etc., etc. I kept asking Bob how this could be. Didn't he check anything? Then I said, "Bob, who's the crazy client who would let you build this monstrosity?" Bob swung his arm around, pointing to himself, and said "I'm the client."

We all laughed at this story and the dinner conversation continued.

The next morning, someone found me and said that Mrs. Wright wanted to see me in the living room. Gads, I thought, just like some 35 years ago. When I entered the room, she suggested I sit down, and proceeded to tell me that when I am in company at Taliesin, I should not raise my voice and should not talk so much. Then she changed the subject. Yes, it was like the good old Fellowship days. Nothing changed.

REUNIONS

At Taliesin West in the early 1980s, during a visit with Mrs. Wright in her living room, we shared pleasantries, during which she brought up a subject that she thought should be considered. Several of the apprentices had suggested a reunion of former apprentices, which had been discussed several times at length.

Her feelings, she said, were that it would require much planning, work, and costly time and effort. She asked me what I thought about it. I told her it could be done easily if they engaged the services of travel and catering firms. These details could be handled by the firms, which would make all the arrangements—it would cost them nothing. I added that I was sure apprentices from all over the world would be delighted to come.

Then, firmly, she stated, "Edgar, the problem with the whole idea for me is that too many would come who I dislike and don't want to see."

Several years after she passed away, a reunion was held—a great success.

Letter to Byron Mosher
from Edgar Tafel

This is a letter the author wrote to Bob Mosher, who was in Spain, on March 5, 1985, after Mrs. Wright's funeral.

Dear Bob,

Wes Peters called me last Friday noon saying that Mrs. Wright had passed away in the Scottsdale hospital, early in the morning about 3 a.m. There was to be a viewing of the body in the living room, followed by a service at 4 p.m. on Saturday, and would I come as a guest of the Fellowship.

Last November I visited Taliesin West and stayed for dinner and when Mrs. Wright appeared for a few moments, it was evident that she was in sad condition—couldn't hear much and could hardly see. We were introduced and though I talked loudly, it was apparent that she didn't hear. Taliesin undoubtedly was making plans for the inevitable, and only a short time ago Wes was given the title of president of the organization.

On the plane ride out I thought back to the many days at Taliesin—not so much at West but about being in Racine during the building of the desert camp. And about a visit a few years ago, after a bout of Mrs. Wright's fury, she kissed me goodbye and said, "Edgar, remember, I am the only mother you have." That reminded me of how many times she or Mr. Wright would say at a Sunday evening, "Edgar, play Bach's *Jesu, Joy of Man's Desiring*." She will never ask again.

Driving from the airport brought back many memories, and my eyes teared all along the way; I remembered along Scottsdale road our "moonlighting-drafting" for the Pauson house contractor who offered us, as payment for some lousy plans, $25 or an acre of his land. We were realistic for that time, and took the money for beer. Scottsdale, now a metropolis, was then an intrusion into or back from Phoenix.

I arrived at about 2 p.m.—there were many cars parked and the sign at the entrance said "closed today"; there was a guard person stationed and if you looked official she let you pass. Many of the guests had already arrived, there was action in the kitchen, and I was led to the loggia between the Wright's quarters and the dining area. The body would be on view until the four o'clock service.

The living room was full of flowers and chairs; the casket was set at a 60 degree angle from the fireplace, the upper half open and draped in Cherokee red velour. Mrs. Wright looked asleep—I had never seen her asleep before. Remember, we had often seen Mr. Wright asleep when taking a nap in the drafting room studios—he could nap for ten minutes and come back refreshed. Here, several apprentices stayed in the room—some wore sun glasses to hide their tears. Somehow, I felt I shouldn't leave. Perhaps it was a dream, I would awaken in New York City and just add the dream to all the others about Mr. and Mrs. Wright.

At four o'clock we all filed into the living room, apprentices bringing more chairs. The apprentice/chorus took their places behind the bier and Bruce Pfieffer led. (He came to Taliesin right out of high-school in about 1950 and is now their archivist.) Bruce led three of Mrs. Wright's favorites—a Serbian hymn, "Deep River," and "Vaya Con Dios." After a few silent moments, Iovanna read haltingly from Mrs. Wright's *Roots of Life*. One Reverent Father Poulos softly gave prayers and we all stood. Lastly, Effi Casey played violin from Mrs. Wright's sonata as Bruce accompanied. After, we all filed out.

Outside clouds had gathered. It was cool—you know, one of those early March days in Arizona. As we stood about, the coffin was brought out of the living room, pallbearers being the closest eight people or so. . . . I couldn't see through my tears who besides Wes and Jonnie the others were. The coffin was placed in a white hearse which drove away to the crematorium.* The guests were invited to stay for refreshments—iced coffee and sweets—and we all visited with each other until the local guests left. Preparations were being made for dinner.

Dinner was in that area next to the kitchen that was a loggia during our time—the foyer dining area is now offices. Tables for eight were decorated with flowers and candles. Selected seating in some informal way, and I found myself with Wes, Wes's son Brandoch, Herb Fritz, his wife, and the Lovnesses—we talked as did all the others about vague things. There didn't seem to be any program to follow, there was no beginning nor ending apparent. Near the end of the meal I suggested that Wes might say a few words, but he didn't respond.

---

*One of the apprentices told me that it was her wish to be cremated, and that it was also her wish to have Mr. Wright's body disinterred, cremated, and his ashes buried next to hers at Taliesin West. I couldn't believe it.

I found myself talking with Elizabeth Lloyd Wright Ingraham (granddaughter), she is now an architect in Colorado and a forceful one with the Wright genes. I suggested that perhaps the "Wright-side" might say something. She asked how to get attention and I tapped my glass as she stood. Betty outlined the importance of the moment, its sadness, and the turning point in Taliesin's history. It was deeply moving. Eric rose and added to her words, then Franklin Porter (the last of Mr. Wright's nephews); then Bisser Lloyd Jones (of the Jones House in Tulsa) finalized the family thoughts. Wes arose—I couldn't hear him clearly—and then Brandoch. You could hear a pin drop; there had been the clarity of finalization. We all seemed pleased, something outstanding had happened, there had been an "end" and clearly a beginning. There were no tears.

Sue Jacobs Lockhart announced that there would be music in the theater, we all rose again and walked out into the dampness of the moonlight—or nature's attempt at moonlight. Music was furnished by apprentices—recorders, violin, etc., and after a couple of pieces I stole out to the car and drove to Phoenix. I'll never remember what went on in my mind during that drive, maybe I felt it was what purgatory could be, or that the past was done.

Kindest regards always. . . .
    EDGAR

The Fires

This album covers a wide range of my memories and experiences starting when just out of my teens. I read Wright's newly published autobiography describing the haunting account of his first fire at Taliesin in 1914. Through my nine years with Wright, all of us had fear of fire—don't let one start, don't leave any of the 17 fireplaces unattended. (Floors, framing, and roof shingles were of wood.) Whenever the dinner bell rang at a time other than meal time, we were all filled with dread of fire. This final chapter deals with the many fires in Wright's life—including the ultimate fire.

Before the Fellowship was begun, two devastating fires at Taliesin had deeply affected Mr. Wright. The first, in 1914 while he was away, demolished the family quarters and killed seven people, including Mamah Cheney Borthwick, the woman with whom Wright had been having a relationship for several years; her two children, who were visiting; and four workmen. The second fire, in

Postcard view of Taliesin I, Spring Green, Wisconsin, Sunday, August 16, 1914. View of courtyard looking northeast from hill-garden area. Note Frank Lloyd Wright (wearing hat, white shirt with dark vest, arms crossed, looking in direction of photographer), along with armed guard (to the right of Wright), whose duty it was to protect the still smoldering ruins and to bar intruders. Photographer unknown. © 1992 Collection of Jerry A. McCoy, Washington, D.C.

1925, was started by a poor electrical system, it destroyed the same area, but nobody was hurt. We apprentices shared Mr. Wright's fear of fire. We were repeatedly instructed in what to do should one start: the exterior dinner bell would be rung constantly and buckets galore would be assembled in a bucket brigade. Water by the bucketful was the only means of fire fighting.

During the first year of the Fellowship, in 1932, a fire started within a two-by-four stud wall. We all acted with dispatch. The dinner bell was kept ringing and a bucket brigade was immediately put into action. From the second floor of the students' rooms Mr. Wright directed the operation. He had us break through partitions from opposite sides with axes. At one point an axe pierced through a wall a foot from me. He thought nothing of that. "Keep chopping away...from both sides," he exclaimed. When the flames were extinguished, he stated again, as he had many times before, that the hollow stud wall was "the invention of the devil." It created fire by conducting drafts; he said he would never again design them that way. At Hillside, we built with solid walls, and later on, in the Usonian houses, he employed the solid wall inside and outside, as he did in most of his buildings.

Another devastating fire, this one at Hillside, was, for all intents, of Mr. Wright's making. On returning from Arizona one spring, he instructed that the fields below the theater be raked, the broken branches assembled, and the debris brought close to the theater section of the building—for burning. He didn't want to start a fire out in the open field. He took what he assumed to be every precaution. The fire was lit, and sparks quickly spread it to the theater. Before the local fire department could arrive from four miles away, the entire theater was demolished.

Another spring, I was living at Hillside with my wife of some six months. On the Fellowship's return from Arizona, Mr. Wright, as usual, gathered several of us to rake all the leaves and debris into one pile. This time he directed us to make the pile about three feet tall and wide, and some dozen feet long. I was instructed to ignite the fire. Mr. Wright then strode off for some other endeavor. For the life of me, even with the aid of kerosene, I couldn't get that fire going. To my dismay, it kept petering out. In about a half hour Mr. Wright returned to assess the operation. I told him of my predicament. He thought for a moment wistfully, wet his forefinger, pointed up toward some heaven, and stated in a deep voice, "Edgar, the wind is coming from the opposite direction from where you are starting the fire. Start again, on the opposite end." Then he looked at me, and with a smile said, "I don't perceive much of a successful marriage for you if you don't know at which end to start a fire," and he marched off again. He was right, the marriage lasted but two years.

"Stuffy's Tavern" was a bar and grill down on the highway along the river beyond Taliesin. Stuffy Vale originally had owned and run a cheese factory near the family Lloyd/Jones chapel. The cheese factory was a point of interest to show visitors, especially if you got there early enough in the day, before the cheese had settled down. Vale was a gregarious fellow who enjoyed company and loved to describe his operation. But as time went on, the big cheese combines bought up the local factories, and Stuffy invested in another endeavor, a tavern. Often, we apprentices would stop by for a drink or two, sometimes more. It was on "our side" of the bridge to town, thus saving us commutation of three miles. Also, it was within walking distance. Mr. Wright often said how much he hated the idea of a public tavern so close to Taliesin (he also wanted no obstruction of the river view). Finally, he assembled enough finances to purchase Stuffy's establishment. After the negotiations, he and Wes Peters went to the Farmer's State Bank for the closing. When they returned to Taliesin, Mr. Wright assembled a picnic at the site of the tavern. Then he instructed Wes to get some rags and kerosene and ordered him to burn down the tavern. After all, it was his, he felt, to do with as he wanted. John Amarantides, Taliesin violinist and apprentice, was directed to fiddle while Stuffy's Tavern burned.

Among the farm buildings at Taliesin, there was a "gas storage room." It had been a one-car garage, but was then being used for storage of gasoline for farm equipment, in two fifty-gallon drums. There was no tax on gasoline used for agricultural purposes. However, gas was often siphoned out for Wright's trucks and cars, thus avoiding taxes, for he was always short of money. One dark afternoon, a new arrival and former city dweller, Ellis Jacobs, and I were to put some of this gas into a truck we had parked in front of the garage door. Jacobs was instructed to go in and draw some gas in a gallon tank. Apparently it was so dark inside that he couldn't locate the drum's spigot, so he lit a match to find it. Suddenly the whole area was on fire, and I yelled to Ellis to get the hell out, which he did. I jumped in the truck and backed it up, just as the big drum exploded. Soon, our own fighting brigade brought the situ-

Tractor shed and garage at Taliesin that burned.

ation under control, and on telling Mr. Wright of the event, he stated, as often, "Something always happens in the country."

*   *   *

The River Forest Tennis Club was designed by Mr. Wright in 1906, and not much was heard about it, except in the drafting room, where we would hear his versions of the origin of the blaze: "The rafters were placed too close to the chimney flue; they caught fire, and the building was demolished. That tells us to keep wood construction away from chimney flues." Nothing ever was mentioned about who designed the location of the rafters.

*   *   *

The Nathan Moore house was originally built in 1895. Moore, we were told, didn't want to have a house that would be a curiosity, or that people would avoid or, conversely, want to see, from, or that would be talked about as another Wright house—he insisted on "English-Tudor." Mr. Wright would tell us that the project came as things were slow and "food and clothing were needed for the family"—so English, somewhat, it was. In 1923, the house burned, and it was rebuilt, with the same British "stance," but with many interesting details that were never before seen in that style: precise Wright-designed stained glass, ornamental effects of creative design, all in keeping with the original house. However, Mr. Wright never referred to it as one of his better works—as it certainly was.

One day, at Taliesin Spring Green, several of us were in the drafting room working with Mr. Wright, and we heard a giant crash outside. Was it an explosion? Perhaps a fire? We all dashed out the back way and ran to the end of the road where it goes under the stable. We saw the whole area strewn with egg crates. A flat-bed truck's load had been higher than the headroom. The truck went through and smashed into a wall on the other side. The driver was in a drunken stupor—possibly always wondering what it was like "up to Wright's," as the neighbors described Taliesin.

Not knowing what to do, I returned to the studio and described what had happened to Mr. Wright, and asked what he would want us to do. He thought for a moment and stated, "Pick up and save all the unbroken eggs, and call the sheriff."

*   *   *

Wes Peters, one time brother-in-law, was a vivid and accurate story teller, and soon after Iovanna's wedding told me this: The second marriage of Wright's daughter Iovanna was held in the Louis Sullivan-designed Greek Orthodox church in Chicago. Iovanna's mother, Olgivanna, had been raised in the Greek church, and Mr.

Louis Sullivan-designed Greek Orthodox Church, Chicago, Illinois.

Wright had worked for his "lieber Meister," Sullivan, in Chicago. So on all counts it seemed a most fitting location for their daughter's wedding. The day arrived, the bride wore white with a long, full veil. At one point in the ceremony the couple stood facing the altar while the Metropolitan walked around them, holding in his cupped hands a flaming brazier. Upon the priest's last encirclement of the bride, he came too close to her floating veil. It burst into flame.

In this church's main floor there are no arrangements for seating, and members of the Fellowship were standing in a quarter circle behind the wedding couple. As the veil flared up, many of the apprentices ran to the rescue. They quickly extinguished the fire and all ended well. But Mr. Wright was seen walking up and down along the outer wall of the sanctuary, cane in hand, muttering over and over, "All my life I have been plagued by fire. All my life I have been plagued by fire."

When the memorial service in Arizona for Mrs. Wright was completed, in 1985, we all followed the casket from the living room out onto the terrace, up the stairs to the right, where a hearse was waiting to take the body to Phoenix for cremation. We stood in silence while we waited for the hearse to leave, and after it departed, we broke into small groups visiting with each other. One of the longtime apprentices then told me that Mrs. Wright's wish had been to have Mr. Wright's remains cremated and brought to Taliesin West to be placed next to hers.

I was terribly dismayed to hear this, for he was a man of his selected base, Wisconsin, deeply rooted in the traditions of his beloved mid-America. It seemed outrageous to me to disturb his body, for it was resting among his family in their own cemetery in the valley of the Lloyd Joneses, near his mother, in those green Wisconsin hills.

Soon, however, news of his cremation broke across the country. His daughter Iovanna had signed the required legal documents, the remains were brought from the chapel cemetery to Madison, cremated, and the ashes were sent to Arizona. Editorials condemning the disinterment and cremation came from all across the country, and former apprentices wrote to others in dismay, but the act had been done and there was no recourse.

His gravestone—an unmarked stone selected by Mrs. Wright after his death, and the adjacent stained glass memorial inscribed: Frank Lloyd Wright, 1867–1959. "Love of an idea, is the love of God" remain in the Unitarian chapel graveyard in his beloved Wisconsin.

Yes, even after death, he was plagued by fire.

Believed to be the last photo of Frank Lloyd Wright.

Cartoon by Maginel Wright Barney, Frank Lloyd Wright's sister.

PHOTO CREDITS

Hedrick Blessing: page 149

Rick Glintenkamp: page 245

Pedro Guerrero: pages 26, 89, 171, 213

Al Krescanko: page 108

Carter Manny: page 144

Byron K. Moser: page 154

Werner Moser: page 94

Joe D. Price: page 97

Charles Rossi: page 59

Edgar Tafel: 31, 33, 34, 35, 88, 112, 118, 125, 130, 131, 150, 160, 161, 174, 176, 191, 192, 193, 219, 222, 227 (top), 231, 239, 273, 277, 314

Edmund Teske: page 262

M. Thorn: pages 135, 136, 137

Stuart Weiner: page 317

Index